A BLESSED GIRL

A BLESSED GIRL

Memoirs of a Victorian Girlhood

Emily Lutyens

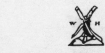

HEINEMANN : LONDON

This book is dedicated to my son-in-law, Herbert Agar, without whose encouragement it would never have been begun, and to my daughter, Mary Links, without whose patient assistance it would never have been finished.

William Heinemann Ltd
Michelin House, 81 Fulham Road, London SW3 6RB
LONDON   MELBOURNE   AUCKLAND

First published by Rupert Hart-Davis 1953
First published in this edition 1989
Introduction copyright © Mary Lutyens 1989
All rights reserved

British Library Cataloguing in Publication Data

Lutyens, Emily, 1874–1964
    A blessed girl : memoirs of a Victorian
girlhood.
    1. Great Britain, 1837–1901. Biographies
    I. Title
941.081'092'4

ISBN 0 434 43914 2

Printed and bound in Great Britain by
Mackays of Chatham

Contents

Introduction

How often can a daughter have been given such an intimate knowledge of her mother's early life and character as I have been given in this book? My mother was nearly seventy-nine when the book was published in 1953 and it was eighteen months before publication that I first read the letters it contains with an avidity that can be imagined. Our backgrounds and upbringing had been so different, hers so conventional, mine so much the reverse, yet my childhood had been far happier than hers. It is, of course, the historical background of the book – English society nearly a hundred years ago – that is part of its fascination. Her description of staying at Hatfield House with the Salisburys during the election of 1892 is an excellent example: Robert, Marquess of Salisbury was Prime Minister three times between 1886 and 1900. She also stayed at Knowsley with the Derbys the following year when their newly installed electric generator – a great innovation – kept breaking down.

Because her mother had been so recently widowed, Emily was brought out at seventeen by her married sister, Betty Balfour, sister-in-law of Arthur Balfour and a prominent member of the exclusive literary and artistic coterie, the "Souls". Her agonies of shyness at dinner parties were not helped by Betty listening to her conversation and reproving her afterwards for not talking enough. All the same, she infinitely preferred Betty as a chaperone to her mother who was forever scolding her for one thing or another. Her feelings during the three years she was in love with Wilfrid Blunt, the poet, who did his best to seduce her, are revealed with an astonishing honesty.

How much did the girl and young woman resemble the mother I was so close to? To a remarkable extent. The great difference was that the girl who was always trying to control her terrible temper and irritability had succeeded so completely that I cannot remember her ever losing her temper. All that she had longed for in her early life she gave to us, her five children (four girls and a boy, of whom I was the youngest) – freedom, trust and never a scolding. Indeed, it might be said that she criticised us too little and trusted us too much.

She had a wonderful gift for reading aloud and a beautiful voice. She complained in her letters that her mother would read aloud to her and her brothers only "improving" books in which her mother was not in the least interested, thereby making them even duller than they need have been. My mother never read us anything she was not keenly interested in herself; in consequence her daily reading aloud was one of the chief joys of my childhood and the most valuable part of my education.

Unfortunately her marriage turned out to be a disappointment. My father was so absorbed in his work, which he was unable to share with her, that he could not give her the companionship she craved; therefore, for the first few years she tried to find an outlet for her passionate energy in various kinds of social work. She kept throughout her life that quality of honesty, so evident in her letters to Elwin, which was sometimes disconcerting to strangers. Dislike of society people, sympathy for the underdog, disregard of public opinion and indifference to physical discomfort and good food were other characteristics she retained, but she conquered her shyness when in 1910 she at last found in the Theosophical Society a cause that absorbed her utterly for the next twenty years; she trained herself to be a lecturer for the Society and became an excellent public speaker.

Although she abandoned orthodox Christianity, her devotional nature was fulfilled in her sublimated love for Krishnamurti, the young Indian who had been proclaimed by Theosophists as the vehicle for the coming World Teacher. When he disclaimed his role in 1929, declaring that he wanted no followers, she suffered greatly for a long time. Gradually, however, her interest in her family and husband returned, and by the time my father died in 1944 they were as close as they had been at the beginning. Her love of babies had never left her and she found great joy in her grand-children.

The publication of *A Blessed Girl* enlivened her old age. She received dozens of fan letters and confidently bought herself a press-cutting album which she almost filled. Two more books followed – *The Birth of Roland*, an exchange of letters between her parents in the first year of their marriage, and her autobiography, *Candles in the Sun*. She died peacefully of an aneurism in her eighty-ninth year, a "blessed mother" as well as a "blessed girl".

Mary Lutyens
London, 1989

Foreword

THIS is not a book of reminiscences in the usual sense but an exchange of letters between the Rev. Whitwell Elwin and myself. Elwin, who was born in 1816, was fifty-eight years my senior. Nevertheless, from the age of thirteen to twenty-three I gave him, in almost daily letters, the entire confidence of a somewhat passionate nature. From him I received a warmth of friendship, coupled with an understanding and sympathy for my youthful problems and heart-aches, rare in the relationship of youth and age. I had preserved and treasured all his letters to me, and almost fifty years after his death his grandson bequeathed his property in Norfolk to me, and those of my letters to Elwin which had not been destroyed came back into my possession.

This seemed to provide an unusual opportunity for making a journey into the past, independent of the frailties and distortions of memory to which reminiscences are subject. Moreover, each correspondent wrote exclusively for the benefit of the other, with no thought of the possibility of publication.

I have thought best to leave the letters exactly as they were written, confining any comment to what is essential for the understanding of the people and events recorded. I have not even disguised the names of real people, and it may seem to their descendants that some of the contents would have been better omitted. If this is so I beg them to remember that they were the outpourings of an inexperienced girl.

I should like to emphasize that during my early years my mother meant everything in my life and my devotion to her influenced all my outlook. After the move to Paris the duties and obligations of official life, which she carried out superbly, became a barrier between us, and my love for her turned to the narrow-minded criticism which is reflected in many of these letters. With the blind, cruel lack of understanding of the young, I showed little sympathy with her in her sorrow after my father's death, or with the trials of a changed social position, more difficult to face in those days than they would be today. After my marriage, however, and until the day of her death my early devotion was never again eclipsed by criticism, and I learnt more and more to love and admire her great and noble qualities, and to take for granted the asperities which sometimes accompanied them.

My criticism of my brother Victor must also be read as the expression of the childlike relationship which so often exists between members of the same family. In later life I learnt to dearly love and appreciate him.

Perhaps I should also here explain the title I have chosen for this book. It is in no way intended to place a halo round my own head, but the epithet of "blessed" was used by Elwin to express his feelings towards those whom he especially loved and cherished. It is an epithet which belongs to his age rather than to the present, when "blessed" and "blasted" have become almost synonymous, and both are terms of opprobrium rather than of benediction.

To live is to grow and to grow is to change, so I have grown very far from the writer of so long ago, with her somewhat narrow-minded attitude towards life. But I cannot repudiate or change her, though I think *she* might disapprove of the greater charity and tolerance which old age has brought to me.

Emily Lutyens

10 June 1953

Chapter One

I WAS born in Paris on December 26th, 1874, and have therefore lived through nearly eighty years of the most revolutionary period of the world's history. There is, of course, nothing remarkable in this fact, for, the expectation of life being so much higher today than in the past, I am not by any means alone in my generation. My only claim to an experience which is somewhat uncommon is that I have not only been a voluminous letter-writer, recording my thoughts and emotions in almost daily letters from the age of thirteen to the present time, but that the bulk of my letters were preserved, and returned to me on the death of their recipients. These letters form a record of my life, not based solely on memory, but on day-to-day recording.

My father, Robert Lytton, was the second child and only son of Bulwer Lytton, the novelist, and his wife, Rosina Wheeler. I am afraid that my grandfather is more remembered today for his unhappy marriage, and the hatred with which his wife pursued him, than for his novels, which are no longer read: He was himself the child of an unhappy marriage. His father, William Bulwer, was the owner of Heydon Hall, in Norfolk. His mother, Elizabeth Barbara Lytton, was heiress to the Lytton property of Knebworth, in Hertfordshire. There were three sons of this marriage. William, the eldest, and favourite of his father, inherited the Norfolk estate. The youngest son, my grandfather, was the particular favourite of his mother, and at her death he inherited the Knebworth estate.

My mother was the daughter of Edward Villiers, younger brother of the Earl of Clarendon, and Elizabeth Charlotte Liddell, the ninth of the sixteen children of the first Lord Ravensworth of Ravensworth Castle, near Newcastle. Sixteen

1

were born alive and lived to grow up; thirteen were married and had families, most of them large ones, so my mother laid claim to a hundred first cousins. Children in those days had a much more spartan upbringing than the young people of today. The Liddell children used to be bathed in the morning in an open tank in the yard of their father's castle; and one winter my grandmother records her joy at the nursery-maid saying, when she came back from the yard, that the ice was so hard it was impossible to break it. The children were let off their cold bath for that morning.

Four children were born to my maternal grandparents, one son and three daughters. My mother was one of twin girls. My grandfather, being a very poor man at the time, when presented with this addition to his family was alleged to have remarked: "Would it be wrong to hope that one of them will not survive?" But his hopes were disappointed, as both twins lived to the age of ninety-five, a very unusual age for twins. My grandfather Villiers died very young from tuberculosis caught from a younger brother whom he had nursed with that dreadful complaint.

To return to my parents: my father wished to devote his life to poetry, but this was prohibited by his father, Bulwer Lytton, on the plea that it was not likely that two successive generations could make a success of literature, and my father was consequently urged to make diplomacy his career. Although this advice may have been inspired by jealousy, the result, I think, shows that it was wise, for my father turned out to be a very distinguished diplomat and remained, in my opinion, but a second-class poet.

My father started his diplomatic career by going to Washington as an attaché to his uncle, Sir Henry Bulwer, who held the post of Minister to the U.S.A. At the time of his marriage to my mother in 1864, he was well on the way to promotion in his profession. At the time of my birth he was Secretary of the Embassy in Paris.

My mother was very beautiful and was always dressed by Worth. The founder of the great designing House told my father that he owed all his success in life to Bulwer Lytton's

novel *Night and Morning*. When he was so poor and un-
successful that he had contemplated suicide, *Night and
Morning* had been put into his hands and had so inspired
him that from that day he had gone forwards to success.
Although he always dressed my mother I do not know
whether he reduced his charges as a tribute to my grandfather.

I was the fifth child of their marriage. My sister Betty was
the eldest of the family, followed by a boy, Rowland, who
died after an attack of whooping-cough at the age of eight.
Next in age came my sister Constance, and then another
boy, Teddy, who died aged eighteen months, a year before
I was born.

Coming after the death of two brothers my sex was
naturally a great disappointment. In one way this affected
my childhood, as my mother was so determined that I should
not be allowed to feel their disappointment, that she was,
perhaps, more specially fond of me for that reason, and soon
after my birth she refers to me in a letter to a friend as
"little Miss Consuelo." I had a passion for her and throughout my childhood and early youth she was my ideal and most
beloved. A word from her did more to influence me than all
the scolding in the world, and to give her pain was the only
punishment I really minded.

My nurse has told me that I was such an ugly baby that
when my father came to look at me he inquired anxiously if
I was all right. I was christened Emily after my father's
beloved and only sister, who had died young.

In November 1874, a month before I was born, my
father had been offered the post of Minister of the British
Legation to Portugal. On May 13th, 1875, my parents and
their three children reached Lisbon. They were not to
remain there long, however, for on November 23rd of the
same year my father received a letter from Disraeli asking
him to accept the position of Viceroy of India in succession
to Lord Northbrook, and the appointment was made public
on January 1st, 1876. My father prepared to quit Lisbon at
once, leaving my mother and the children to follow as soon
as possible.

Writing to my mother from London on January 19th, my father records: "I have seen M. Corry [Monty Corry was private secretary to Disraeli], who touched me much by telling me that when my appointment was finally settled, Dizzy walked up and down before my father's picture, rubbing his hands and saying, 'Ah, my dear old friend, if he could know that I have made his son Viceroy of India, how pleased he would be.'"

My two brothers were born in India during my father's viceroyalty. The elder had the honour of having Queen Victoria as his godmother, and was christened by the grandiloquent names of Victor Alexander. He was born on August 9th, 1876. My younger brother, Neville Stephen, made his appearance eighteen months later, his birth taking place while a ball was proceeding at Government House, Calcutta. I can remember being taken on tiptoe to see the new baby in his cradle.

I had at that time and for many years after a very violent temper, and my father's A.D.C.s used to encourage me in my rages and tell me to stick pins into my brother, which I did. Edward Clifford, the painter, was doing a portrait of my two sisters and myself. Nothing could look more cherubic than my small self in this picture, but my Nannie has told me that Mr. Clifford refused to have me as a sitter unless she was by, as he said he could not manage "the little devil."

Perhaps my most vivid memory of India, in which my brother Victor shared, was when on one occasion we ran ahead of our nurses and found a Hindu temple behind which the carcase of a goat was hanging. We fled back to our nurses in terror and were told by them that if the priests knew that we had seen this they would slay us also. A ridiculous statement, but one which impressed our childish imaginations—so much so, indeed, that when on our return to Knebworth we discovered in the garden a summer-house of rough-hewn stones, we were too frightened ever to go near it lest we should see another slaughtered animal.

In 1880 there was a change of government at home and my father followed his chief out of office. On June 8th, 1880,

Lord Ripon arrived at Simla to take over the viceroyalty from my father, and we sailed for England in a troopship. I remember this very vividly. The captain was a great friend of mine and used to carry me round the deck on his shoulder. There was a bear in a cage which used to thrill me. Every morning, or perhaps only every Sunday, the crew used to be drawn up in front of us for prayers, and the great ambition of myself and my brother was to try and make the sailors laugh by wearing paper spectacles, and by other tricks. Our favourite game, however, was to run round the decks in opposite directions and bow to each other in passing. This was an unfailing source of amusement. There was a prison on board, and the captain used to terrify me by his threats of putting me there. What incalculable harm the foolish and thoughtless threats of grown-ups can do to children, breeding nervousness and fear through all their lives!

Of my father I have few memories in those early days, except as a distant and awe-inspiring figure. My mother I adored and thought very beautiful.

With our return from India the first chapter of my life closes. There followed seven years mostly spent at Kneb-worth, our Hertfordshire home, with occasional visits to London. I have no remembrance of the return to Knebworth, but my mother has told me how the tenants removed the horses and themselves dragged our carriage through the village, and of how my father stood up in the carriage with my brother Victor in his arms, amid shouts of rejoicing, to show his heir who had been born during his absence.

The first summer after our return my parents took a house in Carlton House Terrace for the season. I have a few very vivid memories of that time; such as when our Nannie left us, and I can see myself sitting on the stairs weeping my eyes out with misery. In her place we had a very fat woman called Tassy, whose reign was brief. On one occasion Tassy sat upon some scissors and the point entered a tender spot. She proceeded to lift her petticoats and exhibit the wound for my inspection, and I still feel a horror at remembering the large expanse of flesh exposed to view.

Tassy's reign was brought to a close as the result of the

following incident. My two brothers and I were out with her in the Green Park, Neville in the pram, and when she turned aside to gossip with a friend, Victor and I—aged four and six respectively—decided to cross the Mall by ourselves. We stepped boldly into the midst of the traffic, and I still remember our pleased surprise when the carriages and horses held up, like the Red Sea before the children of Israel. Victor and I, hand in hand, walked across, graciously bowing right and left to those who had so kindly allowed us to pass. For this neglect of her charges Tassy was dismissed.

As I have said before, my temper was easily aroused and very violent. I can remember on one occasion turning upon my brother Victor and biting him in the shoulder, and the satisfaction it gave me to feel my teeth meet his flesh. My mother, coming in at the moment, asked what the row was about. I replied with vindictiveness, "I have bit the little beast."

But a far graver offence, and one with more lasting consequences, was committed one memorable Sunday morning of that summer. My grandmother, Mrs. Villiers, had for some reason a partiality for my brother and an antagonism to me. On this particular Sunday morning Victor and I were with Grannie in the drawing-room. I was looking at some book which Victor also wished to see. I refused to let him have it, but Grannie encouraged him to go and take it from me. I promptly boxed his ears, whereupon Grannie called him to her side, presented him with half a crown, and said she would herself fetch the book. But I treated her as I had treated Victor, and boxed her ears with a resounding smack which gives me satisfaction to remember to this day. For this heinous crime I was taken to the nursery and put to bed. Getting up and peeping out of the window, I saw Grannie and Mother going off to church in a four-wheeler, Mother crying bitterly as Grannie no doubt recounted my sins.

This incident naturally did not help my grandmother to like me better, and indeed she never forgave me and took every opportunity of showing her affection for Victor and her dislike of me. She would never allow me to visit her at Ryde, where she lived. When my mother suggested bringing me, her answer was: "Bring her if you like, but I shall have detectives in the house all the time."

The only punishment I ever remember was being put to bed early, for my mother took the very sensible view, "If you are naughty, you must be ill, and bed is the place for you." My answer to such measures was: "There is nothing I like better than tea in bed." ·

The smell of brewing still recalls that summer in London to me, for there was a brewery nearby. I recall the hot nights when sleep would not come. For some reason we were not allowed water to drink at nights, and we used to creep out of bed and drink from the jug. Neville, being the youngest, was helped first, and sometimes we were interrupted before my thirst was quenched.

But my chief memories are of Knebworth. Knebworth was originally a very beautiful Elizabethan house in the form of a quadrangle of red brick. My great-grandmother pulled down three sides of it and whitewashed what was left. Her son (my grandfather, Bulwer Lytton) turned it into a pseudo-Gothic castle, covering it with stucco and sham battlements and turrets and griffins and other monstrosities.

The main "oak" staircase was in reality made of papier-mâché. An enormous picture at the foot of the staircase was labelled "Sir Rowland de Lytton," but was as a matter of fact a very poor copy of the portrait of Charles V by Velasquez in the Prado in Madrid. But to me, as a child, Knebworth was a real castle, filled with all the romance of chivalry.

A wide park surrounded the house, and a lime avenue led to a small lake half a mile away. This lake was a never-ending source of delight. On it we boated in summer and skated in winter, and fished for perch and roach and pike. It was a proud moment of my life when I landed a ten-pound pike single-handed. I also had a curious experience in catching a fish with its own eye. I had caught a small roach and in removing the hook brought out the eye with it. The fish, being small, I threw back, and then for fun baited the hook with the eye. A few moments later I had a bite and landed the same small fish with a gaping socket to show where the eye had been.

2

The domestic staff at Knebworth was a large one, as was usual in those days, and the etiquette observed was very rigid. The head servants took their meat in the Hall with the lower domestics and that part of the meal was eaten in complete silence, but with the advent of the pudding, the head servants took up their plates and solemnly marched with them into the Housekeeper's Room. Then, and then only, might the underlings speak. Our great amusement as children was to peep into the Hall during the solemnity of the meat course and try to make our special friends among the lower staff giggle. One of the housemaids, called Mary Ann, was promoted to be my maid as I grew older, thus joining the ranks of those higher beings who had their pudding in the Room, but she often told me of the hard time she had after her promotion as the senior domestics looked down upon this upstart risen from the ranks and made her life a misery.

When I passed from the nursery stage, I had a governess called Miss Plaistowe—more familiarly, Paisy. I do not think I learned anything from her except how to avoid learning at all. Competition stimulated me and I believe I would have benefited from school on that account. I attended a weekly French class in London, presided over by M. Roche, which I found both stimulating and exciting.

I cannot say that I enjoyed my childhood. On the contrary, I look back on it as a time of much unhappiness, mingled with streaks of joy.

My unhappiness was chiefly caused by my own temperament. My father used to suffer, as did my grandfather before him, from moods of black melancholy for no apparent reason, and all his children have, I think, inherited this tendency. Certainly my moods of depression were very severe. I had a sense of being a prisoner, caught in a long tunnel of childhood which would never end. I resented bitterly my helplesssness, my dependence, the fact that so many people in the shape of nurses and grown-ups stood between me and my mother, and that no child was believed, or treated with respect. I had a great sense of my own dignity, a terrible shyness, and a horror of being laughed at. I could never enter a room full of grown-ups without extreme self-consciousness and a sense that I was helplessly at their mercy, that they could talk of me before my face as if I did not understand. Some incidents increased this shyness and self-consciousness. My mother had a great idea that we were not to be brought up in luxury, and three dresses—bad, better, best—for winter and summer was my allowance in clothes. In winter I can remember a horror in the shape of a dress of red, and another of yellow plush, while for summer I had two cotton frocks and a white flannel one made like a sailor suit. This last frock I loved, as at that time I had a passion for the sea and meant to run away and be a sailor. But when the yellow plush dress was almost new, I had the misfortune to spill some ink down the front, and thereafter I was made to go on wearing it, with its ink stains, until it was worn out.

As far back as I can remember, I was always a very religious child, of a devotional type. I had a passionate love for Christ, and a firm belief that I should live to witness His second coming. I can see myself now, seated on the nursery floor, hugging my doll while I read *The Peep of Day*. Religion held no terrors for me. I was too convinced of the goodness of God to worry about hell, although I did refrain from calling my brother a fool—much as I should have liked to have used that epithet!

The happiest moments of my childhood were spent in an imaginary world which I created for myself. There I pretended to be whatever was my favourite character at the moment. I was a voracious reader, and never so happy as when, curled up in an armchair, I was devouring a favourite book, or, perched on the top of a ladder in my father's library, could browse among the books there. Happily, both my father and mother believed in giving us full liberty to read whatever and whenever we liked. I was never forbidden but once in my life to read any book, and that was by my stupid governess, who forbade me to read *Old St. Paul's*, by Harrison Ainsworth. I waited till she had departed on holiday, when I promptly got out the proscribed book and read it with a feeling of deep disappointment because it contained nothing I did not know already.

I was an inquisitive child, especially about the facts of sex —but it never occurred to me to ask my mother any questions on the subject. I pestered the servants with questions, however, and pretended to know more than I did in order to draw them out. A cousin and I made a bargain to find out all we could and report our discoveries to each other. I can remember my excitement when she told me that babies were born from their mother's bodies, through the navel. For years I regarded this part of my anatomy with hopeful awe, hoping that a baby might appear, for even in my very young days I had a passion for babies. I can remember provoking much mirth because on one occasion I was asked in company what I intended to be when grown-up, and promptly replied, "A wife and a mother."

I was a great tomboy and also a romantic. My father on one occasion called me a hoyden, which hurt me deeply. I longed to be a boy, and in my games I was always a hero of some kind. Never have I known happier moments than when, sallying forth into the Park, armed with bow and arrows, I pretended to be Robin Hood, Ivanhoe, or Richard Cœur de Lion. The only drawback to these games was that I needed a foil to my merits, an enemy to conquer, and my brother was not always ready to act the part of John, Friar Tuck or Brian de Bois-Guilbert.

We were allowed great freedom, and wandered about the Park at will or fished in the lake. On one occasion I fell into the lake from the bank and though speedily fished out I asked anxiously, "Shall I be drowned?" believing that death as a result of immersion was death from drowning. But I only gave cause for more ridicule to be poured on me by my unfortunate remark.

As I grew older I joined in all my brother's games, being especially fond of cricket. I was a fast underhand bowler and captained a side calling itself the Knebworth Bounders. I was always a little bit in love with my brother's boy friends, but my first really sentimental attachment was for a French boy named Catulle whom I met when we were on a visit to Berc-sur-Mer. I was discovered tenderly embracing him at parting.

My favourite books were historical novels, and of these my

grandfather's works took first place. Of all his works, *Harold*
was my favourite. I was passionately Saxon and hated to feel
that my ancestors had come over with the despised Conqueror.
I was tremendously proud of my grandfather and of my own
descent from a `long line of distinguished ancestors. I read
my family tree and pondered over the names recorded in
stained-glass scutcheons in the hall windows—Robinson,
Stroud, Pole. I had a tremendous sense of *noblesse oblige* and
felt myself to be an aristocrat to my finger-tips—and very
proud of it I was. In my favourite novels noble birth was a
necessary qualification for knightly deeds.

I was very sociable in those early days, and loved to go to
parties and to have other children to stay. I resented it
bitterly when I heard my mother telling a neighbour that
she did not allow us to go to many parties as it upset us.
Few children came to stay, and my natural sociableness was
soon killed by the agonizing shyness from which I suffered.

My two sisters, being respectively eight and six years
older than myself seemed to me almost grown-up. I was
devoted to my sister Betty, and still remember the excitement of the tea-parties she gave us in her room, and the
thrilling stories with which she used to beguile the long
Sunday afternoon walks. My sister Conny I actively disliked,
and this dislike was heartily reciprocated. She has since told
me that she once registered a vow never to speak to me.
She had a vein of sarcasm which I hated, and I also resented
the fact that when I had been particularly odious to her she
would cry—for which I was much reproved. I used often to
cry myself—but no one seemed to think that mattered. In
after years Conny and I became the most devoted friends.

My chief companions were my two brothers, so nearly of
my own age. I cannot say we were fond of each other in our
early days, and certainly we were not kind. My brother
Victor and I were always more or less on opposite sides, and
Neville would be played off by each of us against the other.
Victor and I bribed him by turns to be on our side. Neville
took all the bribes and was ever smiling. He had an unfor-
givable habit of making up to the grown-ups. His merry
smile took them in, but we were never deceived by him.

He had a nasty way of making presents with apparent generosity, but he always took them back afterwards. On one occasion which I well remember, Victor and I decided to combine against our common enemy. We took Neville into one of the empty spare bedrooms, bound him hand and foot, gagged him, and then cheerfully left him, hoping that he would starve to death. Unfortunately, as we then thought, he managed to remove the gag, and his cries summoned a housemaid to his rescue.

On one occasion Victor fell into a well in the garden while fishing for frogs. I hauled him out by his arms and he complained that I hurt him in the process. So *he* was put to bed for falling in the well, and *I* was put to bed for pulling him out, which struck me as monstrously unjust. I vowed that the next time he fell into the water I would leave him to drown.

I think I always had a strong sense of justice, and one of the reasons why I so bitterly resented being a child was that my sense of justice was constantly being outraged. And there was no appeal. One had just to endure the wrongs in silence and grow bitter with brooding over them. Perhaps that is why I have always had such passionate sympathy with the underdog.

From all that I have said it will be seen that I had not exactly what is called "a sweet disposition." I had strong passions of all kinds and found it very hard to control them. I used to be shaken with a tempest of rage when irritated, but I was equally passionate in my affections, though I strove to hide them under a mask of indifference. When I was considered too old to share the night nursery with my brothers, I pretended to be delighted that I was to have a room of my own, but when they retaliated by saying they were glad to be rid of me, I wept my heart out. I was always amenable to affection, but no one could drive me. I was then, and have ever been, a rebel against authority.

I was given to walking in my sleep, and would often dream that I was shut up in a room in which there was no door, and I would wander round and round my room until something woke me. I was not allowed a night-light, but I had a luminous matchbox which used to bring me to my senses.

Two events occurred when I was nine years old which left a great mark upon my character—the first unpleasant, the second pleasant. I had always been given to telling stories to my brothers and to myself, and some of these I wrote down. But at the age of nine I perpetrated a novel, a really serious work, tragic too. And tragic for me were the consequences! My governess found my precious MS. and, without my knowledge, passed it on to my father. The family were then in London, having taken a house in Portland Place—one of those houses in which the drawing-room is divided by folding doors. I had gone up to London for the day and was waiting in one room, when from behind the folding doors came peal after peal of laughter. When the lunch bell sounded, my father and two sisters came from the adjoining room and Betty said to me: "Father has been telling us about your novel and how good it is." A chill went to my heart. So this was the cause of their ribald laughter! My tragedy, showing, as I thought, such a profound knowledge of life, had only provoked mirth. I was cruelly hurt, and for years I was not allowed to forget about that wretched novel. On whatever subject a conversation started, it always seemed to veer round somehow to my novel, and I was covered with confusion. Not only did this incident cause me severe pain but, who knows, it may have killed a budding novelist? Henceforth, when inspiration drove me to set pen to paper, I invariably destroyed my manuscripts before they could be discovered.

The other thing which had an immense influence on my life was the advent of the Rev. Whitwell Elwin. My father was engaged in writing the life of my grandfather, Bulwer Lytton, and for this purpose was getting into touch with the few remaining men who had been Bulwer's friends. Amongst them was Whitwell Elwin. Elwin, born in 1816, was a clergyman living in Norfolk on his own estate. For many years he had been Editor of the *Quarterly Review*, which post he inherited from Lockhart, Sir Walter Scott's son-in-law. This position had brought him into close touch with all the distinguished literary men of his day. He had been the friend of Scott, Lockhart, Dickens, Thackeray, Forster, and many

others, and his stories were thrilling and unending.[1] My
father wrote of him, to Mrs. Earle,[2] soon after meeting him:

"Elwin is the last, or one of the last, true men of letters left
to us. Scholarship, style, tenderness, discrimination, a vast
knowledge of books, and unlimited leisure—he has them all.
A more sympathetic companion does not exist among men.
He has a wonderful flow and charm of conversation, which
wells and bubbles up with great spontaneity from a richly
stored mind—a mind in which a wide field of literary culture
has blossomed into those flowers of thought and expression
which enliven and beautify human intercourse. And the
foundation of his character, which gives colour and atmosphere to his mind, is a *genuine* goodness and rare benignity.
His is, I think, one of those natures which are lovable because
in them is a great capacity of loving. But to me one of his
chief charms is a quick sense of humour, which I think a very
rare gift even amongst intellectual people; the majority of
mankind seem to be utterly destitute of it."

To hear my father and Elwin talk was a rare treat. He
soon became the friend and confidant of every member of the
family. My mother told him of her distress over my father's
flirtations, while my father told him of his irritation at her
somewhat nagging and disciplinary attitude.

Elwin was what was then called a "Broad Churchman."
He accepted the Bible as the word of God and was never
troubled by doubts. He disliked extremes at both ends of
the theological scale. He had a genius for friendship, especially with members of the opposite sex. He was very suscep-
tible to female charms and became the close friend and
mentor of a succession of "blessed girls," as he was apt to
describe them. In our family my eldest sister, Betty, was his
first favourite and friend, and after her marriage in 1887 he
adopted me as second choice, and I also became a "blessed
girl."

In the summer of 1887 Betty became engaged to Gerald
Balfour, brother of Arthur Balfour and later second Earl

---

[1] Some of his really remarkable letters about them, not written to me, form
the appendix to this volume.

[2] My mother's sister, author of *Pot Pourri from a Surrey Garden*.

Balfour. Soon after their engagement, Gerald became ill at Knebworth with typhoid, and we passed through many agonizing weeks while he hovered between life and death. In December my father was appointed to the Embassy in Paris, and on December 21st, five days before my thirteenth birthday, we had the double excitement of my sister's wedding and our departure for Paris. Gerald being still very much of an invalid, the marriage took place in the house, Mr. Elwin performing the ceremony. My sister Conny and I were bridesmaids, and I still remember my pride in my dress of white nun's-veiling with a green velvet toque. Later we all left for Dover, where we spent the night at the Lord Warden Hotel.

Chapter Two

THE move to Paris naturally brought about a great change in my life. I now had to live in a town in formal surroundings, seeing many more people and, in fact, learning to grow up.

My English governess, Paisy, who came with us, did not remain after the first year. I then had a French and a German daily governess. The German lady was one of those rare people who are born teachers and inspired in me for the first time a desire to learn.

I also attended some French *cours*. For exercise I went to a riding school, and the Military Secretary, Colonel Talbot, often took me riding in the Bois. I also had a small pony and cart in which I could drive myself. All the same, I spent much time alone in my room reading or writing to Mr. Elwin.

I greatly enjoyed the gay atmosphere of Paris, and yet my puritan conscience was always telling me that it was a frivolous and sinful city. I was crippled with shyness, but yet enjoyed meeting the interesting people who came to the Embassy and listening to what was very often brilliant talk. As I was not expected to join in the conversation, I could listen and observe.

We had a fortnightly box at the Français, to which I was often allowed to go; and as I have always loved the theatre, I was able to enjoy acting at its best. I also much enjoyed an evening dancing class with a French family, which was more like a party than a class, and for which I had my first evening dress of pink embroidered crêpe-de-chine.

I was terribly shy of my father, who, although he was kindness itself, was rather apt to be sarcastic, which I think young people mind even more than being scolded. Before I could summon up courage to enter my father's room, I had to pray for help.

16

It was from this time that I began a more or less regular correspondence with Elwin, whom we all called familiarly "his Rev".

During the years of 1888 and 1889 there are many gaps in the correspondence. At that time I was concerned because his Rev did not write to me often enough. My mother said that it was because my letters were so dull, but his Rev was kind enough to tell me otherwise, and writes to me from Booton on January 2nd, 1888:

Booton Rectory, January 2

I intended to have been the first to write, but the course of events has hindered me. I am glad now that I was prevented, on account of the pleasure it gives me that you should have written on your own impulse, without any stimulus from me to set your pen going. And it is not a stupid letter as you imagined, but very entertaining. I could conjure up some of the scenes, and laughed heartily over them. The perfection of a letter is to let you into the thoughts and doings of the writer. What we should see and hear if we were present is what we wish to be told when we are away.

Remember this and you will never want for topics. Put all you can into your letter of Emmie and of the things around you as they appear to Emmie's eyes. I shall prefer it to the newspaper.

It may seem strange that such an intimate friendship should have sprung up between a girl of thirteen and a man of seventy-one, which was Elwin's age when our friendship first began, but he was remarkable in his understanding of and sympathy for the young, and it was for just that sympathy and understanding that I craved. My beloved sister Betty had gone out of my life by marrying, and much as I loved my mother, at that time she did not encourage intimacy and would have had little sympathy with the problems of adolescence. My extreme shyness made me inarticulate when in company, but on paper I found it much easier to express my thoughts and feelings. I think the extraordinary thing is that Elwin was willing to devote so much time to writing to me.

In the early days of our friendship my letters are brief and childish. Elwin, on the other hand, wrote at some length in order to interest and stimulate me.

In later years my letters become longer and fuller, recording not only my emotions but also my increasing consciousness of people and events around me.

*   *   *

At this point I think I should give a fuller description of my sister Conny. She was in some ways a misfit in the family, as I do not think she had much real sympathy with either my father or mother. The spirit of Bulwer Lytton, in some ways difficult to explain, seemed to hover over Knebworth. The sham medievalism, the romance, the rather maudlin sentimentality were very alien to Con's nature. She was not a reader. She never fell under the spell of Elwin or became "a blessed girl." As if to mark her disapproval of Bulwer Lytton, she resolved when she grew up to seek out and assist his illegitimate children, of whom there were reputed to be several.

She loved music and was a brilliant pianist, having learnt from an Austrian lady, Fräulein Oser, who was herself a pupil of Madame Schumann. Fräulein Oser became not only her teacher but a devoted friend, and it had been planned that Con should accompany Fräulein to Vienna and learn seriously to become a professional pianist. Had this plan matured, my sister's whole life might have been changed and she would most certainly have been a happier woman and might have fulfilled herself as an artist. But several circumstances combined to upset this plan. The first of these was Betty's engagement to Gerald Balfour and his critical illness. Betty was the only member of the family to whom Con was genuinely devoted and she fully shared in her anxiety.

Then my father's appointment to the Paris Embassy put an end to all Con's hopes of a professional career. With Betty married, Con had to take her place and assist Mother in the official and social duties of the Embassy. These were martyrdom to Con, but she never complained. An additional sorrow also at this time was the death of her dog, a Chinese spaniel called Punch, which had been given to her in India. Punch had been her beloved companion in a way that only dog-lovers can understand.

I think her life from that day forward was one of uncongenial duty uncomplainingly performed, until in middle age she emancipated herself from domestic bondage and joined the Suffrage Movement. She was three times imprisoned and her health permanently impaired by forcible feeding. But through imprisonment her spirit at last found its freedom.

The following letter written to a friend gives Con's impressions of my character at this date:

Paris

You say no one ever tells you about Mimmel.[1] I will try and make up for this in future. If I didn't loathe the word, I should be inclined to call her an interesting person. She is what I call *safe*: one in whom I feel implicit trust that she cannot fail to come right in the end, no matter what she does. She has greatly improved since the summer, when her somewhat boyish ways and brusque manners attracted Betty and Gerald's attention and shocked them not a little. When they were here the other day, they both noticed the marked alteration for the better. From being rather less though still *very* shy, her manners are more gentle and respectful to grown-up people now. A few months ago she felt that she wasn't acting up to people's expectations of her, that her abrupt manner prevented people from loving her, and instead of trying to change herself she most naturally felt at first: If my natural way of talking and doing things offends people so that, even if they don't show it, I *feel* their reproach, it is no good trying to make them know me better—if they can't take me all round they won't like me at all. Then when the boys' holidays were over and her life settled down into a more quiet groove, she grew less excitable and had more command over herself.

She has made desperate struggles to become more sociable, to control her temper—and in every way possible

[1] Con's name for me.

to make herself more lovable. Once she felt she *could* please, she really tried to do so.

She still writes to his Rev every week, but I think he does not write so often to her. Probably he finds it difficult to keep up so frequent a correspondence with her, for I know her letters are as yet not at all interesting. She is still quite a baby in giving herself out and expressing her feelings, whether in talking, writing or anything else, but on the other hand she is far beyond her age—she is only just fourteen—in the receiving, taking-in way. The amount she reads seems to me something *extraordinary*, and she *remembers everything* she reads. Also her understanding of other people's characters, motives, etc. seems to me marvellous for her age. She is still very fond of coming down whenever we have people, which seems incompatible with the fact that she is desperately shy, but the truth of it is she is not so shy before several people whom she hardly knows as face to face with one who knows her pretty intimately. She is much more talkative on these occasions when there are people than she used to be, and the other night she chattered away to Mr. de Bunsen[1] for quite a long time. In spite of this love of seeing people, she has nothing of a flirt in her, and I think never will have. She always liked Paris, but I can see she is much happier here this year than she was last. She has given up the Cours—sort of French class—she used to go to and instead a young Frenchwoman comes to walk with her and teach her French. She is very nice and Emily seems to like her lessons with her. She says that Emily has hardly any English accent, which is quite true. She also goes to a private house for dancing lessons once a week, instead of to a public class, as she did last year. These take place in the evening at 8 o'clock, which makes it almost like an evening party.

My mother also reports to his Rev her opinion of my character at this date:

"Emily is still fat and stoops her head terribly, but I am going to make her have dancing lessons. She is wilful and

---

[1] Secretary of the Embassy.

often very cross to Paisy and Neville. I am in hopes she
will get all right.

"Emmie reads a great deal of anything and everything, but
gets it all mixed up in her head in rather wild confusion and
does not concentrate her thoughts as Betty used even at her
age."

In the Spring of 1889 my father was troubled with a
growth in his nose. He was at first inclined to think nothing
of it, but his Paris physician advised him to get further
medical advice when he went to London. A microscopical
examination was made which proved the existence of a
tumour of a malignant nature, and an immediate operation
was necessary. This operation, which took place in London,
proved perfectly successful, but the pain and slowness of his
recovery was increased by a curious oversight on the part
of surgeons so eminent as those who attended him. A
new surgeon, Dr. Butlin, being called in, a wad of lint was
discovered which had been stuffed into the cavity of the nose
and later forgotten.

I record very little of my Paris life during the early months
of this year. In one letter I mention that my father was very
superstitious about sitting down thirteen to dinner, and to
my great annoyance I was kept in reserve upstairs ready
dressed to be sent for if the failure of a guest reduced the
party to thirteen. On nights when there were no other social
activities we played whist, which I enjoyed, or paper games,
or my father read aloud. He was a beautiful reader and I
enjoyed much of what he read, but I have to confess that I
got terribly bored by his own long narrative poems, and
pinched myself hard to keep awake while the reading went on.

During the Paris years we would spend two or three of
the summer months in England, which included the boys'
holidays. During this time I always paid a visit to Booton,
staying for about a week.

I must now give a few particulars about Booton and his
Rev's home-life and surroundings. His Booton property
consisted of the Rectory and several acres of farm land. His
Rev was both squire and parson of the village and was also

constantly called in by the villagers to doctor their small ailments.

Booton was only about ten miles from Norwich but was completely rural in character. I have no idea of the size of his Rev's income, but it must have been a fairly large one, as he built the Rectory and rebuilt the Church entirely out of his own money. The Rectory was a copy of an Elizabethan manor-house, somewhat austerely furnished and without any particular beauty or comfort. The original Church had been a very cold and cheerless building, and his Rev decided to pull it down and build something more worthy of the worship of God. He was his own architect and clerk of the works, taking all his designs from books. The result was, as may be imagined, somewhat of a jumble and much too big for the parish, and yet it really did seem to embody the spirit of love and devotion in which it was erected.

To me as a girl, knowing nothing of architecture, it always seemed next to St. Paul's Cathedral to be the most beautiful building in England, and I loved to hear from his Rev every detail connected with it as it progressed. My husband, when he saw it in later years, maintained that it was "very naughty but built in the right spirit."

Mrs. Elwin was a sweet and lovely old lady. Her name, Fanny, seemed to fit her exactly. She had a delicious smooth, pink face surrounded by a lace cap tied under her chin. I think she suffered a good deal from his Rev's friendship's with "blessed girls," although I know that he was entirely devoted to her and desolated after her death. Whatever her feelings, however, she was always sweetness itself to me, and I was very fond of her, though a little afraid of her at the same time. I always found a packet of sugared almonds in my room to greet me and one or two exciting novels such as those of Wilkie Collins.

Meals at Booton were at rather peculiar hours. Breakfast was at 9.30, and lunch, the chief meal of the day, at 2.30, followed by tea at 4.30, high tea at 6.30 and a light repast of coffee and biscuits at 9.30. I used to think the food delicious, though my father maintained that it was uneatable. I remember that we usually had meat balls for high tea.

At breakfast on Communion Sundays his Rev would cut the bread into small squares, some for the communicants and some for his canaries.

The long mornings were devoted to work, the dining-room being used for this purpose. His Rev was very short-sighted, but he never wore glasses and would sit writing with his face turned sideways close to his work, one eye almost on the page. Every day he and I went for a walk hand in hand before tea—sometimes to the nearby market town of Reepham, but invariably to look at the progress of the Church, which took several years to build.

After the 6.30 meal we would settle down to the enjoy-ment of the evening, by a fire when it was chilly. His Rev always sat in a green velvet armchair with wings, and on my visits I would sit beside him, holding his hand while he read aloud or discoursed on some interesting topic. As Fountain, his grandson, used to say, "If only the green arm-chair could speak!" Mrs. Elwin would sit as far away as possible, occupied with her sewing and often muttering to herself, "May God forgive you," when she disapproved of some sentiment of his Rev's.

There had been three sons and a daughter of the marriage (his Rev acting as doctor and midwife at all four confine-ments). The daughter had died young of tuberculosis; the eldest son was also dead, but this son's son, bearing the strange name of Fountain, had been adopted by the grand-parents. He had married Amy Singer, a lovable and delight-ful person, and this marriage had brought much happiness to the Elwins, but unfortunately Fountain was very delicate and had to spend every winter away from Norfolk in some warm climate. During my summer visits, however, Fountain and Amy were usually at Booton, and added much to my happiness there.

The two other sons still living, Warwick and Edward, were both clergymen and both belonged to the extreme High Church party. Edward became a Cowley Father and died as a missionary in India.

After my visit to Booton this year of 1889, I write to his Rev:

3

"I am afraid you must think me very stupid that I don't talk to you more, but it is always difficult to do at first what one is not accustomed to. I never talk out what I think to anyone, not even to Mother, but rather more try and keep what I think to myself, so when I would like to talk out it seems difficult at first."

To which his Rev replied:

Booton Rectory, September 2

I told you that man for the most part has only the germs of qualities. Their development depends on himself. Babies, I believe, suck by instinct, but they have to learn to speak and walk, just as they later learn to read. So it is only by practice that you will be able to unfold to others your ideas. Often they are vague to ourselves until we begin to try to put them into words. I consider that we made a satisfactory beginning. I chiefly fear lest I should tire you when I talk to you by guess without any intimation from you of what you wish to hear. But you will soon repair the deficiency, if only in self-defence, and say to me, as Carlyle did to one Alingham, who frequented his house, "You have a tendency to be a bore, and should be on your guard against it."

His Rev paid us a visit to Knebworth later in September. Up to this date I had always addressed him as "Dearest Mr. Elwin," but on the 15th I write:

Knebworth House

My Darling Rev

I feel that I know you so well now that I cannot still call you "Mr. Elwin," I am sure that you will not mind my having put what I have. I wish I could tell you how immensely I enjoyed your visit and all the talks. You need never think that it tires me, for I think that I could hear you talk for ever and only enjoy it. But I hope that you will never say or think again anything about me having a better friend, for I never, never could have a dearer or a better one than you.

It is quite true what you said about my not liking Paris so much. I feel somehow that I want something more than I

can get there. In Paris there are always people in and out, and
it always seems to be one rush. I should like it very much if
it was only for a short time. I begin to feel at last that I want
something more. Even Sunday is not quiet, and we have not
got a nice church in Paris.

Booton Rectory, September 18

I like my new title far, far better than the old. "Rev" is
pleasant to my ear, "Mr." painfully formal. I hope for
beginnings without end similar to the last. You are only too
good to me.

Knebworth House, September 22

Father has said several times lately that he thinks I ought
to come out now. Mother will not hear of it, and she has
been saying that she would like to send me into a French
family when we get back to Paris. She has often said that she
would send me to school, when I had been extra naughty,
but as she has never done so, I do not feel afraid now that she
will send me into a family. She was very unhappy the other
night at the boys going back to school, but said that she
only wished that she could be sending me off to another.
Mother seems to think that I have determined not to do
lessons when we go back to Paris or to learn French; that
is why she suggested that I should go into a French family.
Even if it were possible I should not like to come out now;
for one thing I don't think that people would speak to me.
It makes me so angry in Paris; sometimes people are very
nice to me and then they ask how old I am, and when I say
fourteen, they talk a little in a patronizing sort of way and
then turn their backs. If they found that I was good enough
to talk to before they knew my age I can't see what difference
it makes when they find I am only fourteen. I don't see why
I should not come out when I am sixteen. I think I probably
shall.

Booton Rectory, September 30

I went last week to dine and sleep at the house of the
Lockers[1] at Cromer. I usually go from home reluctantly, and

[1] Frederick Locker had held posts in the Admiralty and was also a minor
poet. He had married in 1874 the only daughter of Sir Curtis Lampson, whose
name he added to his own. They lived at Cromer.

though the social part of the visit was very enjoyable I managed to extract a lot of discomfort out of a small mishap or two. My shirt collar is fastened to my shirt by studs, and lest I should lose one or both I always carry spare studs in my portmanteau. It is only for a single night (I said to myself on this occasion), and foolishly concluded that spare studs would be a superfluity. So I took none. Of course when I dressed for dinner, and was about to put on my shirt collar, one of the studs had disappeared. I searched for it everywhere and in vain. Dinner hour arrived and I grew desperate. The house was full of company, and with an establishment not equal to the occasion, I was aware from experience that I should ring the bell to no purpose. Nobody would have come. I went to the glass to see how I should look without a collar. A single glance was sufficient to decide the question. I perceived that if I went downstairs in that state I should be "the observed of all observers." The bright thought occurred to me that as my door opened upon a passage with a line of rooms I might catch sight of a benevolent lady's maid who would fetch a needle and thread and fasten my collar with a stitch or two. I looked out, and fortunately, as it seemed to me, there was the identical lady's maid I was in quest of, just stepping from one of the rooms. You must bear in mind that I was in a half-frenzied condition, and am short-sighted, and you will not then be surprised that the supposed lady's maid should be a young lady, a total stranger to me, who, having finished her toilet, was on her way down to dinner. What I said to her when I hailed her at the distance of some feet has entirely gone from my recollection. I expressed to her in some fashion that I wanted her, and instead of responding she fled like a greyhound. More confused than ever I once more searched my room for the missing stud, and came upon a bit of string in a corner. With this I made shift, in some loose imperfect muddling manner, to tie on my collar, and hoped that the top of my waistcoat would hide the string. I hurried downstairs, holding my waistcoat tight round my neck, resolving that I would contrive to get a place at dinner where I should not have to talk, and be able to give my whole attention to my collar and string. At the door

of the drawing-room I was met by Locker, who told me that
Mrs. Locker had asked Lady Darnley (the principal guest)
whom she would like to sit next at dinner, and she had said
she would like to have me. She must have had a presentiment
of my condition, and showed it by the persistence with which
she turned to me throughout the dinner, looking hard, as my
guilty conscience informed me, at my peculiar neck tie.
With one hand engaged I had a very meagre dinner, and
must have talked at random, my thoughts being centred on
my string, and altogether I had an uneasy time, the result
of the absurd deference we pay to conventionalities. All my
agitation might have been saved if I had had the courage to
say, I have lost my stud, and have come down without a
shirt collar. More mishaps followed, which I meant to tell
you when I began, but my paper is full and you have a story
without its end.

After I got back to Paris, his Rev wrote to me:

Booton Rectory, October 9

I have a word to say on the method of reading books in
general. Multitudes have no other purpose than to amuse
themselves, which is often purpose enough. We have a need
to be entertained. But it is folly to lose sight of the higher
objects of great works, and you should note as you proceed
any beauty of thought or language, any wise reflection, any
excellence of any kind, and then pause upon it, and try to fix
it in your own mind. What merely glides over your mind in
rapid reading, in which your sole aim is amusement, does
not stay there. Some sort of deliberative process is essential to
appropriating ideas so as to retain them. Much will vanish,
do what you will. But if you adopt the simple method I am
suggesting you will go to bed every night richer than you
got up in the morning. We oldsters learn nothing. The
ground has become stony, and the seed will not root itself.
Young brains are the fruitful soil, and happy you for whom
all you see, and hear, and read will, if you please to have it
so, produce a harvest.

Chapter Three

My letters during 1890 were also somewhat scrappy, with occasional reference to activities or to my thoughts and ambitions.

British Embassy, Paris, January 31

I feel it is beastly of me not to have written to you for such ages, but it is so difficult to write to you in the holidays. I always want a long time to write to you because I like to have a good talk with you, and I can't do that when the boys are in and out every minute. Then I feel quite a different person in the holidays. I can't write to you about things I don't think and care about, and in the holidays I don't think and care about anything. It is rather difficult to explain what I mean. I like to talk to you about my inner self and about things I can't tell to anyone else, and then sometimes I don't feel this want and it all seems outer self, and then I can't write to you. I feel so frivolous in the holidays, and I think of absolutely nothing but amusing myself. These holidays I have been worse than ever. I have been tremendously happy, but still I don't think it is right to let all the serious things go. I was not a bit good to the boys, and I only thought of myself. I could not think about Religion or even try and be anything but a beast. It may make one very happy for a time doing just what you like best but it does not last. It is much worse afterwards, for I have all gone back and I must begin at the very beginning again. I loathe myself so intensely and I get worse and worse instead of better.

However, I have made a good beginning by writing to you, I feel different already. When I am getting extra sick of my own badness it is so delicious to know that I am friends with somebody who is as perfect as you are. It seems to put new life into me only to think of you. The worst of Paris is, I either become like everyone else and think only of amusing myself, or else I am sick of it all and am miserable.

My mother once more sends his Rev a report on my character:

"Ems is improving very much, I think, and if it was not for a silly little way of grumbling about living abroad and putting up her back against other people and their opinions, I think she would be very charming, and is perfect with me and a good sister to her brothers. I think and hope she will be very nice looking."

In April, my mother, with my youngest brother, Neville, and myself made a tour of the castles of Touraine, which was rather suddenly interrupted by a telegram announcing the death of my grandmother, Mrs. Villiers:

Gd. Hôtel de l' Univers, Tours, April 16

Mother had a telegram last night to say that Gran is dead. I do my best to help Mother, but I am afraid I get very cross and speak so sharply to poor little Nevs. He is so very helpless when there is anything the matter with him, and makes such a fuss. I never can help being terribly aggravated with sick people who are not very bad. I always feel they make more fuss than they need. I know it is very wrong to feel this and I always make a fuss when I am ill myself. It is so hard, when you feel quite well yourself, to believe that other people are feeling ill. I am afraid my temper is getting worse again. The smallest thing seems to aggravate me so. As I told you last time, I like telling you everything that comes into my mind. It seems so despairing when I know what it is to be good, and I seem to be farther off from it every day. Sometimes I get to feel that it is no good trying any longer, and then I think of what you told me, that though we may seem to fail at first, it will get easier after a time. You can't think how I love telling you just these sort of things. I always feel better after I have been thinking of you and writing to you. I never can be thankful enough for my visit to Booton, and the joy of knowing you so well now goes on increasing. I should like to get a letter from you, but don't bother if it is an effort to you to write.

I forgot to tell you that before I left Paris I went to a play alone with Father. I felt that I got to know him a great deal better even being alone with him that short time.

The play was a French adaptation of *Much Ado About Nothing*. It was very badly acted and rather dull.

A great event to me that Spring was my confirmation:

> *British Embassy, Paris, May 2*

It is quite settled now that I am to be confirmed here. It is nice to be confirmed in the same church that I was baptized in, though I would rather have gone to England. I am now going to some confirmation classes once a week. I began yesterday. I don't think they will help me very much, but still it makes me think about those things and I like going. It may also suggest questions to ask you, though I have got plenty already.

The Bishop of Lichfield[1] and his wife were staying here the other day, and one evening they were talking with Con, and he said something which, if I heard aright, seems too absurd for words, but I was not paying much attention. He said that Nature had been made simply that our Lord might draw similes from it. That when He wished to teach the disciples by pointing to the comparison between His words and something in Nature, that He did not think of it as something new, but that Nature had been made from the beginning for the purpose that the Blessed Lord might compare it with His word. I don't think I can have heard aright, for it seems to me so utterly absurd.

Poor Father is not at all well today, and he gets so low. I do feel so unhappy sometimes that I can't get to know Father better. The boys talk to him quite easily and he talks to them and takes such interest in them, and I know it would be the same with me if I could only not be so silly. But I suppose it will come some day if I go on trying. I do feel, as

----

[1] Later Archbishop of York.

you so often tell me, that I am perhaps a little Mother's
favourite, and I do love her also better than anyone else and
I appreciate her love immensely, but still I wish so that I
could get to feel as easy with Father. I feel he must think I
don't care to talk to him and be with him. But however
slowly, I have got to know you so thoroughly that I feel the
day may come when I shall know him as well. I will hope so,
at any rate.

British Embassy, Paris, May 15

I think it is very naughty of you never to write to me. It
is so difficult to write to you when I never get an answer.
But I love writing to you, even when I have not much to say.
I hate writing letters generally, but when I write to you I
just put down what my mind is most full of, and then I like
writing. I am thinking a great deal about my confirmation
now, and I am sure you don't mind me telling you all I think
and feel about it, and I do love it so. I am so very, very glad
that I have got to be able to speak to you about religion and
those sort of things. Because I feel that I want to talk to
somebody and there are so few people whom I like to tell,
or who would care to hear. But I feel that you understand
me thoroughly and that it does not bore you to hear me.
The Bishop of Lichfield has been staying here again, and
he asked to have a talk about the Confirmation Service. It
was very nice of him to ask, and he spoke to me very nicely.
He said that we had all got our duties to God in everyday
life. I think it is often so difficult to see that there is any
duty at all in many things one does, when they seem quite
useless. But if one can feel that even in the most simple
things God has given us a duty, there is a reason for doing
it well.

As Knebworth House was let, we spent the summer
holidays at Bramfield, near Hertford, which had been lent to
us by my mother's aunt, Lady Bloomfield. From there I
write on August 8th:

"One of the chief delights of England is the thought that
you are here and that it is possible to see you. I think if you

came once to Paris I should think it a nicer place ever after. Each time I leave it I feel to hate Paris more. I wonder if we shall ever come and live in England for good again. It seems as if it was too delicious ever to be. I think it is a good deal always living in a town which I dislike so much, but it never feels really home anywhere but in England. Even a walk for exercise in the country is delicious. For one thing you can always go in comfortable clothes and no one ever sees you, and there is always something new to see in the trees and flowers. But in a town you have to be smartly uncomfortable and walk as everybody else does. And a walk cannot be really enjoyable in a crowd of people. We generally drive up to the Bois de Boulogne and take a very slow walk nearly always in the same place. It never seems to stretch your legs, or be any real exercise. I simply love sometimes to run or do something difficult. I think the pleasantness of a walk greatly depends upon whom you are walking with. I am always perfectly happy when I am by myself, and I am sure I could walk for ever with you to talk to me. I do try to make the most of Paris when I am there, but I sometimes get to hate it all more than I can say."

After the usual visit to Booton we spent a fortnight at Folkestone, and I write from there on September 22nd:
"We are going back to Paris tomorrow, and I feel as if I was going back to prison. Though now Knebworth is let I feel we have no home here, and Betty and Gerald are away, and we have been to Booton, so there is nothing left for us to do here. Also this is the nicest time of year, and I love the long winter evenings, for I can sit in my room and read and I love that. But still I cannot help feeling rather low, so I thought I would like to write to you, for I know you understand what I feel. I do love to think of Booton and of you when I am depressed, and then I feel that it is wrong to be depressed about anything when I have got something so far more precious than anyone else in having you for a friend. I love to tell you just what I feel, for I am sure you will understand. I will try and make the best of the nice things and not think about the rest. I feel it has done me good just

to write this to you. I long to give you a good hug to end
up, but as I cannot I must be content with telling you so, and
have an extra one when I see you next."

British Embassy, Paris, September 26

Everything here looks very comfortable, and I enjoy my
room more than ever. It is really quite Autumn here. Some
of the trees are quite bare and others are shooting again with
little green leaves. I am so glad, as it shows winter will be
here soon. I am an exception to most people and like winter
better than summer. Con says I like everything that is
disagreeable. I had a delicious evening to myself last night,
as there were some people to dinner. I have been reading
some of Wordsworth, as I love reading over the bits you
talked about at Booton. I think *Tintern Abbey* is quite lovely.
It seems to me that Wordsworth has got a most wonderful
way of putting into words feelings that one can't explain.
Mother has been reading the *Excursion* lately. She wanted
me to ask you if you cared for that much. It makes me feel
as if I had found a treasure when I come across a bit like
some in *Tintern Abbey*. You feel it has just said what you
wanted to say so much and could not.

I have already begun to have that horrid feeling here that
I am tied down on all sides. I hate feeling that however
much I want to be alone, I cannot, and that there are crowds
of people on every side. Father is very depressed again and
does not feel well. I don't think we are ever all of us well
together. Sometimes everyone seems to be ill and cross at
once, and then it is so delicious to think of Booton, where
no one ever seems to know how to be cross. I try not to be
cross, too, but it is so hard. I can't think what I did before
I knew you well enough to tell you all these sort of things. I
feel now as if I could not do without it. However cross I
feel, it helps me not to be when I think of you.

Booton Rectory, October 4

I see with great delight that your mind is developing
rapidly in all directions. You will get a finer education from

books rich in ideas than from millions of mechanical lessons in a school room. The lessons are a necessary prelude, but the moment you are ripe for self-education the Paisy routine is a waste of precious years. Your power of breaking an old habit, and of forming a new one, is grand. Your hands, your feet, your back, your head bear witness to what a resolute will can do for the bodily frame. The sweet temper with which you combated and conquered the provocations of the boys bears testimony to the firmness with which you can govern your moral nature. Now I perceive that you have taken your intellect in hand, and you will make it as submissive to your determination as the rest. You can only acquire the literary instinct young—that intuitive insight into its nicer beauties of which you have splendid examples in your own family, and upon which its fascination depends. What is an exquisite dish to a palate that cannot taste the refinements of flavour which constitute its excellence? Any common dish will do as well or better. I regret now that we did not snatch an half hour or two while you were here to go over a few short specimens of immortal prose or verse that we might mark the characteristics which distinguish them. You quickly in this way catch their peculiarities, and ever after recognize the same or the like whenever you come upon them. At our next meeting we will repair the omission, and in the interim if it does not displease you, we can do a little by letters.

British Embassy, Paris, October 7

Your letter was simply delicious and I will try and do my best in everything and think of what you say. Mother says that what you say is a real help to all of us, only it is so difficult to live up to. One part of your letter in which you say you are sorry we did not "snatch an hour or so to go over a few short specimens of immortal prose or verse" Mother read as "immoral." She says she felt confidence in you, but still wondered what you were going to read to me, and if you would begin with some of the worst parts of Zola!

When I write to you I almost feel as if I were back at Booton, and you were in the dear green chair and I was sitting by your side. Only I can't feel your hand which is the best part of the talk.

British Embassy, Paris, October 19

Mother has had an invitation from Lady Pembroke to go to Wilton at the end of November, and as she and Father both think it would be good for Con, they have accepted, and Con will go to England with Mother when she goes to Betty. I shall stay here with Father. I do dread it. I am sure Father will be very dear to me, but I can't amuse him a bit, and it is perfect agony to know how to talk. I daresay it will help me very much to get over my shyness with him, but it is so awful the beginning. What I dread most is that he will always be having people to dinner, and I never know when to stay upstairs. However, the time has not come yet and it may be much easier than I think, so it is no use grumbling now.

Though I don't get into the same tempers I used to, things seem to get on my nerves, and I speak so crossly and sharply. I think there is nothing so hard to control as one's tongue. I feel that if I could only keep my mouth shut I could bear anything, but it is having to say something gently when you are feeling irritated that is so hard. It seems to take away the only hold you have on your temper when you are obliged to speak. It is not the people themselves that irritate me so much, but I feel cross for no reason whatever and then when I open my mouth it all seems to come out. It is much easier not to do things when you have had time to strengthen yourself beforehand, but when I am tempted to say something cross there does not seem to be time to control it. But I *will* try and get over it.

British Embassy, Paris, November 11

I have just been reading a little of the *Religio Medici*. Just at the beginning he is talking about the Mysteries of Religion, and how he loves to lose himself in one. I think that if to think of all these mysteries only gives you a deeper faith, it is all well and good, but it seems to me that people who are always puzzling their heads about them and trying to find them out are very wrong. Because they can't understand

everything in Religion, they lose all their belief. Religion
would become so poor and mean if it all came within the
bounds of man's understanding. God has plainly revealed
everything that it is necessary for us to know, and why
should we try and find out what He has hidden from us? For
instance, people are always giving reasons and trying to
find out the origin of Sin. They would not be one shade
better for knowing it. It is sufficient that Sin is there. We
have got to fight against it, without trying to find out why
it came. People think it shows their cleverness by giving
explanations of these things, or trying to, but I think it only
shows their ignorance, and how very little they know about
them all. Though to think of all these mysteries never
tempts me to disbelief, still they puzzle me, and I think it
far better to let them alone.

British Embassy, Paris, November 25

I am getting on very well without Mother, though I miss
her very much. It is very funny, that though I no longer feel
so shy of Father, yet I still feel I can never say a word to
him. I think it is chiefly that he does not talk to me. You go
on talking to me, and then at last I feel I can answer you.
But I am always so afraid of boring Father, so I never seem
to know what to do, for if I don't speak I feel it bores him,
and also if I do. And then he very seldom begins talking to me,
and so I never know what to say. He has taken me to a lot of
plays, which has been nice. Tonight he is going to take me
to a little theatre where marionettes act, and I am rather
dreading it. First because we are going to dine with a lady
who is a great friend of Father's. For one thing she is French,
which always makes me shy, and then I feel so out of it, as
I can never talk and I feel such an idiot. She has got a
husband who I suppose will fall to my share, though as I have
never seen him and he is also French I shan't feel much
better off.

Second. They are going to act a play on the Nativity. I
don't know whether it is meant to be serious or not, but
anyhow I think it is horrible, and I hate going, but I don't
like to refuse Father when he asked me to go.

You see I am getting nearly as bad about writing as you
are. I have quite given up expecting letters from you, but
I know you have been ill and so I don't really want you to
write, only I can't help grumbling a little, as I do love your
letters so tremendously. A letter from you seems to wake
me up and make me better for a long time. I get into a sort
of sleepy state sometimes and I seem to do everything badly,
and then when I wake up it is only to see how bad I am, and
then I quite despair of ever being able to change all the
amount of bad there is in me. It seems to take out some of
the bad to write to you, only then I want your letters to put
good into me. I know it is difficult to begin writing again
when there has been a long break, but do begin again if you
feel well enough. Just write me anything so that I may see
your handwriting. Your handwriting is so like what you
are, so big and good and kind, that it does me good to
look at it. Sometimes I get to feel so wretched, because I
think I never can do anything right or good. Con is such an
angel and seems to make everyone happy and I feel I can't
do anything. I am not in the least jealous of her, for I love
her, only when there is someone very good near me, it seems
to make me feel extra bad. I seem to be just the opposite of
Con in everything; she is the most unselfish person I ever
saw, and I am horribly selfish. I do try not to be, and to
think of others, but Con has always done all the unselfish
things before I even think of them. Then it makes me so happy
when I have a letter from you, for I feel you understand me,
and love me though I am bad, and you know I try to be
better. I think I should actually become quite good if I were
to live long with you, for you are so good that you make
those about you good. Then that longing for someone to
love me gets so strong at times, and I feel extra cross and
selfish. I can't tell you what a comfort it is to me to feel you
understand all about that, for I sometimes feel I ought not
to feel it, and people would say I was much too young to
think anything about it. But one can't help one's feelings,
and you know there is nothing wrong about it. I wish I
could tell you how I love you for being such a dear perfect

friend to me and understanding me as you do. If only I could fly to England every now and then and have a good talk with you, how much happier I should be. I don't want always to be bothering you about writing to me, for I should hate to feel you did it if you did not want to, but still it would make such a difference to me if you would just write me a line sometimes.

You must think me frightfully discontented and grumbling, for in every letter I complain about something. But I think the real thing to complain of is myself, and it is because I am bad that other things seem bad. You say the right thing in a letter is to talk of oneself, so I think my letters ought to be right, for I talk of nothing else. I hope my grumbles won't make you think I am unhappy, for I am not a bit really. I do hope this cold weather has not made you ill again, and you won't take care of yourself. I like the cold so much and it makes me feel so well and in such good spirits. We have had skating for the last two weeks, and it is delicious.

Chapter Four

I always feel so thankful each year as this time [Easter] comes round again. Sometimes I get so careless and sleepy, and then when a time like this comes it seems to wake up all the good things in me, and to draw me up to God, and then I feel so much happier. How is it possible for anyone to feel indifferent to religion at this time? I cannot understand it. The account of the Blessed Lord's death in the Bible is one of the most beautiful parts, I think; there is something so touching in its simplicity which no other words could give. I do think it is such a great mistake the way people dwell on the physical sufferings of our Lord, as if they were anything compared to the mental agony. Last Sunday the clergyman said in his sermon that the fear of death was a very dreadful fear, but even in this our Lord could sympathize with us; that He had had a great fear of death, and had lived face to face with it all His life. I never feel that the Blessed Lord had any fear of death, or of pain, but that He only suffered from the agony of our sins which He was bearing. I think it is saying He was a coward to say He feared to die. And I never see any use in dwelling on any of the physical pain, for it does one no good, and it is so awful. I always feel that no one should fear to die, and yet so many, many do. I think life would be miserable without the thought of death, and it makes me happy to think I am not going to live for ever. People seem to think it is very dreadful that you should want to die, but I think it is right. I think to look upon death as the going home to God, and to long for it that you may be with Him for ever, is a right thought, and which ought to make you live a better and holier life. Of course there is the thought that we are sinners, and we do not deserve heaven,

and then one would fear to die. But that thought would never
make me better, for I could never be good through fear of
punishment, but only from love of God. Therefore the hope
of heaven helps one to try and be good.

British Embassy, Paris, May 14

Poor Mummy was very unhappy about the boys these
holidays, especially Vic. He is so rude and cross to her.
She says they never care to be with her and talk to her, and
that it is so hard they should be nice at school and horrid at
home. Of course it is very hard but at the same time very
natural. At school you can't be cross, as the other boys
would never stand it for a moment. You would never gain
anything by sulking but be laughed at, while at home if
you are sulky you find people give in to you and then you
naturally do it again. About the boys not liking to be with
Mother, it is really not true. Of course they like it, only
they are really quite children and like their games better.
They are very selfish from never thinking, and do not try
and be nice to Mother. Boys always hate talking, as they have
nothing to say, except about their games and their own
pleasures, and Mother wishes them to be interested in books
and more serious things. I am sure that as they grow older
they will enjoy being with Mother more and more. The
dreadful thing, though, is Vic being so rude. He had to go
to a French lesson every afternoon and that made him so
cross. I think it was trying at first, and afterwards when he
got to like it better, as I know he did, he was too proud to
say so.

I cannot understand Vic. At night when I go in to him he
sobs and says he is so miserable because he has been rude to
Mother, and he sees he makes her miserable. I tried to help
him as much as I could, and told him the things that help me,
and next day it is just the same, he is rude all day and cries
over it at night. I think he is very delicate and very nervous
and that has a lot to do with it. One mistake I think Mummy
makes is to talk about him to others when he is in the
room. I think you should never scold a person before others
or talk about them. The best way, it seems to me, is to let

him alone, and not notice his being in a temper when others are there, and then speak to him alone. I am awfully sorry about it, because poor darling Mum gets so unhappy.

What a dreadful thing a temper is and how miserable it makes everyone. Sometimes it seems to come over me like a cloud, the thought of how much misery and wickedness there is in the world. And then what a great blessing it is to feel that God is over all, and so everything must come right.

I think some explanation is needed here of the critical attitude which my mother now seems to have developed towards me, and mine towards her.

In my childhood, as I have stated before, she meant everything to me, and I loved her with all the strength of my rather passionate nature. She suffered much with migraine headaches, a complaint which I have inherited, and would often have to lie up in a dark room, speechless with pain. I loved just to sit in the dark by her side, wanting nothing except to be near her.

As I grew older, a natural reaction set in, especially after we moved to Paris. My mother had to lead a busy official life. I was a large ungainly girl, still wanting to cling round her neck. She would push me away and tell me not to bother her, and I would retire to my room in tears. I cried myself to sleep night after night and gradually hardened my heart and grew bitter. My favourite song was that of the Miller of Dee: "I care for nobody, no, not I, and nobody cares for me."

I resolved never to show my feelings to anyone and cultivated a hard exterior, so a rift grew up between us, as is evident in my letters to Elwin. I also became more conscious of a side of my mother's character which I had never noticed in my early youth. She had a very strong personality and liked to rule those about her. My sister Conny, who had a sweet and pliable nature, immediately yielded to opposition, preferring disappointment to a row. I was by nature a rebel, and opposition and scolding roused the devil in me. I am happy to remember that the day came when once more my love for my mother reigned supreme, and to the end of her life we were near and dear to each other.

In August we were in England, the last holiday that we
were all to spend together, and as Knebworth was still
let, a house had been taken near Ascot. But before the
holidays began I paid a visit to Booton. Back at Ascot I
write:

Frognal, Sunninghill, Ascot, Berks, August 2

You said you did not mind how often I wrote to you, and
I have such a longing to tell you all the little things. I feel it
will take all the sting out of my troubles if I can only tell them
to you. I am feeling much more cheerful now and think this is
a really nice place. There is one great drawback, however,
which is that it is very cockneyfied and there are so many
people about the roads that Mother says we may not walk
about alone. I always think that if there was any danger at
all it would be lessened rather than increased by the numbers
about. However, the grounds are very large and so we can
go for nice walks without getting run away with! I am sorry
to say that Mother is taking the opportunity of our being
here alone without the others for a good many lectures,
and it seems more impossible than ever to do anything quite
right. Besides the reading in the evenings, Mother insists
on the boys reading something well written every morning
for an hour, much to their disgust. Though she thinks it
will be instructive for the boys, it evidently is too dull for
her to bear, as she says her household duties will quite
prevent her reading to them herself, and so I am obliged to
do it. I asked her what book we were to read and she said
we must settle among ourselves. She did not mind if it was
even something amusing so long as it was well written, but
she thought a little poetry would be the best. Imagine me
sitting down to read the boys good poetry for an hour! Not
content with this Mummy also read them a lecture of
Froude's on the conduct of boys, at breakfast. The contrast
between what Froude thought boys ought to be, and what
boys are, called forth another lecture from Mother. You see
we are being well drilled. Mother asked me if you read out
loud much in the evenings when I was at Booton, also if you
talked about politics and books always at meals. I was able

to tell her that the subject of conversation was much more amusing than that.

It also strikes me more than ever what a very small amount of food is called stuffing. How shocked Mother would be at the generous helpings at Booton. It is difficult to know how to answer when you are accused of stuffing gooseberries when you have eaten six. I either have to stop eating them or call down a storm upon my head, both of which are extremely disagreeable. I see it was a good thing that I indulged well in strawberry mash at Booton, as I should have no chance of any here, even if there were any strawberries left, which there are not.

Mother has just been talking to me about the boys, and she seems so distressed because they do not care more for reading. I told her I think there is nothing to grieve over in that, it will all come in time, and it would be most unnatural in a boy always to be sitting down to a book. Mummy says, though, that nothing can come without practice and unless they try and read now they will never care for it. But I know they read a certain amount at school and they naturally prefer playing games to reading in the holidays. Anyhow, you cannot force a boy to read, and I think it is a thing that can only be done when you love it. The master says Neville's English is so very bad, and Vic has not at all a good report either, so I'm afraid they will have to bear a good many lectures.

Frognal, August 5

Betty and Con arrived here yesterday, and Father this afternoon. Betty seemed to bring sunshine into the place at once, and to put everyone in good humour. Father has also arrived in excellent spirits, looking very well and seems pleased with everything. I never can help feeling rather low, though, the first few days of the holidays. First, because as I told you, Mother seems pushed into the background when Betty and Father are talking, and they either don't listen to what she says or else are rather inclined to laugh at it. Then I never can help feeling it when Father laughs and scoffs at things which seem to me so sacred, and he always seems glad to have an opportunity of running down religion. I don't mean that he openly talks against it, but there is that sort of feeling running through so much of what he says. I know perfectly well that Father does not mean half that he says, but it makes me unhappy all the same. Con once said to me what I think is true, that some men from their very love of truth feel anything is better than the sort of hypocrisy of what are called religious people. But still I feel it is so easy to tell real religion from what is put on, and there is no reason to put away the real thing because you do not approve of the false. Anyhow there are some things which Father seems doubtful about, therefore cries down, and which seem to me so very easy and natural to believe. For instance with prayer. Father talks as if it was no use praying because what is to happen will happen whether we pray or not. I feel the very fact of the Blessed Lord having told us to pray contradicts that idea. But besides that, though we believe that God knows all things and what will happen to us, it does not force us to act one way or the other. I feel it is rather stupid to be unhappy about this, for I feel Father does not mean what he says, and also, as you often tell me, it is sure to come back to him one day. But still it always makes me sad to think of people who cannot make religion a part of their lives.

On August 7th his Rev wrote to me:
"I begin to reproach myself with not having properly cultivated you while you were here. The more carefully flowers are tended, the more liberally they are treated, the more they flourish. So do weeds, and in the application of the system to human beings everything turns upon the question whether you are a flower or a weed. Each develops according to its nature. Fostered weeds get bigger, and flowers likewise. I have settled to my own satisfaction that you are a flower, and act in some measure accordingly, only I ought to have done better. The Methuselahs justify their perversities by saying, "I am too old to change." Old Methuselah as I am, I am hoping to mend. This is the thought uppermost with me as I read your letter, in which there is

as much of your presence as a letter could contain. After all the great subjects we talked out fresh topics spring up, and would do to the end of time. You are right in your confidence that they do not bore me; they have the extremest interest for me, and I have a boundless delight in telling you all I know or think about them. I bless you for the place they have in your inmost being. I would have added something to what you say of prayer if I were not expecting to speak it, the tongue being a preferable instrument to the pen. I ought not to leave home, but I have a longing to see my dear Lady,[1] and the rest of the magic circle, which is irresistible, and from Tuesday the 18th to Friday the 21st I will try to forget that I have any duties and responsibilities, and will abandon myself to pleasure. In the meanwhile, the more letters you write me the greater debtor I shall be to you, and the bigger the debt the more I shall delight in it, as I do at this moment in the account as it stands, with a monstrous balance against me. You must fill up the blanks in my shabby, disjointed notes, the best you can."

Frognal, August 8

I feel so happy today to think that you are really coming that I don't know what to do with myself. I have not been able to settle down to anything, but long to rush about and shout with joy. Do you ever feel that your happiness is so great that the world will hardly contain it? That is how I feel always when I am at Booton, and I have felt it today at the mere thought of seeing you again.

I see more and more how false it is when people say that you ever tire of what you love. I have just had a delicious long bit of you, but I only feel more longing than ever for more.

Frognal, August 12

How delicious to think that in less than a week now, I shall see your dear face again. Everyone has a lot of troubles and we are counting on you to put everything right. Mother is rather worried about the expenses and also about the boys.

---

[1] As he always called my mother.

She is distressed because Father does not notice them more, and they him. He was speaking about it to Betty the other day and said he really could not take any interest in cricket and what they seem principally to care about. I think it is far better to leave them alone and in no way force the boys to go to Father. I am sure that directly they want him or have any interest which he can enter into they will go to him. I feel you will help all this so much and tell Mother that she need not worry.

Father, for no reason at all that I can see, except that he was feeling very well and in excellent spirits, which doctors always seem to think a sure sign that you are very ill, has been taking a cure since he came here, which is making him wretched. He has got a sort of nettle-rash on his face and hands which irritates him very much, and he says he is certain he will get yet worse. So I am sure you will help to raise his spirits too. I don't know if Betty and Con have any troubles but I am sure no one wants you as much as I do.

Booton Rectory, August 14

Your letter which came yesterday would have made a sick man well had I needed the restorative. There can be no better practice in style than letter-writing. And as advances in youth come by starts it is a fact that you have just made a stride forward. You have in a high degree the two qualities which are the basis of all good writing—you know exactly what you want to say, and you say it with perfect clearness. The finish will come of itself as you get older. Already, and probably without your being conscious of it, there is great improvement. Letters are best not composed; they should be the free runnings of the mind; and the force and nature of your letters to me are worth a million artificial exercises which have neither a fault nor a merit.

Some qualities in books are appreciated by all persons, educated or uneducated, such as a thrilling story. Other merits are more subtle and can only be relished or even perceived by cultivated tastes. The faculty of judging will rapidly spring up in you, and you will henceforth be able to thread the labyrinth for yourself, and intuitively pronounce

upon whatever comes before you. You are precisely the
right age for the process. Too young, the mind has not
attained to sufficient intelligence; too old, its plasticity is
gone, and you never acquire the insight which is a natural
growth at its proper season. I enjoyed what you said on the
subject—enjoyed especially that priceless honesty which
makes you refuse to adopt the conventional chatter that
pronounces on books without understanding them. Honesty is
your habit in all things, and is a treasure beyond reams of
literature. But literature is a treasure also, and that too you
will possess.

Frognal, August 14

Gerald [1] was so dreadfully shocked with the way the boys
behave in the evening, as they generally throw themselves
on to a sofa and go fast asleep. Mother was vexed with me
because she said I encouraged them, which I'm afraid I had.
What I do think rather hard in the evening is that Betty and
Father play a game by themselves, or else talk, and if anyone
else speaks above a whisper they are immediately scolded.
Betty says let the boys go and amuse themselves somewhere
else, or go to bed if they are sleepy. That is, of course, quite
true, but I feel they are by themselves all day, and hardly
ever see Mother and Father, and in the evenings is the only
time to make them sociable. I think it is a good thing to
make them talk more and interest them in what the others
are talking about. Of course if they never do talk they will
not get into the way of it. Betty had a talk with Vic yesterday, and she says he was very nice, and he certainly did try
much more yesterday. I think Gerald is very easily shocked,
and he has such a great idea of what the boys ought to be.

After the visit from his Rev to Frognal, I write on August
21st:
"I cannot tell you what a gloomy day it has been to me
without you. I can only go and sit in the places where we
sat together and think of all the talks until I could hardly
bear to think that you were gone. I think we made as much

[1] My sister's husband had now joined us.

use of our time as we possibly could have done and we did not waste a minute.''

Booton Rectory, August 24

I have always found that when I see the persons, after an interval, for whom I have a special love, they appear more delightful than I pictured them. It is probable that they have actually grown in charm, and the power of appreciating it may have also grown in myself. That is a speculative question which I need not try to settle. The important point to me is that every member of the family appeared more fascinating than before, with the result that the enjoyment of seeing and hearing and living among them was intense. My history of the two days and the bits of a first and fourth has been the staple talk for three evenings, and we have not done yet. To be sure we get into digressions when we find ourselves in Windsor Forest, or on Ascot racecourse, or, above all, when we are in the midst of personalities, each of which spreads out into a species of biography in three volumes. We continue to talk lovingly of your love of fun, which I love also. Youth without merriment is ghastly.

Frognal, August 24

It is a great bore, whenever I try to do anything useful I fail utterly. A little time before you came here I was left to make the tea as Con was out. No sooner did I touch the kettle to pour the water into the teapot than it tumbled over and the boiling water took all the polish off the floor. On Saturday we had some visitors to tea, and Con having gone to Woodlands [1] Mother said I must make the tea again. I was just saying to Betty I wondered what would happen this time, when as I touched the kettle the whole tray fell over on the floor. The boiling water went all over poor Betty's foot, the milk jug was broken and its contents spread all over the floor, and, to add to the confusion, the spirit out of the lamp for boiling the kettle was all on fire. Betty and I tried with all our might to blow the fire out, which only made it much worse. The visitors rushed about calling

[1] Mrs. Earle's house in Surrey.

"Smother it, smother it." Of course there was nothing to smother it with. I rushed to get something and tumbled down, which I always do when I am in a hurry. I hoped no one would see me in this confusion, but when it was all over everyone asked if I was hurt, which annoyed me very much. The fire was at last put out with a shawl, and no damage had been done. Thanks to the visitors I escaped a scolding which I am sure I should otherwise have got. I am determined never to make the tea again if I can help it. It was a very comic scene and I laugh now when I think of it, but still it makes me angry with myself that I can never do anything properly. The more care I take the clumsier I am. If I am told to take a message I invariably forget it, and the very fact of trying to remember it drives it out of my head. I never can help laughing when I do these sort of things, which only makes it worse, as people think I don't care in the least. But I feel I don't half so much mind being scolded now I can tell you the little things. The joy of having someone who will never scold me gets greater and greater. With most people it seems to me that getting more intimate with someone means that you have the privilege of scolding.

To this letter his Rev replied:
"In early boyhood I read a story called, I think, the *Bashful Man*. The precise incidents have faded from my memory, but they ran something in this style. In his nervousness at a party, the bashful man upsets an inkstand. In his fluster he hastens to sop it up with his pocket handkerchief. His agitation of mind has thrown him into a perspiration, and instinctively he wipes his face, smearing it with ink, and the company bursts into fits of laughter at the ludicrous appearance he presents. What follows I forget, but his trials did not end here, and the moral of the whole was that however becoming may be a certain measure of bashfulness, too much of it leads to awkwardness and mortification. Instead of resolving not to make tea again, you should ask as a favour to be allowed to make it every day for a week. You would never be scared by a tea-kettle any more."

Frognal, August 29

This morning Vic came down to breakfast grumbling that there were all the same things for breakfast and he could not eat them, and why could there not be more. This made me so angry, as it always does when I hear the boys grumbling over their food. I told Vic that I thought it was absurd that he should grumble about the food when everyone else was contented with it. This made him angry and he said he was not speaking to me, and if he did not like the food, he did not see why he should not have some more. Mother told me afterwards that I had irritated him, which I ought not to have done, that it was just what Father would have said, and that the boys could not help imitating him. As I said to her, in many things they could not do better than be like him, but one should never try to copy people's faults, and grumbling over food is certainly a fault in Father, and would be a much worse one in boys. I daresay I ought not to say anything to the boys though, as my being so near their own age makes them angry, but I simply cannot help it when I see them doing the things, and Mother never says anything. I don't in the least mind their being angry with me, if I think I ought to tell them about things, but sometimes I think it is not my business and makes them worse. Mother always tells me to talk to them and help them, and then if I tell them they are not perfect she does not like it. Do you think it is wrong of me to interfere? There is another thing in Vic which always makes me angry, and that is the way he speaks to the servants and those whom he thinks beneath him. I am sure it is a great deal Eton that gives it, but it is a great fault. They were both asked to go and play cricket with another boy here, and came home so cross because two *cads*, as they call village boys, had played too. I asked why that made a difference, and they said they could not bear to play with boys who wore dirty shirts, and who talked the whole time. I only tell you this as an instance, and it seems to me so wrong. Betty says that though she also thinks it a great mistake, it is a good thing for the boys to keep their position and not be too familiar. I quite see that, but I can't see why either thing should be done. It always makes me so angry and ashamed when they speak rudely that I don't know what to do. But in spite of all these things both boys have been most wonderfully better this holidays and I only tell you about the things as they concern me.

On August 28th, I write that Mother, Vic and I have been staying for a night with the Blunts [1] at Crabbet. This is my first mention of a family with whom I was later to become very intimate. I describe their only daughter, Judith,[2] as she appeared to me on first acquaintance, as being: ". . . rather a peculiar girl. Her only amusements are riding and driving, shooting and wrestling. I went there with a quaking heart, as she particularly likes wrestling with her friends. She being very strong they generally come off badly. I determined to own myself a dreadful coward, and refuse to amuse myself in her way. This morning they all went out to shoot rabbits and begged me to take a gun. I refused, as I was afraid I might hit a rabbit by mistake."

Booton Rectory, August 31

The distinction between courage and foolhardiness is important. Courage is shown in braving dangers for a worthy end. Foolhardiness is running risks needlessly for an insufficient purpose or none at all, and is expressly condemned by our blessed Lord: "Thou shalt not tempt the Lord thy God." The cowardice which shrinks from foolhardiness is an instinct implanted in us for our protection. Not to obey it is a vice. I respect the moral courage which avows that it is afraid to play with edged tools, with upsetting spirit lamps, with reckless driving, or any of the other rashnesses of harebrained men. No one would be numbered in the list of heroes for pranks like these. Such persons have a nearer affinity to lunatics.

Frognal, September 1

Vic says he wishes his sisters would go out shooting with him instead of always saying "How horrible" whenever he

---

[1] Wilfrid Blunt, the poet, and his wife, Lady Anne, who was Byron's grand-daughter.
[2] Now Baroness Wentworth.

kills anything. Todd [1] was to accompany him this morning, and he asked me why I would not go out shooting with them. I replied that I did not like to kill rabbits. He then said, "It is very wrong not to enjoy the fullness of the earth, which the Lord has given us; to show you I am right, it puts in the Bible—'O rise, Peter, kill and eat.' We are the salt of the earth and rabbits were made for us to kill and eat, and it is a waste of nature if we do not do so." I nearly choked with laughter.

Booton Rectory, September 2

I shall answer no more Biblical questions. I refer you to Todd. I was afraid to read aloud his interpretation at breakfast for fear Fountain,[2] whose sense of the ludicrous is extreme, should choke and be ill afterwards. I kept the fun for the evening, and laughter being contagious, we kindled fit after fit in each other till we were exhausted. When at last one grows grave, it is curious to reflect that Todd seriously believes that one of the primary purposes of religion is to stimulate the bloodthirsty and gluttonous propensities of man, and that to the ordinary pleasure of the sport he joins the self-satisfied conviction that he is discharging a duty.

Booton Rectory, September 3

A woman's fullest ambition might be satisfied in the exercise of feminine qualities. I have in mind at the moment Wordsworth's little poem beginning, "She was a phantom of delight." He describes her under three aspects—as she appeared at first sight, "upon nearer view," and upon thorough knowledge. The verses are not perhaps equally felicitous in expression throughout, but take it as prose or poetry his summary of the endowments he ultimately finds in his "perfect woman" are a splendid model, true to life. She has

"The reason firm, the temperate will,
Endurance, foresight, strength and skill;

[1] My father's valet.
[2] His Rev's grandson.

A perfect Woman, nobly planned,
To warn, to comfort, and command;
And yet a Spirit still, and bright
With something of angelic light." '

In the first couplet you have the qualities of the woman, in
the second the service they render to the man in her special
relations with him, in the third the estimate he forms of her:
though human she is more than mortal and has something of
the angel in her also. That is the aspect in which a superior
woman invariably appears to the man who can estimate her
rightly.

Frognal, September 4

Your letter which you seem to think was dull could not
have been more delicious than it was and you have shown me
clearly what you intended to. I think nothing can be more
disagreeable than a woman who tries to be like a man, for
she loses all the charms of a woman without gaining any of
the advantages of a man. And instead of always grumbling
that she cannot do what men do, I think women might feel
proud of the power they have over men, and determine that
it should be put to a right use. I have often read the bit of
Wordsworth that you quote, and am very fond of it, and now
I shall love it more and feel all that you have told me as I read
it. You are the only person who ever made me feel how
grand a woman's life may be. I used to think that men were
the only ones who ever did anything great, and I wished
that I was not a woman, but since I have been friends with
you, I feel that a woman can be as great in her way as any
man. And you made me long to be a perfect woman, and
though I know I shall fall far short of the model, yet in your
letter today you have shown me so clearly what a perfect
woman ought to be, that I know now what to aim at, and
will try very hard to come somewhere near it. I am afraid I
have not made a very good beginning, and as I told you, I
get clumsier every day. There being a few people here today
I took the opportunity of falling in the garden on my knees,
which made me feel very silly. My ankles have a horrid
habit of giving way just when I want them most to support

me. I can't help laughing when I do these stupid things, but all the same they make me very angry with myself.

Booton Rectory, September 4

I ought to have told you yesterday that I noticed this year how much your abruptness had diminished, not to me only, but generally. It would probably wear away of its own accord, almost without your being conscious of the change, though it would not be safe to trust to this, and your efforts will be speedier in their action. Personally, I often contract a liking for the peculiarities I associate with one who is otherwise dear to me, and I had grown to be rather pleased when you answered me with a snap. But the effect upon the world at large in matters like this is the proper test, and no doubt your intonation ought to be in harmony with your mind, or it misrepresents and calumniates you.

Frognal, September 5

You made me miserable by saying that I snap at you, even though you say you like it. If I am snappy to you, how awfully cross I must be to people I don't care for. I suppose the only thing is to watch myself and try very hard not to do it.

We went out to tea the other day and so I began to try then. Mother said I was to try and gush a bit, as they were relations and our relations always gushed so dreadfully themselves. But it is a thing I cannot do. I say all the right things, how delighted I am to see them and how beautiful their house is and a few other things of the same sort, but try as I will, they always come out in a tone of voice which is anything but cordial. The people we went to see the other day had seen me some years ago in London and asked if I remembered them. I said "No, I don't," as I always make a point of never saying I remember people when I don't, as it leads to such endless muddles and they always find you out in the end.

Mother says it is very rude. I think that was the only wrong thing I did the other day. When I go out to tea, I don't have the chance of upsetting a kettle, but I generally manage to upset my teacup into my lap.

Strong expressions in familiar letters must not be interpreted too literally. I did not mean that you snapped at me
with the feelings of a dog who intends to bite. You never
spoke one unloving word to me, not one in the days before
your words grew loving. The thought I had in my mind in
calling your abrupt intonation a snap was to let you know
that personally I liked the manner at its worst because it
was yours, and carried with it an impress of the speaker.
Other people who have not the same associations with you
that I have would be apt to fancy the manner was an index
to your feelings, and might misjudge you altogether. I am
not under any concern about it now. Next to Wordsworth's
"She was a phantom of delight" is a little poem in which he
compares the song of the nightingale and the coo of the
stock-dove, and he gives the preference to the coo. I fully
believe that with a little practice you will speak in the tone
of a stock-dove. Already the final stanza of Wordsworth's
verses fits you exactly.

> "He sang of love with quiet blending,
>   Slow to begin, and never ending;
>   Of serious faith, and inward glee;
>   That was the song—the song for me!"

Wordsworth says that the stock-dove's song blended with
quiet, because he selects a spot with quiet surroundings, and
"his voice was buried among trees." "Never ending" love
is not always "slow to begin," though it may have a better
security for endurance when it has satisfied itself that the
qualities which attract it are themselves lasting. Never
ending, however, it was with the stock-dove, and he sang
not only of love, but "of serious faith, and inward glee."
Love, serious faith, inward glee, are not these Emmie's
characteristics, the life of her life, the essence of her being?
These were the characteristics which in Wordsworth's
estimation constituted the charm and excellence of man.
"That was the song—the song for me!" Strike out the
"serious faith" and what becomes of the other two? The
faith is the foundation of all the rest, and I never cease

5

rejoicing with all my heart and mind that you have it to the full.

Have you discovered that Booton has not materials for a Daily News? Would not a weekly be preferable? Or shall we try a monthly? Last year it was an annual and even that did not answer. To open your paper expecting news, and to find a dry rambling dissertation upon a stanza in Wordsworth's poems, must be a severe exercise of temper. It would be to me. I have an unwritten volume awaiting our next conversation, but it is too big for a periodical, and the smaller matters are not big enough. Only perhaps as there is love at the bottom of the whole you will make out with that and decide, while you are in England, for a Daily News, with fitful interruptions after all.

Frognal, September 7

Of course I decide for a Daily News. Whatever you tell me is most delicious, whether it is about Booton or Wordsworth's poems. I think on the whole I prefer the Booton news, for it seems to bring all you are doing more closely before me. There is only one thing in your letter today which made me unhappy and that is when you say I shall decide for a Daily News while I am in England. Do you mean to stop writing to me when I get back to Paris and shall want your letters more than ever? Now that I have so many from you, the thought of getting none is awful to me. My only hope of bearing the life in Paris bravely now is that I shall have your letters to help me, and if they stop I don't know what I shall do. I shan't feel happy now till you tell me that you will go on writing whether I am in England or in Paris.

Booton Rectory, September 8

My paper this morning would make a hypochondriac happy. I have no intention of dropping the correspondence. Wherever you go my letters will follow you as long as you care to have them. The pleasure of writing to you is one great motive, but I have another, and if possible, a stronger. You are at the age when minds commonly take their final bent. Some stagnate, some grow frivolous, some expand and

develop the qualities of heart and mind which ennoble man.
All your aspirations are towards what is good and lovely,
and considering what I could best do, in my small way, to
help you to mature your gifts I could see but one thing,
which was to write to you constantly, not for what I could
say to you, but for what my letters would lead you to say to
me. Education resolves itself into self-education. Nothing is
of the least avail except in so far as you exert your own
powers, whether intellectual or moral. You and I have
endless sympathies, and let me touch ever so lightly upon
any one of them, and it sets your mind working in the same
direction, and you pour out your thoughts to me in your
replies, which thus becomes mental exercises which bring
you forward apace. It seems essential to your progress that
you should have one writing friend to draw you out, and
since you, in your loving kindness, find me sufficient for the
purpose at present be sure I shall not abandon you. My big
love for you would not deserve the name of love unless I had
always in view your lasting welfare, and was bent upon
doing my utmost to advance it.

Frognal, September 8

Wonderful to say, I passed the day yesterday without
doing anything very clumsy or saying anything very rude.
One visitor was a young man, who had been out to the Cape
with the Lochs [1], and of whom they were very fond. I felt
I ought to ask a lot of questions about them, but it is very
difficult to show interest in people when you do not feel it
and I cannot take much interest in the Lochs. The girls do
all the right sort of things, they play and sing and draw
beautifully. The more I hear of other people's accomplishments the more proud I am that I have none. I can never be
asked to show off before people for I have nothing to show
off, unless it is my stupidity, and I generally manage to
show that off without being asked. I think Mother is rather
distressed at this. She was saying to me last night that she
was sure I would do nothing if left to myself, and that I
should get so bored with myself, and that I never found

[1] My mother's twin sister and her husband. He was Governor of the Cape.

things to interest me. I told her that when I was obliged to have governesses and to do things which did not interest me, I then had no time to make interests for myself, and so of course I was bored. But that now I should have the whole day to myself I could do no end of things, and should never get bored.

I don't believe that a governess has ever taught anyone a single thing that was worth knowing. I can't think where Mother has got the idea that I will not do anything if left to myself; it is just because I hate wasting time that I want to get rid of the governesses.

Frognal, September 9

As Father and Betty were talking so much about it, I am reading *Martin Chuzzlewit* again. I read it once before, but have forgotten a good deal, and I think I always enjoy a book more the second time than the first. I think it is delightful and quite one of the best. I hate Dickens when he tries to be pathetic, but all his comic parts are simply excellent. Mother and Con both say they cannot read Dickens, he is so dreadfully vulgar, and the people seem to do nothing but drink. But I suppose in Dicken's time people used to drink far more than they do now, and very few of the characters are meant to be real ladies and gentlemen, and so I do not mind their being vulgar. I am sure they are not half so vulgar as a great many modern books which people delight in, and I think all modern books horribly dull, which Dickens certainly is not. What I do not understand is that Mother reads all the new French novels and Rudyard Kipling, and those sort of books, and though she says they are so horrible she can hardly get through them, she will go on reading them. I suppose it is because she likes to read what everyone else is reading. But how if you cannot read Dickens because of the vulgarity you can enjoy Rudyard Kipling is more than I can understand.

Booton Rectory, September 10

I have always held *Martin Chuzzlewit* to be Dickens's masterpiece. When the vulgarity of a character is part of the

comedy it does not offend. It adds to the fun. But it revolts
when the intention of the author is to pass it off for good
manners and fine feeling. All the persons in his books, high
and low, who are supposed to behave with propriety, repel
you. Their sentiment, their pathos, their bearing, their
habits and especially their love-making have a taint which
disgusts you. Like the perpetual drinking, the vulgarity
belonged to the class from which Dickens sprung and was
deeply ingrained in him. He never got rid of it. He could not
even relish the company of gentlemen. His chosen associates,
the people with whom he hobnobbed, were nearly all of the
type he describes in his books. But I must confess to enjoying
the farcical humour of his characters when it is at its best.
And though he sacrifices truth of character to heighten the
fun yet there is usually nature at the bottom, and that of a
species which we are willing should be made ridiculous, or
good-naturedly comic. Continue your enjoyment, and if fresh
reflections occur to you, continue your comments; which
are enjoyment to me. I tried Rudyard Kipling and broke
down.

Waste no time in considering what you shall read. Fasten
on the first book that promises to interest you. You will
gradually work your way into a just estimate of authors, and
will be carried on from book to book till you are saturated
(not satiated) with literature. You are reading already
with new intelligence, and nothing which is not worthless
will be thrown away upon you. I was surprised to find how
many poems you were acquainted with, and how keenly and
justly you appreciated their beauties. You have quietly and
unobtrusively done more for yourself than people would
imagine until you began to exchange minds with them as
you have done with me. I believe it would be advantageous
if you and I always kept a book in reading, and wrote about
it to each other. Is there any you fancy? I would gladly adopt
it. You ought to be Wordsworth's perfect woman before you
marry; the undertaking is great, and you may have only a
short time in which to prepare yourself. We cannot begin
our mutual instruction plan too soon, or persevere in it too
steadily.

Frognal, September 11

I am delighted to hear you say that you broke down in Rudyard Kipling. I thought his books so dreadfully vulgar, besides being dull. People seem so fond of horrors now and such unnecessary horrors. All the new French books which are so much talked about, I believe are perfectly dreadful, from what I have heard said about them. *Martin Chuzzlewit* is a very grim book, and yet it does not disgust you, and you feel there is some reason for the horrors, but the French writers seem to try and make it disgusting, by collecting all the misery and wickedness they can think of, and then piling it up together, with nothing to relieve the horror.

When Aunt T.[1] was here yesterday they were talking about Dickens and saying how impossible he was to read now, and I said I thought some of his books were delightful. Aunt T. said, "Oh yes, that is quite the right feeling at your age, just what you ought to think." This is a stupid little thing to tell you, only it made me angry. Of all the things in the world I do hate being told that I do things because of my age. It seems to imply you like reading Dickens because you think it is the right thing to do. For one thing I have no idea of reading him because he is supposed to be a good writer, but because I enjoy his books, and then if I did what everyone else did I should abuse Dickens and read Rudyard Kipling. It seems absurd to notice it but I hate being told my reasons for doing things especially when they are quite wrong.

Booton Rectory, September 11

You must judge your letters by their effects, and to know their effects you must be told them. I revel in them, and most of all in that which I received today. I will go on to say why I delight in them, and then you will perceive that I have good reason for my glow. For they are the transcript of your mind, of a mind drawn to whatever is holy, praiseworthy, and beautiful, full of generous emotions, teeming with activities, eager to attain to what it admires, and in and over all there is the bloom and fervency of youth. When a nature

---

[1] Mrs. Earle.

like that spreads itself out without reserve day by day, no
character in fiction depicted by a master's hand could rival
the living example in interest and charm. Add that you owe
the daily history to the fact that the letter-writer has chosen
you to be her familiar friend and helper and that the
whole comes steeped in her love expressed or implied, and
manifestly no one with a heart or a conscience could read
your daily letter with any other feeling than daily gratitude
and joy.

When we are greatly loved we do not believe we deserve
it, but are stimulated to try and deserve it.

Frognal, September 15

I had to make the tea again yesterday as the others were
out, and though I did not succeed in upsetting the kettle, yet
I went out of the room and forgot all about it, and it boiled
all over on to the table and floor, for which I was much
scolded when the others came back. Poor Con said nothing,
but looked a great deal at the mess I had made. Mother sent
me with two messages during the day, both of which of
course I quite forgot to give. She said, which is quite true,
that I was of no use whatever. There are very few things
which I can do properly, and those few are of no use to
anyone.

Father is still very low and unwell, I am afraid, and he says
the food is too nasty to eat. I suppose he cannot help it now,
but it makes me feel unhappy each time I hear the food called
filthy. And it makes me feel angry too. I try not to be but
I cannot help it. I don't mind so much when it is only
Father, for I feel he cannot help it, but when the whole family
begin saying the food is disgusting and uneatable, I long to
get up and leave the room. I am glad that I can eat anything
and enjoy it, for then wherever I am I can be happy. It always
makes me angry to hear people complaining, whether it is
about food, or pain or anything else, though I know I do it
myself.

Frognal, September 18

Though I laugh to you about my carelessness and stupidity,
I do feel that it is **a** great fault, and I will try my best to get

over it. I am always angry with myself when I do stupid things, but being scolded for them does not help me to do better another time, and so I tell you about them, and you always help me. I enjoy the way you scold me, and like telling you all my faults for the pleasure of the scolding. When other people are angry with me, it only has the effect of making me angry in return, for they always talk as if I had done the things on purpose. But when you tell me in your dear way to conquer a fault, I determine to try with all my might to do so. I know I forget messages because I do not think, but I seem to upset kettles when I am trying hardest not to do anything careless. My hands and feet seem to get so dreadfully in the way when I want to use them, I seem to lose all control over them. Last night at dinner I just put out my hand to get something and of course knocked over a glass and smashed it to pieces, which made Mother scream. The funny thing is that I can hold a baby in any position whatever without letting it fall, and yet if I take up a cup or a glass it is sure to drop from my hands and break. But I will try and wake myself up, and be more careful, especially as you have told me to. I can always remember things which no one will want to know, but directly I am told to remember anything it goes clean out of my head. I don't think I have yet learnt to hold myself up, or to walk properly, for only yesterday Mother gave me a lecture about it. She says I slouch along as if I was too lazy to lift up my legs. I know I often feel too tired. She wants me to do exercises in my room in the morning. I used to do them but they never did me any good, and I much prefer lying in bed, and I am sure it does me more good.

Booton Rectory, September 19

You think it curious that you can hold a baby without letting it fall, but not a glass. There is no mystery in the matter to me. You are attentive to the baby, and not to the glass. The power of attending to what you are about, be it ever so trivial, is a faculty to be cultivated. Many small graces which subsequently appear natural to us are in reality acquired arts, like walking and talking, only less difficult. I

not only hope but expect you will end by being as graceful
as My Lady in walking, in handicraft, in everything. These
accomplishments have a peculiar charm in a woman.

Frognal, September 24

One of our visitors was saying this morning that no life
was well arranged except in a convent, and that nothing ever
happened as it ought to do. I tell you this because it seemed
to me so ridiculous. Of all the places in the world, I think a
convent is the place where a life is worst arranged. What can
be more selfish or miserable than a life shut up by itself,
under the pretence of living solely to God. And it seems so
cowardly to shut yourself up from all the temptations of the
world. If you look at some lives from a human point of view
you may sometimes feel that they might have been differently
arranged. But it makes me so angry when people talk in that
sort of positive way about things which they cannot understand as if they knew better than God who had ordered it all.
And the way they seem to think that they could have done
things so much better than He could have done them. I think
those people must have very little minds who think that
because they cannot understand all that God has done He
must be in the wrong instead of themselves. And fancy
daring to say that they could do better than He has done in
His infinite wisdom. I know they only say the things to be
thought clever and original, and such poor and ridiculous
things they are that I only wonder how they ever dare say
them. And I think that all the ridiculous things men say
against it only makes religion seem greater and grander and
more blessed than ever. People seem so wilfully to shut
their eyes to all the grand truths, for no one could ever feel
really convinced by the absurd things they pretend to believe.

Booton Rectory, September 25

Here is another most delectable letter. Without it the post
would have come in vain for me. We were looking at breakfast at the portrait in the *Daily Graphic* of the new Postmaster-
General, Sir James Fergusson, and we agreed that unless the
artist had done him an injustice we should not like to entrust

our letters to him. I am sure his rueful face would not approve of my correspondence with you. He would pronounce it infectious and steep it in vinegar.

Backs were made among other purposes to be beaten and to be patted. There are reprobates who can only be restrained from evil by fear, and beating is salutary. But when there is reasonable hope of drawing good out of people, patting is the more promising.

In October my father paid what was to prove his last visit to Booton, and it is thus described in the following letter from his Rev:

Booton Rectory, October 2

The arrival of your father and Conny yesterday evening was like a page out of a romance. Your father came in with the manner you know, and Con darted in after him with a beaming face, and loving words, and a kiss and embrace in keeping with them. We immediately settled down in the old fashion as if there had not been an hour's break in the intercourse. We had a charming evening. Your father was at his best, every trace of ill-health and low spirits disappearing, each of us enjoying his talk, and no one happier in it than Fanny. She said to me afterwards that his description of the French people, of French society and of European politics taught her more than one should have expected to learn of any subject in a study of years. This morning he came down to breakfast looking well and vigorous, the lovely weather aiding, and it will be grand, though I can hardly hope it, if his ailments will give him a respite to the end. Thus far there is nothing left to desire.

I said when we were sitting down to dinner on Sunday evening that I hailed the arrival of evening because it was (socially) the pick of the day, to which Con replied, in her delicious way, that she liked breakfast here from the thought that she had now a whole day before her, and lunch because there was still half the day to come, and dinner because she did not care that so much of the day was gone since the prime of it remained. Did anybody ever express a delightful idea more delightfully?

I would say that I meant to take all the pains in my power
to make your visit a blessing to you,[1] were it not that I shall
have no opportunity to take any pains whatever. I shall do
it without any, irresistibly and without an effort, and I am
certain for myself that breakfast, lunch, and dinner, and
the hours between and after, will be the best by a long way
I ever had with you. My sensations at present are yours. I
should wish Time to run himself out of breath with his
extra speed till Thursday afternoon and then I should wish
him to halt, and rest till we bid him go on again. As far as I
was concerned he would not have to complain that I over-
worked him and cut short his holidays.

After this visit to Booton we all returned to Paris for the
last time, and I write from Dover on October 14th:
"I cannot help being so wretched that the time in England
is over, for it has been such a perfect time and so full of
happiness, and the Paris life seems to me drearier than ever
to go back to. It is not really, for I know I shall be living out
of it all with you and with my books and none of the empty
things will be able to take away my peace and joy in having
you for my friend. But just now I can think of nothing but
that it is over. The holidays are over, the times at Booton
are over and I have got to go back to the empty formal life
with the luxuries which I loathe, and everything looks black
to me."

[1] I was going to Booton for a final visit before returning to Paris.

Chapter Five

On October 19th I write:

> *British Embassy, Paris*
>
> Poor Father arrived here last night so dreadfully unwell. He had suffered agonies of pain that day and, of course, the shaking of the train made it much worse. The doctors could give no reason for the pain, or, anyhow, did not give him any.

This was the beginning of the illness which was to prove fatal.

My letters to and from his Rev had now become daily events, but, as in all daily letters which record the small details of everyday life, there are many repetitions and mine give day-to-day bulletins about my father's illness which could be of little general interest.

From his Rev's letters to me I quote two passages which I found helpful or amusing:

> *Booton Rectory, October* 19
>
> I have your letter of Friday. I repeat again that you need never excuse the smallness of the events. The story of your life is what I relish. Our principal farmer has a little boy of nine with bad eyes who sits in a darkened room, and his mother said to me today, "We read him Homer and Virgil; that is what interests him." You can take him for a correspondent when you write in an heroic strain. You will cease to interest *me*. You yourself are my heroine, and the closer you keep to yourself and your immediate surroundings the better I am pleased.
>
> I will end my letter by telling you again that I delight in

yours. The fifteen decisive battles of the world (there is a
book with that name) is not a hundredth part so interesting
to me as the battles you fight with yourself. I enjoy reading
of your successes and failures of every kind, and live them over
with you as if I had been present. They are as real to me as
they were to you. The identity of our natures is the source
of human sympathy. Like answers to like.

Booton Rectory, October 20

Locker told me a witty remark of Tennyson's friend
Brookfield on *In Memoriam*: "Tennyson kept his tears ten
years in the wood, and then bottled them for posterity." If
this needs elucidation, your father will supply it.

My shyness of my father was somehow increased by his
illness, and I write:
"I do feel it is so dreadfully difficult to go in and see him.
To begin with, I am always afraid he may just have got to
sleep, and then when he is awake there is always someone
with him and so I cannot get out a word and it seems so silly
to go in and say nothing. But I will take every opportunity
I can of seeing him."

British Embassy, Paris, October 27

Father was much cheered this morning by a letter from
Mrs. Wagstaff, the fortune-teller, as he had written to
consult her about his case. She says there is no sign of tumour
and it is merely a temporary thing. But he must be very
careful of anything surgical. Suppose the doctors think it
necessary, I wonder if he would believe them or Mrs. Wagstaff? It is curious how he believes all that these people tell
him, and Mother is just as pleased about what she says as
Father.

British Embassy, Paris, October 28

People so often seem to think that if you try and take
people with their good side, and find good in them when
others only find bad, that you approve of the evil and think
that it is good. They seem to think it a proof of particular

virtue to pick others to pieces and that it shows you are so good that you cannot bear any evil in others. People seem to take a real pleasure in making out that their neighbours are very bad. In Society everyone talks of the badness of every-one else and rejoices in it, and you hardly ever hear a kind word said of anybody, which is what I think makes Society talk so dreadful. Of course, you get to think everyone bad if you never even try to find any good in them.

A lady who came to lunch the other day said that it annoyed her so in Society how if a husband was devoted to his wife, everyone said "how silly," while if anyone else was devoted to her they said "how touching," and it is so true. In Paris no one seems to think it a possible thing that a husband and wife should care for each other. Every woman has an acknowledged lover and the husband is pushed entirely into the background. He is asked out to dinner with his wife, but no one takes any notice of him, but it is considered absolutely necessary to ask the lover too, and no secret is made of it. Girls know absolutely nothing until they are married. They are taught that everything is wrong, and then suddenly plunged right into the middle of it. I think it is most awfully wicked. I never can be grateful enough to you for having taught me all these things so clearly.

British Embassy, Paris, November 3

Father said yesterday that I was to tell you that he was now so much better that he has made Con read out to him again yesterday Oscar Wilde's essay (*The Decay of Lying*) and that he thought still more highly of it than before, and that it was very true and wonderfully well done. He was most anxious for you to read it at once.

Oscar Wilde came here to luncheon yesterday and we all thought him very amusing and not so odious as we expected, though he is evidently fearfully conceited. He talked chiefly about his own health and his books, but he was certainly amusing. He has just written a play which he wants to have translated into French and acted at the Français; nothing less would be good enough for him.

I am very anxious to know whether you think his *Decay of*

Lying is as brilliant as it is supposed to be. I cannot help
hoping that you will not. Taken seriously, it is an absurd
statement that there can be no such thing as art without lies
and there is no fun in it, taken as a joke.

British Embassy, Paris, November 11

I am to tell you from Mother that Sunday was Father's
birthday and she likes to think that you got back to the
Church [1] on that day. It may seem odd to you, but I give this
message particularly from her, but she was asking me this
afternoon if I had told you, but I said "No" and I thought
birthdays were most uninteresting things, especially to other
people. So she said she was very fond of them and as I had
not told you myself I was to tell you from her.

Christmas and Easter and any general time of rejoicing I
love, for everyone rejoices together, but birthdays I hate.
When I was a child I hated other people's because they got
all the petting and I was always supposed to give in to them,
and I hated my own because it comes the day after Christmas
when everyone is tired and cross and I never got as much
petting as I wanted. Now I hate birthdays because they mean
that everybody's cross all day. I am glad to say my own is
not taken much notice of now.

In one letter I mention that my father asked me to read
him "Locksley Hall" and my delight because the book could
not be found, because to read poetry aloud to my father would
have been an awful ordeal. Here is his Rev's note on that
work:

Booton Rectory, November 14

I have been speculating as to whether the lost Tennyson
has been found, and you have taken the precaution to rehearse
"Locksley Hall." Locker, who has lived a good deal with
Tennyson, and is not disposed to underrate him, said to me
the other day that he thought the popular estimation of
"Lady Clara Vere de Vere" and "Locksley Hall" was somewhat beyond their merit. The poems ask the reader for more

[1] The first day the service was held in his new church at Booton.

sympathy than he can render, for they leave the feeling that probably the girls were not much to blame, and might certainly be right in their ultimate decision. So far Locker. The "foolish yeoman" who commits suicide because Lady Clara declines to marry him does, I confess, alienate my sympathy by the excess of his folly. It was not a dignified employment for Lady Clara to be carrying on a flirtation with a small farmer, but he must have been a conceited idiot to imagine that she was in earnest, nor was she likely to suppose he did.

I write on November 18th:

British Embassy, Paris

I have read "Locksley Hall" as you asked me to (not aloud) and I think some parts of it are quite beautiful. I think, in Tennyson, in the midst of the most lovely things you suddenly come across something so fearfully common-place that it gives you quite a shock and this spoils the beauty to a great extent. I think in "Locksley Hall" the rejected lover makes himself out to be a perfect beast and I feel the girl is quite right in what she did, as her husband can, at any rate, not have been more odious than the lover. He says of her love, "No, she never loved me truly. Love is love for ever-more." But I do not think his love can have been worthy of much to turn round and abuse the woman he loved in that way. She may have treated him badly, but as he still loved her, he should respect her too. He may have thought her unworthy of respect from the way she behaved to him, but he might still respect her as the woman he loved. "Woman is the lesser man and all thy passions matched with mine are as moonlight unto sunlight and as water unto wine." For these words alone I feel he deserved his fate or rather worse. It is a strange love that thinks the loved one in every way inferior to himself.

My father's illness was complicated by the fact that the French and English doctors disagreed in their diagnosis. I record in my letters that when in great pain he was dosed with morphia, and when he showed signs of collapse he was

given brandy. A French doctor said that he could not tell
how long the illness might go on:
"but we must expect Father to be laid up at least three
months. The nurse says she has known it to go on for six.
I do not believe the doctors really know what is the matter
with him. The nurse says she has known people as bad after
six months as Father was last night, so that is a dreary
prospect."

In the same letter I then return to my own personal
struggles:
"I think the hard part of conquering sins is that perseverance
is wanted and not strength. Anyone could gather together
sufficient strength to fight one battle, but when one follows
upon the top of another it is hard not to give in. And to know
that all through life there will always be something to fight
against, and if you conquer one thing another will appear,
makes one feel desperate at times. If it was only one struggle
against sin, you could put all your strength into the one
struggle and then there would be a certain amount of excitement which would help to carry you through. When I have
determined to conquer some sin, for the first few days I feel
worked up to it and feel strong enough to do anything, but
after several failures and I seem only to get worse, I get
depressed and all my strength seems to go. But I will not
get discouraged but only go on trying harder and harder, if
you will go on helping me."

British Embassy, Paris, November 21
A thought came into my head this morning in church
which I tell you because I thought of it. I have read in books
and heard people talk as if the Blessed Lord had lowered
Himself to the very depth of human weakness by becoming a
child, that He was not content only to take the form of man
but He would stoop yet lower and become a child. I think it is
just the contrary and that in His infinite mercy He stooped to
become a man. Surely there is no degradation in being a child,
for children are angels compared to most men. No one, I
think, realizes how much God is present with children, or

6

they could not talk of them as they do. People laugh at children's amusements and think they are simple, but there is a great deal more behind them than people think, for children's imaginations make great realities out of trivial things. I think in looking back to your childhood you still feel the fascination of the things that amused you then and you never look at the amusements themselves but to the ideas they gave you and to the great things they represented to your mind. And though outsiders, looking on at children's games, see nothing in them, yet looking back to those they played in their own childhood, they must feel that it was the things behind that made the fascination of them. So I feel that the Blessed Lord was born in man's holiest state, that year by year He took upon Him all man's infirmity and degradation.

British Embassy, Paris, November 24

I have never yet been severely tried, and I can't say what I should feel if I was, but I never, never yet have doubted for one moment the infinite mercy and love of God, and I feel as if I never could. I have never felt as if His face was turned away from me. I think the chief joy of prayer is the knowledge that God will never give us what is not for our good. I think that if all our prayers were answered in the way we wished, I should never dare pray at all, for fear that what I asked might turn out to be an awful curse. We cannot know the future, and so we cannot know what things will turn out for our good. But now I feel that I can pray in perfect confidence, for God will not grant my prayers unless they are for my good. And so I pray for everything I want as earnestly as I can, knowing that He will answer my prayers in the right way. And sometimes when I have prayed very earnestly for a certain thing, and it all turns out contrary to my prayers, I feel as if God came to me and said, "I have heard your prayers and answered them in my way and so be in peace and feel that all is for the best." I do not mean to talk of my faith in God as if it was any merit of mine, but I think of it as a proof of His great love in having so taught me about Himself that I am never troubled with any doubts.

My father died very suddenly on November 24th of cerebral thrombosis. I was summoned from a children's tea-party and rushed back to the Embassy to find him dead.

It was the first time in my life that I had been brought close to death, and I felt at once as I have so often felt since that in the presence of the dead a little corner of the veil is lifted which separates us from the Great Unknown. We do not see enough to make all things plain, but for a short while our values are changed and the things we usually count as so important seem suddenly to matter very little, and we understand for a moment the meaning of St. Paul's words: "Now we see through a glass darkly, but then face to face."

My mother met this crisis in her life as she had met many others, with incomparable courage and dignity. My sister, Betty Balfour, my two brothers and my aunt, Mrs. Earle, arrived the following day. I went to the station to meet them, and it was a great shock to me on our return to be greeted by my mother already in her widow's dress.

Elwin's response to the news of my father's death was as follows:

Booton Rectory, November 25

It was good of you to send the telegram.

I had your letter of last Friday on Sunday morning, and my own inferences told me that the crisis was at hand. But the doctors did not seem to say so, and as I could not set my own little knowledge against their full knowledge I might be mistaken. Divided between these two views I could not tell how to act. I longed to telegraph to Betty, "Go at once, or you will be too late," and dared not. I tried to effect my purpose by an intermediate course, which never answers, and when it failed I was glad, thinking that the doctors must surely have spoken out if my fears were well grounded. Finally, I settled down into the opinion that since the doctors alone were in a position to judge with certainty I ought to be guided by them, and not utter a word that could create the misery of a false alarm. But though I took this for the rule of my conduct my real conviction did not change, unless now and then for a few minutes when I had my pen in my hand,

and I and Fanny since your Sunday letter have talked of little else than of what would be presently. Yet when the expected intelligence came it moved us as much as if we had not been waiting for it. Now we talk of the sorrows of heart, and the many attendant miseries of the situation, which are oppressing my dear Lady, and all of you in your degree. And we like to dwell on the qualities in your father which won our love, and find some comfort in his having been here so recently, every virtue in him manifesting itself in its utmost perfection. His goodness to us at all times knew no bounds. But I cannot dwell on this topic now. I could talk to you for hours, and cannot write.

"I can render no further service to the dead; my duties to the living remain." This is what James Watt, famous for his inventions in connection with the steam-engine, wrote when he was broken-hearted at the death of his wife. I have always admired the wisdom of it since I first read it years and years ago. Grief will have its way; love, magnificent love, for the dead will remain; but the duties chiefly appertain to the living, and we should throw into them, if possible, redoubled zeal. Darling Emmie, be an angel to mother, and sisters and brothers. Link your hand tighter than ever in theirs. Irritations will come. They are likely to come especially to sensitive and wounded hearts in the many ruffles attendant on the changes death brings with it. But when tried, struggle hard to let the angel in you prevail. I read what you said of your efforts in this morning's letter with moist eyes. The frankness of your self-accusations is always pathetic, and your endeavours are so honest, so earnest that I cannot but praise them when they fail.

My mother was anxious to have a post-mortem examination, in order to make sure of the cause of my father's death, as the doctors had disagreed, and she wished to make sure whether there had been any return of cancer.

In a letter to Elwin, I write:

"Mother has just had the doctor's report. There was absolutely nothing of cancer, but the inflammation in the bladder had mounted up and both kidneys were affected. In the right

one there are two abscesses which have not yet come to a
head, though they say he must have died in about a month
and he would have suffered tortures now that the morphine
had lost its effect to such a great degree. What really killed
him was a clot of blood on the brain. They find he had a weak
heart, about one inch less thick than it ought to have been."

Booton Rectory, November 26

My latest memory of your dear father was the best of all
our loving memories of him. No words could express too
strongly what he was in his final visit. Fanny and I feel alike
about it, and yet I think it was in my own particular talks
with him that his rarest qualities shone out most radiantly.
I see him walking up and down the room, hear his voice,
recall his words, and these pathetic visions of the past, which
have also their comfort and gladness, and speculations
respecting the condition of things at the Embassy, have
almost exclusive possession of my mind. I cannot write of
them.

It is a just thought of yours when you say, "If all our
prayers were answered in the way we wished I should never
dare to pray at all, for fear that what I asked might turn out
an awful curse." And the whole passage is right, and while
you keep it alive in you, your path on earth will be directed
and maintained by the power of heaven. I read your words
with delight.

British Embassy, Paris, November 29

Mother said to me this morning after she had read your
last night's letter how perfect it was and that every single
word was what she most wanted. And she said she hoped
you would always go on writing to me. And she said I was
to thank you for having made us what we are, as we are such
a comfort to her. My darling, you know I always bless you
for having taught me what you have, and it is only my fault
that I am still what I am. Don't give up teaching me because
I am slow to learn, will you? I want you now more than ever,
for I have so much more to do.

Mother also told me to tell you how glad she was that
Father had been to you in the summer. She says she felt
then how very ill he was, and had doubted for a moment
whether she should let him go, but afterwards she thought it
might be for the last time, and that if he was to die, nothing
could sanctify him more than to go to you, and she is so glad
now that he went.

Last Sunday was the last day I sat with Father. I stayed
with him about three-quarters of an hour before church.
He seemed worse that day than I had seen him before. He
hardly spoke a word to me, but kept on dozing. He had his
poem by him and kept thinking it out. Then I got up and said
I was going to church, and he said, "How happy for you
that you like it." I keep on thinking of his dear face afterwards, and the peace of it puts peace into my heart.

Booton Rectory, December 1

What is good should increase and not decrease. I shall not
love you less but more, or if less then my love is not worth
having, and you will have no cause to regret it. I have
pledged myself to you that while you feel I can help you to
fulfil your own ideal, can help you to conquer faults and
improve virtues, can help you to better your life and brighten
it, I will strive, from duty, from inclination, from my
associations with him you have lost and with those that
remain, to be your friend in the highest sense of that word
as I have interpreted it out of my own heart and out of the
writings of some of the greatest intellects and noblest
dispositions that ever adorned the world. My dearest Lady's
messages to me would of themselves bind me to be zealous
in the service of her children.

That little Sunday bit with your dear father is inestimable.
Never forget it—never forget that he said to you on his death-
bed, "How *happy* for you that you like it"—like the Sunday
services, the faith, the prayers, the eternal hopes, all that the
Sunday service involves. Never forget it.

By the side of what your father said to you, I place the
words which the dying Walter Scott spoke in his very last
moments of consciousness to Lockhart. He sent for Lockhart

to come to him immediately, and said, "I may have but a
minute to speak to you. My dear, be a good man; be virtuous;
be religious; be a good man. Nothing else will give you any
comfort when you come to lie here." It is when standing on
the confine which separates the two worlds that men can
often judge best the world they are leaving and the world to
which they are going. They see with a more single eye when
they are divested of the ambitions, the passions, the distrac-
tions which went before.

My father's body was brought back to England and was
given full military honours on the way through the streets
of Paris, as he was a representative of the Queen. I write of
this:
"Everyone says that it was perfectly wonderful yesterday
the signs of respect and affection that were shown him. The
troops lined the streets from the church to the station, and
the crowds everywhere were quite tremendous. People had
even climbed up into the trees. The last public funeral here
with all these honours was Victor Hugo's. It has pleased
Mother very much, and she loves the respect to have been
shown to him."

I write from London to Elwin a description of my father's
funeral at Knebworth:

Stratford Place, London, December 2
There was nothing yesterday to jar on our feelings.
Nothing painful, nothing that was not all love and peace. At
first, the sight of the dear old place, the house, the gardens,
the church, made me feel very, very sad, as I had longed so
for the time when we should all come back there together.
But when we got into the Hall where his coffin was, it
seemed as if he was waiting for us to welcome us home, and
I no longer felt sad. It was all so simple and so peaceful.
The coffin was covered with the Union Jack and just
Mother's little wreath of bay leaves on it. The service itself
was very beautiful and very impressive. Eight of the strongest
gardeners carried him and the chief tenants held the ropes

of the Union Jack. There was no hitch anywhere, as the same undertaker who managed all in Paris came over with the coffin and arranged all yesterday. He has done it all so quietly and respectfully. It is very curious that he is the same man who brought little Teddy [1] over from Paris seventeen years ago, and Father showed him round everywhere himself then, so he knew the place quite well.

The choir came up to the house to meet the coffin and went back singing "Lead Kindly Light." Their white surplices and the cross and their voices in the open air were all so beautiful and so impressive. The West door of the church was opened and it was wonderful when they all passed in, singing.

Lord Salisbury came himself and went first to the church and then came out to go up to the house and meet the coffin just as it was coming out of the gates. This has pleased Mother more than anything, first, that he should have come himself, and then that he should have met Father instead of following him.

I had never seen the Mausoleum [2] open before and had always had a horror of it, and it seemed such a cold, dreary place. But, instead of that, it looked so cheerful and comfortable. There was not room there for more than ourselves, and it was so nice that in the last part of the service they read alone to us quietly.

There is a slab which hides the coffins of Grandfather's mother and Grandmother, and besides there are only Aunt Emily's [3] and little Teddy's. Father was put beside Teddy and quite close to his sister, and it was so touching, one of Father's wreaths fell on the little coffin beside him.

It made me happy seeing Aunt Emily's coffin, for I have always had a kind of adoration of her, though I don't know much about her life, but when I was a child and very miserable I loved her as I knew she had been treated very unkindly, and I thought I would give her all my love, and

---

[1] The little brother who died before I was born.

[2] This Mausoleum was built by my grandfather's mother, the heiress of Knebworth, and she herself was buried there.

[3] My father's sister.

I used to hope that I should die young as she did. It makes me happy still to think that I have got her name.

Kipling [1] was telling us yesterday that seven years ago Father went alone with him into the Mausoleum and put a wreath of rosebuds on his sister's coffin. The lock of the gate outside was rusty and he could not open it. Father jumped over the railings long before he could get over himself.

[1] The Knebworth gardener.

Chapter Six

WHEN we left Paris we went straight to Bramfield House, near Hertford, which my great-aunt, Lady Bloomfield, had put at our disposal, and I write from there on January 5th, 1892:

"Mother is now reading out to us in the evening Lord Rosebery's *Pitt*, and I cannot help laughing at the whole scene, though I think the reading is a bore. No one takes in or understands a word of what is read, Mother least of all. She might read all over one evening what she had read the evening before, and no one would know it. Victor settles into the most comfortable chair in the room and goes to sleep, pretending the light hurts his eyes and so he must shut them. Poor Neville is most terribly bored, not understanding a word of what is said, and keeps asking eagerly if the chapter is yet finished. Con occasionally breaks in with her quiet remarks which make us all laugh. Betty last night was very interested, and asked lots of questions about what we had read the night before, which of course no one could answer. To be interested in a book seems quite out of place. The boys love being read to, if they are allowed to ask as many questions as they like and if the book is rather more exciting than the life of Pitt. I think the chief mistake of Mother's reading is, first, she will only read a book which she thinks she ought to read, secondly, she will never allow one question to be asked, and thirdly, she never reads as if she was really interested herself. I tell you the little things as I used to, for they have not changed, but you know that I love Mother with a far bigger love than ever before, and no one in the world can admire her more than I do. Each day I feel a new wonder and a new love for her."

Bramfield House, Hertford, January 7

The last two evenings Betty has read the *Life of Pitt* to us, and she being interested in it makes everyone else so. Neville gets quite excited. He does take much more interest in things than Victor, and he is very amusing in the way he talks about them. Neville is far more original than Vic, and I think he has a good deal more in him. And these holidays especially I do think he's a real angel. He is as unselfish as Con, and I hardly ever see him in a temper. He is still very fond of teasing, but as I no longer feel so irritated by it, I see more what a dear he is. Vic is trying very hard to be good-tempered, and he certainly is ever so much better, but he is very selfish, and never thinks it a bit wrong that everyone should wait upon him. He makes Neville a perfect slave. I tell you this as I feel I am always complaining about them, and I do think this time that Neville is an angel of unselfishness. Vic tries to be, but he does not quite realize what an angel is.

Con knocked over a chair yesterday after lunch, and poor Mother was so nervous and began to scream. It frightened me so I longed to begin too. She was miserable afterwards and said it was so dreadful when nerves got beyond one's control, and she was so afraid of doing it again. Con says she is glad she made the noise, as Mother is so marvellously brave that one is apt to forget in a kind of way all that she is suffering. It will teach us all to be more careful. When I am trying hard to be quiet, I always manage to knock over the biggest thing in the room.

Booton Rectory, January 8

Yesterday our farmer came in with a long face and said he had very unpleasant news to communicate. After he was seated, his eyes filled with tears, which increased to crying, and I supposed he had lost a relation. Though I had some feeling of compassion for him I remained placid, but when I heard that the loss was pecuniary, and that we should be involved in it, the brutal thought came over me, "Now his news is growing serious." So inhuman is human nature in certain persons when it obeys its first impressions. However, the brutality lasted only an instant or two, and when, the interview over, I repeated the facts to Fanny, she immediately said, "Depend upon it we shall be the better for the loss; I can't tell how, but we shall be." That is her under all circumstances—a faith which nothing disturbs, the unshaken belief that events adverse as well as prosperous have blessing at the end of them. If we can but set our farmer up again we shall be triumphant.

Bramfield House, January 11

I love my Sunday more and more. I look forward to it all the week, and I am never disappointed. I love the service and I love the peace, and above all I love passing my day in communion with God. And that is a joy which increases. The little church here is not beautiful, and the services are dull, but it cannot take away from the beauty of them, or the joy of being with God. That always remains, and Sunday is always a blessed day. To sit still in a church and read the Bible gives me the keenest pleasure. When the disturbing part of life is put aside, I can read it so much better, and the beauty of it grows upon me. The words seem alive, and I feel while I am reading as if I were lifted into another world. And passages which I read over and over, instead of their seeming stale or tiresome, each time I feel the beauty of them more keenly, and each time I feel more lost in wonder at it.

On Saturday we trudged out for our two-mile walk. The ground is covered with snow and very slippery, which adds to the difficulties. Mother had decided we had to walk for an hour. We went up and down every lane, trying to make long rounds, but the time would not pass, and we were at last obliged to come in. I should enjoy the walks far more if I was not every minute being told to hold up and to walk properly. When I am just getting along so comfortably, Mother says to me: "Oh dear, you walk worse than ever, it is perfectly dreadful."

Booton Rectory, January 11

You will find something about biting your nails on the back page of my letter. According to this authority if you wish to keep well you will have to give up your favourite diet. Seriously, there may be an element of truth in it. There are

many reported cases of death from persons swallowing
habitually minute fragments of material which from their
nature stick to the coats of the stomach, and which the gas-
tric juice cannot dissolve. When you are here we will try
and get you into right courses.

On the back of the letter was written:
" ALARMING INTELLIGENCE: 'Biting the finger-nails is a
prolific cause of death, according to a medical correspondent.
On one occasion, at a post-mortem, he observed the entire
coating of the stomach bristling with bits of finger-nails.'"

Bramfield House, January 12

The newspaper cutting is certainly most alarming, and it is
dreadful to think my health may depend upon my leaving off
biting my nails. I have tried so often and never yet succeeded,
but you have given me a new reason for trying again.
Luckily I'm coming to school soon, and you will have to hold
my hands tight to prevent me biting. I love your way of
curing me so much that I shall have to keep on biting, to give
you a reason for holding my hands. I wish for my own comfort I could leave off the habit, for I generally bite till my
fingers are dreadfully sore. In spite of this I simply cannot
leave it off, so I feel at least, for of course I could if I tried
properly. I will set about it with a new energy now, and I
hope when I come to Booton I shall have quite a respectable
set of nails to show you. You will still have to hold my hands
though.

Had I known that to bite my nails might injure my health,
I should have tried harder to leave off doing it, for I never
intentionally do anything to make myself ill, and I think, on
the contrary, it is very wrong not to do everything in one's
power to keep well. However patiently you may bear
suffering you still cannot be of as much use as if you were
well, and you are generally a great nuisance if you are ill,
so for that if for no other reason I think one ought to try and
keep well. I assure you I realize the necessity of caring for
my health as much as anyone. I try and bear pain patiently
when I have it, though I am afraid I grumble dreadfully, but

I always try and keep free of pain if I can. I am never afraid of being ill but I try to keep well.

Mother has been suffering so much with irritation in the head, which nearly drives her wild, and last night and this morning it is all over her back and chest. There is no rash and apparently no reason for it. Vic has also had it the last few days. Mother asked Dr. Moore [1] about it when she was in London, and he said it was from a low state of health, and the only thing to be done was to hold a very hot sponge to the head when the irritation was very bad. He said that anything else would only make it settle in one place, and it would be far worse. If it is from a low state of health, why should Vic have it too, as he is particularly well? Mother wanted me to ask you about it, and to tell you that since she has been in England she has entirely given up all mineral waters, of which she used to take a great deal, and all alkalis, and now only takes lemon and hot water and an apple before lunch (this is the newest remedy). Since she has taken these, she has suffered much less from headache and neuralgia than she used to do, but she thinks either this or the cold may have something to do with the irritation. Can you suggest anything that will relieve her?

Alas for my poor mother, the origin of her complaint was revealed when my brother Victor was sent back from Eton with what is technically called "a dirty head," and Mother was found to be suffering neither from acidity nor alkalis but from the same parasites as my brother. She felt this as a dire disgrace and, with her beautiful long hair, it was something more than a nuisance. She came to the conclusion that she must have picked up her enemies at one of the many French churches which she had visited in Paris after my father's death. This thought at least put a halo of sanctity upon her head, and was of some comfort.

Bramfield House, January 18

Betty goes today, and the boys leave on Thursday, so this will be a sad week. Though the boys are in some ways a

[1] A friend of Elwin's, recommended by him.

nuisance and often irritate me very much, I am always
unhappy when they go. There is always something for me to
do when they are here, and I feel quite lost at first without
them. However, I have much more time when they are away,
and if they were always at home I probably should not be so
fond of them. Neville was rather funny the other night. He
said, "I think I should like to be a Stoic, that is a person
who is never afraid of any danger and always keeps quite calm
and cool." Seeing I was smiling, he added, "I don't mean
that I am never frightened. I should like to be *very* sarcastic.
I always get so excited directly and lose my temper, while I
should like to keep quite cool, and just say some very
sarcastic thing which would rile the other person terribly and
put them into a great rage." And last night during the
reading it said that Pitt was sarcastic, so Neville broke in,
"Was Pitt sarcastic? Oh, I am so glad." It is rather funny,
as his character is so very much the opposite.

I am reading to him *Night and Morning*, and he gets so
tremendously excited over it. I do think it is a very delicious
book and some parts are excellent, but in most of Grandfather's books, that is in those I have read, there is a good
deal of false sentiment which spoils them very much, it is
so very false and made up. Still I think most of his books are
delightful, and the boys care more to have them read to them
than any other books, and get simply enthusiastic over them.
I remember one passage in particular in *Night and Morning*
which makes me angry to read, I think it is so false. I copy
it for you and tell me whether I am right or not:

"The funeral was over; the dead shovelled away. What
a strange thing it does seem, that that very form which we
prize so charily, for which we prayed the winds to be
gentle, which we lapped from the cold in our arms, from
whose footstep we should have removed a stone, should be
suddenly thrust out of sight—an abomination that the
earth must not look upon—a despicable loathsomeness, to
be concealed and to be forgotten! And this same composition of bone and muscle that was yesterday so strong—
which men respected and women loved and children clung
to—today so lamentably powerless, unable to defend or

protect those who lay nearest to its heart; its riches wrested from it, its wishes spat upon, its influence expiring with its last sigh! A breath from its lips making all that mighty difference between what it was and what it is!"

Every word of it seems false to me. It is talking as if the body is the only thing which made a man, or anyhow the chief thing. While in reality the body is a very, very small part, for it is the grand qualities and the soul and mind that make a man, and the body is only a covering to the real man. And it is not the body which you love and respect but the grand qualities, and death can make no difference to these. They never die. Death means only that they are removed to a place where they will become yet more beautiful, where there is more room for them to develop, and death cannot take away your love and respect for them. The body has its use and its beauty, and we love it as belonging to the qualities which we love, but when we are called to the higher state, we no longer need the body. It is with all reverence and all love that we bury it, not to hide it away, "as a despicable loathsomeness to be concealed and to be forgotten".

Booton Rectory, January 19

Your comment on the extract from *Night and Morning* exhausts the subject. I have not a word to add, and subscribe to every word you write. It is an old remark that we call the body "mine, not me," say *my* hands, *my* feet, *my* head, and this from the instinctive consciousness within us; neither separately nor combined do they constitute *us*. They are but appendages to the actual man. Your grandfather could not be insensible to the fact, and I cannot explain why it was that he constantly indulged in false and morbid sentiment in preference to what was true. No one equalled him in the construction of a plot, or surpassed him in the management of his story. But his predilection for artificial and often unworthy aspects of human nature has kept people from returning to his novels with renewed and inexhaustible pleasure. The first excitement over, the impression of lasting charm does not equal that of their power.

Bramfield House, January 20

Lord Rosebery mentions that Pitt had many friends whom he loved like brothers. Betty said it was such a wrong way of putting it, for a friend's love was so much greater than a brother's. I did not contradict her there. Several of Pitt's letters were given as specimens of his deep affection for his friends. When we had read them Conny remarked in her quiet way: "Yes, I think Lord Rosebery was right in saying he loved his friends like brothers." The letters were as cold and formal as any letters could be. I never knew anything of Pitt before, and I certainly think he must have been a splendid character.

Mother scolded me again the other night for being so positive, and giving my own opinion in such a decided way, instead of asking gently other people's opinions, and going by what they told me. This was after the discussion about the sentence in Pitt. Certainly Betty is not the person whose opinion I am always to take no matter what it is. Mother told me I frightened people by being so positive, and when I asked who I frightened she said Betty and Gerald and you. She was obliged to laugh, though, as she said it. I told her that you nearly always agreed with me, so my opinion must be right. She could not answer that.

On February 12th, after I returned from a visit to Booton, his Rev writes to me:

"When we are together, I do most of the talking, and am disgusted with myself afterwards. When we are separated, you do most of the writing, and again I am full of self-reproaches."

This was perfectly true, for I always found it much more difficult to express what I wanted to say by word of mouth than by my pen.

There are no letters from me during this month, so I do not know what called forth the following letters on Macaulay [1] but I imagine that I was reading his Essays.

[1] See Appendix.

Booton Rectory, March 4

Macaulay's face was round and flabby, and his general build was in keeping with it. I only knew from meeting him at parties, and could judge of nothing beyond his conversation which was uniform in its nature as far as my experience extended. There was no brilliancy in it whatever, either of language or ideas. He talked in an easy, unpretentious, almost negligent style. In substance, he mainly confined himself to dealing out scraps of his reading, and what was remarkable was the vast extent of his reading, and his memory in retaining it. In these particulars I never came across anyone else who approached him. It was truly wonderful. But there was a deficiency which, in a man of distinguished talent, was not less surprising. There appeared to be nothing, or next to nothing, of his own mind in what he told. You got facts, and circumstances, and quotations as he found them, and that was all. You would have expected him to be rich in reflections, deductions, acute observations which were the product of his own understanding, and for these you listened in vain. The source of the defect was evident. He had spent too much time in reading and too little in thinking. I should infer from his talk that he thought out nothing unless he had to write upon the subject, and his works show that then he did not go deep and was content with hasty, scanty, and superficial conclusions.

His talk, like his knowledge, was inexhaustible. Whoever was in the company he practically monopolized the conversation in his neighbourhood, and only allowed the brief observations of others to be a text for his own profuse outpourings. This garrulous habit has its foundation in self-conceit. A modest man would take for granted that the company would like to hear others besides himself, and he himself would wish to profit by the conversation of others. And the practice too implies an insensibility to good fellowship. If a little discernment was mixed with the self-conceit very loquacious people would soon discover that they were bores. Nay, mere reflection would tell them it must be so, were they not too satisfied with themselves to look further. The range of Macaulay's knowledge was a curious exhibition

to witness now and then. For a constant or frequent companion he would have been oppressive, and as his talk was
not of the luminous order you were not rewarded by the
wealth of ideas you brought away. I have only answered
half your conversation. I will speak of his writings another
day.

Booton Rectory, March 6

Macaulay's written style is artificial and cost him much
pains. His conversation was widely different. It had no
brilliancy whatever, but, what was better, it was easy, natural,
and, as I have said, almost negligent.

That his written style is attractive is shown by its popu-
larity. Its merits are certainly great. The English is pure,
the sense clear, and leaves on the whole, when not over-
loaded with insignificant details, a vivid impression. But the
constant effort to be over-pointed renders his style in my
opinion radically vicious, and I cannot read much at a time
without its palling upon me. Nothing gives me lasting
pleasure except simplicity. Worst of all, he loved effect
better than truth, and to sustain it he systematically dis-
torted and over-coloured facts without scruple. His favourite
artifice was what is called antithesis, or setting one half of a
sentence in opposition to the other, as for example, "Many
of the greatest men that ever lived have written biography:
Boswell was one of the smallest men that ever lived, and he
has beaten them all." The course of events not happening
regularly in such violent contrasts he could only keep up the
trick by adapting the circumstances to his style instead of
his style to the circumstances. When the construction of a
sentence was not in question exaggeration was still his
method of making his descriptions telling. In his characters
he paints men better or worse than they were in reality,
abler or stupider. In depicting the usages of past times he
picks out exceptional incidents and generalizes them. The
failing accompanies him in everything. Although numerous
passages in his works show that his vast reading was superficial, and his deductions from it often false, he was exceedingly dogmatic in his assertions, and could not bear to

be corrected, and Sir James Stephen, in his book on Elijah Impey, gives a painful instance in which Macaulay, being convicted of misrepresentation, fabricated an untrue statement to refute the charge. When I was younger I was captivated by his style, and too ignorant to detect his errors and what I now think his want of principle. The moral blemish in his works seems to me far worse than the literary, and has rendered them so distasteful to me that their great talent has ceased to charm. And the talent itself being more showy than solid is not of the kind that suits my present desires.

Chapter Seven

WHEN the boys returned to school, my mother, Con and I
moved to London to a house in Elm Park Gardens which
belonged to the Lochs and which they had either lent or let
to my mother.

In the early months of this year my letters seem to be
missing, but I write on April 11th:

44, *Elm Park Gardens, April* 11

I felt very cross yesterday afternoon, for we all went with
Betty and Gerald to Kew Gardens. This means going some
way in a stuffy train and when you arrive walking about for
hours on horrible gravel in the boiling sun, in and out of
hothouses, each hotter than the other, and loaded with wraps
for when you sit down, which you never do. Yesterday it
was better than usual, for with the exception of Mother and
Gerald, who faithfully trudged all through the Gardens and
into the hothouses, we sat down on the grass at once and
remained there. Of course at the end we spent about half an
hour looking for each other and then ran for the train,
which we did not catch. I should not mind all this if anyone
enjoyed it, but I don't think anyone did. However, it was
rather fun all the same, because there was something so
ridiculous about it. I was cross chiefly because I would so
much rather have been in church. I tried though as hard as
ever I could not to seem cross and I succeeded well enough
to be satisfied with myself. Probably to the others I could
not have seemed more sulky than I was, but I was satisfied
with myself because I know I succeeded in keeping back
some of the cross feelings, though by no means all. It is
impossible, by simply wishing, to change my whole nature in
a minute and become sweet tempered and gentle when I

feel in a towering rage. I know that before I arrive at this result I must go on trying for a very long time, and I will try till I succeed. I will try and not get impatient with myself.

44, *Elm Park Gardens, April* 20

I sometimes wonder whether I really am as hard as people think me. The reason I say this is that I never remember a day of my life when I did not feel that in everything, sorrow, pain, trouble of every kind, there was more blessing than anything else, and that always and in everything there was room for endless rejoicing and thanksgiving. I have not known many troubles and perhaps when I have I may change, but I do not think I shall, for my reason for rejoicing is a reason which can never change, for it is based upon truths which are eternal. I have never been really ill or suffered much pain. I have never suffered anything which I would not gladly suffer again. At the time I sometimes feel I would give much to be rid of my pain, but on looking back afterwards, I think of it with as much pleasure as anything else, because of the blessing which I feel it has brought to me. Perhaps the reason is that I have never really suffered. This year I have learned what a real sorrow is, but I have learnt at the same time that the blessings which accompany it are so great that I can but rejoice and be thankful. When Mother and Betty say the lovely weather makes them miserable because Father loved it, I have just been rejoicing in it, chiefly because he loved it, and the sunshine seems to bring him to me. The others are sad because life seems so dull and lonely without him, and I rejoice because the happiest part of my life is made happier because he seems now to live it with me. Mother says our sun is gone from us; I feel that our sun shines brighter and warmer in heaven. I would not change for all that the world can give me, but I often wonder if the reason that I always feel happy is more because I have a hard and unfeeling nature than anything else. Other people seem always unhappy and each thing that happens seems to make me happier. I cannot sympathize as I ought in people's sorrows because I do not feel them in the same way that they do. If I am right I feel more people would think as I do. I feel like Mark Tapley; I am always wanting to come out strong and there is never an occasion.

Con and I go off to Terling [1] after lunch. I enjoy going there, as I do not feel shy, and Betty and Gerald are coming on Friday.

When we get together, can you guess what we shall talk about? I feel so much luckier than she is, for I have a Booton visit in front of me, and hers is past.

Terling Place, Witham, Essex, April 21

I told you yesterday that I liked coming here because I did not feel shy. I wish I could say the same today. We had hoped no one would be here, and there is a party of dreadful relations. A Mrs. Paley, sister of Lord Rayleigh's, who is very vulgar and seems every inch a relation. That is, always on the look-out for something she can abuse. Then there is her husband, who is nearly as silent as I am, and looks as morose, and a son who is just growing into a man. He is the most solemn-looking youth I ever saw, which is saying a great deal. When he occasionally opens his mouth to speak, he looks straight in front of him and without the smallest expression in his face or voice, utters some sentence. Then there is a sister-in-law of Lord Rayleigh's, Mrs. Richard Strutt, who is also vulgar, and very talkative, and laughs profusely at everything that is said. Evelyn and Lord Rayleigh evidently have no great affection for these relations and are quite shut up by them. I hope they may leave before we do. Betty's babies are here, which is a great joy, and Betty herself comes tomorrow, so if the relations left I should be supremely happy. As it is I enjoy it all and love the Rayleighs and this house, if only my tongue would not so obstinately refuse to make a sound. The more I try the more impossible it seems to open my lips. I grin in an idiotic kind of way and try to look pleasant till my jaw aches. I not only cannot wear my heart on my sleeve, but I do not feel to have a heart at all, or an idea in my head. I begin to think I am fit for nothing but to nurse babies. I get so angry with

[1] The home of Lord and Lady Rayleigh. Lord Rayleigh was a distinguished scientist and was married to Gerald's sister.

myself for being stupid and shy, and that only makes me worse. I have at present only been here one evening, so perhaps before I leave I may get over my shyness a little. I will try at any rate.

We were let in last night for a village concert, which was as funny as village concerts usually are. A deafening band performed, and Evelyn played the piano accompaniment, but bang as she would no sound could be heard. The conductor made almost more noise than anyone else by exclaiming "Hush" every few minutes and then banging on the top of the piano with his stick in a most alarming way. Then there were young ladies who sang very sentimental songs, and a comic man who recited a very pathetic story. The audience was as funny as anything. Not an expression of any kind was to be seen on any face. The performers went through their pieces with perfectly stolid faces, and the audience applauded loudly but never changed their expressions. The whole thing was very comic.

Terling Place, April 22

I am beamingly happy today. It is a glorious day, and last but not least the dreadful relations have all gone today. And Betty and Gerald come instead of them this evening. So altogether I feel ready to shout with joy. My shyness is also beginning to wear off a little. We had rather a dreadful day yesterday at Southend, which is a sea place Lord Rayleigh and his brothers and sisters used to go to when they were children. It is not an attractive place, with mud instead of sand. We were fourteen people altogether and we all crowded into a third-class carriage, where we began our first meal. It was a very hot day and we were obliged to sit on the top of each other, which was not pleasant. A brother of Lord Rayleigh's came with us, and he is more vulgar than all the rest put together, and yet there is a dreadful likeness between him and Lord Rayleigh. Lord Rayleigh has got a most delicious chuckling laugh, and it is so exaggerated in the brother that every time he looks as if he had got a fit. It was rather inconvenient when we were packed so tight, as he made the whole carriage shake with his fearful laugh. We passed our afternoon in walking to the end of the pier and back. It is a mile and a quarter in length. We then had another meal, and drove most of the way home in a brake which felt as if it was coming to pieces every minute. We ate some more on the way, and arrived home in time for dinner. It was a lovely day, and it would have been much nicer staying at home. I am too lazy to enjoy expeditions. I would always rather remain quietly at home. I have nothing amusing to tell you, for the conversation has not been brilliant, as far as I could hear. I escape upstairs whenever I can, and there I am happy in thinking of what I am avoiding. I am afraid I am very unsociable, but I try to look interested when I am downstairs. I wish I could learn to enjoy myself in company, but I only enjoy thinking of it afterwards when I am alone. I daresay I shall grow sociable in time. I have always spent most of my day alone, as I hardly ever come downstairs except at meal times and in the evening, and I think that is the chief reason why I do not get on well in company. People sometimes pity me for being so much alone and having no sister or companion, and the very idea of it makes me feel life would become too tiresome to be endured. I am never so happy as when I am alone, for then I can choose my own companions.

Terling Place, April 23

There is quite a party here now and I am shyer than ever. Betty and Gerald came last night, with a Mr. George Talbot and Doll Liddell, who is a cousin. You seem to know about everyone, so perhaps you know about these. Betty is very fond of George Talbot, and from all accounts he sounded an ideal creature. From what I saw of him last night I thought he was a horrid prig, but I am told I shall change, as he is not a bit of a prig. Betty says he has a splendid face, and I think it is the most priggish part about him. One reason I dislike him, perhaps the only reason, is that he is an enthusiastic admirer of Rudyard Kipling. He has a charming smile, which is the only good point I have yet noticed about him. But it is a fact that I never by any chance like people whom other people are fond of. Perhaps I am difficult to please.

Doll Liddell is rather amusing, but I do not know what else to say about him. Some more charming people come this evening, to my horror. Betty's charming friends frighten me to death. I did enjoy myself rather last night though, for I managed to get out two or three words at dinner and I tried to look very interested, and during most of the evening I played a game with one of the Rayleigh boys, and then had a delicious Booton talk with Bets when everyone else went into the hall to hear Con play. The rest of the evening was awful, for talking of Booton I could think of nothing else afterwards, so I sat in a corner and sulked and thought of all I would give to be able to get away, and for five minutes to be with you. And it all seemed so intolerably dull, compared to the evening I pictured to myself, that I could hardly stand it. And I thought with dread of two more evenings to be lived through. I went to bed feeling cross with myself and everyone else, and feeling that no one had ever been quite so stupid as I was. This morning I am more sensible and quite happy and I feel that it will be just possible to get through the day feeling tolerably happy. It's useless for me to attempt joining in general conversation, for I should not add to the interest of it, and if I did get a remark out so as to be heard by everyone I should certainly die of shame the next minute. I will be content to look interested and answer when I am spoken to. I had a drive with Evelyn Rayleigh yesterday afternoon and talked a good bit to her, and she was so charming to me, and the conversation got round to shyness, and I told her I was fearfully shy, and she was so nice and said the only plan was to say out everything that came into your head, no matter how silly it might seem to you. I said no doubt that was the wise thing to do, but it was not easy all the same. I can generally talk pretty well to one other person, but it is joining in general conversation which seems to me so utterly impossible. I think no torture can be quite as fearful as great shyness.

Booton Rectory, April 24

I should think your shyness of no consequence if it was not a trial to yourself. It will wear off without any effort of yours. Never trouble whether you have a chance to talk or not. Simply bide your time. "Everything comes to those who wait." I am greatly pleased at your talk with Lady Rayleigh. She is the person that is the most important to be impressed with your winning qualities. You must be known before you can be loved, and she will help you to opportunities of making acquaintances. You will be telling me that I am as bad as a match-making mother. Yes, but suppose one is a match-maker on good and not on sordid principles, and it is as much a duty in regard to a girl as to seek a profession for a boy. Marriage is a woman's testing and highest function, and it is a culpable remissness not to use the means for the end. My love for you says this much to me.

Terling Place, April 24

I notice that whenever I expect to be happy and at my ease I am always miserable, and when I expect to die of shyness and misery I am quite happy. Last night I went into dinner with Mr. Crawley [1] and he actually talked to me about Paris and things which I understood. I shall feel grateful to him for ever after. I do not know what I said about Paris, but I talked and made long sentences when I might have said what I wanted in two words. Doll Liddell sat on my other side and he even deigned to say a few words to me. I like him, but he always nods when you are talking, and looks as if he had heard quite enough before you have begun to talk. After dinner we all played the most exciting game that ever was invented, called Tiddleywinks. It consists in flipping counters into a bowl, and being a good number we played at two tables, one table against another, and the excitement was tremendous. I assure you everyone's character changes at Tiddleywinks in the most marvellous way. To begin with, everyone begins to scream at the top of their voices and to accuse everyone else of cheating. Even I forgot my shyness and howled with excitement. Con darted about the room snatching at counters, screaming and trembling with excitement. Lord Wolmer flicked all the counters off the table and cheated in every possible way. George Talbot was very

---

[1] Ernest Crawley, a well-known amateur cricketer.

distressed at this and conscientiously picked every counter up again. Even Gerald got fearfully excited and was quite furious because someone at his table knocked over the bowl just as all the counters were in. Sidney Colvin, whom they nicknamed the Bard because he wrote a prize poem at Cambridge, also got excited and thought he played beautifully. He was at Gerald's table and whenever a counter dropped on the floor G. turned to him and said, "Oh, now you can pick that up," and coolly went on playing. Even he began to scream. I assure you no words can picture either the intense excitement or the noise. I almost scream in describing it.

Betty was talking to Con and me today about Gerald's mother, and said she was so wonderfully sympathetic and always seemed as if the person with whom she was talking interested her more than anyone else. I said that certainly was a wonderful quality, upon which Betty laughed and said, "You talk as if you had been trying it so hard just now," meaning that I had been trying to seem interested in what she was saying and that I was not a bit really. Now, in reality when I made this remark, I was thinking that no one ever seemed interested in what I said. I never can make myself understood. Betty always thinks I am snubbing and contemptuous, when I am generally thinking that I am snubbed myself, or deserve to be. She always thinks I want to say something sarcastic or contemptuous, and so she turns my words, and puts a meaning into them which I never intended. It may be my tone of voice. In old days when I hated everybody and thought everyone hated me, I cultivated a kind of don't care manner to hide how much I was wounded by what people said. I suppose I still have something of it, as I always try and hide whenever I am hurt, as it is so silly, and so I give exactly the opposite impression from what I intend. I get nervous fits on me sometimes, and feel things in a ridiculous way, and to control this I keep a tight hand over myself, and push my feelings away.

Booton Rectory, April 25

Now you are home again you can take a view of your Terling visit in its entirety, and tell me your general

impression of staying out. In old days I have heard men say
that it was delightful, that you were divested of home bothers,
that you fared sumptuously, that everything was done for
you, that you had only to enjoy yourself. I have heard others
say that the tread-mill was preferable, and there were as
many of the last opinion as of the first. I suppose women
differ on the subject as much as men. I am of the stay-at-
home-party, and always was. The small degree in which I
went out was for the purpose of meeting friends that I could
see in no other way. I submitted to a general state of boredom that I might keep alive individual attachments. If it
should chance that visits to country houses are not on the
whole a gain in pleasure to you, there remains an overwhelming motive why you should give in to them, and,
more than that, should court them, for they offer the best
opportunity of making acquaintances out of which to pick
the one that is to grow into a second self. This is the
thought that may always reconcile you. You can take visits
as a duty, though a disagreeable duty. The one that promises
least is often the visit that pays. I put the case at its worst.
But the probability is that if some parties are dull others
will be pleasant, and in the matter of parties a single
swallow will often make a summer.

Booton Rectory, April 28

Those who live near railway stations soon cease to hear
the puffs, and screams, or to feel the vibration of engines.
Lord Lyndhurst [1] told me that when he was an undergraduate
at Cambridge he lodged close to the University church, St.
Mary's, where the curfew was rung daily at 9 o'clock at
night, and the sound of the big bell boomed into his room
as if it had been the belfry. In a few days he ceased to hear
it. I, as an undergraduate, lodged in similar proximity to the
bell, and my experience was precisely the same as Lord
Lyndhurst's. I did not know whether the curfew had rung or
not. People who live in noisy streets enjoy the like immunity.
The mind takes no notice of the sounds when once it has got
accustomed to them. This provision of nature appears more

[1] Lord Chancellor under Peel (1834-5).

admirable when you couple with it the fact that if the mind
has a motive for hearing, then the repetition of the same or
kindred sounds, day after day, has not a deadening effect
but the reverse.

The mention of Cambridge reminds me that I said I would
tell you a fine instance of self-sacrifice in friendship. W. H.
Maule, afterwards a distinguished judge, took his degree
there in 1810. The three highest honours to be attained at
Cambridge were those of Senior Wrangler, first Smith's
prize-man, and Senior Classical Medallist. The first and
second of these honours were for mathematics, the third for
mastery of Greek and Latin. Maule was trained for college
by an uncle who took pupils, and among the number was one
Brandreth. He and Maule became friends, went to Cambridge
the same year, and soon showed themselves to be superior
to all the other men of their standing. Brandreth recognized
the extraordinary talents of Maule, but thought him rather
idle, and was confident that he himself would be Senior
Wrangler. Maule, on the contrary, came out first, and it was
subsequently known that while Maule got 1600 marks at the
examination, Brandreth, who was second, got only 900.
Being so much the profounder mathematician of the two, it
was a matter of course that Maule should be first Smith's
prize-man, and there now only remained the third grand
distinction, that of Senior Classical Medallist. In the entire
history of Cambridge University these three honours have
only three times been won by the same man. Would Maule
make the fourth? It was a foregone conclusion. No one had
a chance of being Senior Classical Medallist except Maule
and Brandreth, and it was certain that Brandreth in classics
was Maule's inferior. You must have been a Cambridge
man to realize the glory, however fleeting, that waits on
Senior Wranglers and Senior Classics. The homage and
enthusiasm are immense. And to carry off all three distinc-
tions is to be raised to more than mortal height of University
fame. Think of Maule's elation in the prospect of his triple
crown. The day of examination came, and he did not appear.
The reason of his absence remained a mystery. He gave no
explanation, and I believe no one guessed the cause. Years

My father, the Earl of Lytton, while Ambassador in Paris

My mother, the Countess of Lytton, 1895

Emily　　　　　　　　Con　　　　　　　　Betty

From a painting done in India by Edward Clifford

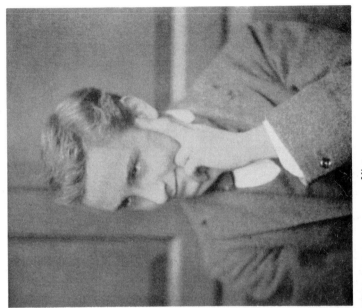

Victor

Neville

The Rev. Whitwell Elwin

Constance and Emily in 1891 at the Paris Embassy

afterwards, his friend Romilly, who became Lord Romilly and Master of the Rolls, wishing to get at the truth, said to him, "I can't understand why you did not try for the medal?" What follows I give in Lord Romilly's words: "I shall never forget, as it is impossible to describe the peculiar expression that came over his countenance. It positively worked with emotion, and he said at last, in a low voice, '*It would have killed Brandreth.*'" It was a sacrifice to the weakness of his vainglorious friend. I am proud to have seen Maule sitting on the bench in his old age. Merely to have seen him was a distinction.

44, *Elm Park Gardens, May* 2

I think I should often give up trying to be better if I did not have your letters, for I feel so miserable and discouraged till you write to me, and then I feel that I will try harder than ever! When I read all you say to me I feel it was so foolish of me to get discouraged before, but I cannot help feeling miserable when I am trying hard and I am always told that I am so hard and snubbing. I will try hard to remember that other people only notice one's faults without seeing one's struggles, which is only natural. What I hate especially is being always noticed and told what I am and what I ought to be, as if I had never thought of it myself. When I am trying hard to be good-tempered Mother sometimes says when I have been cross, "You know you should not give way to those little tempers, you must control them." As if you had only to try and you would succeed. People always seem to think that you do not know your faults and therefore they will be kind and tell you of them and tell you that you ought to conquer them. I cannot help getting irritated at the time, but of course the right thing is to make up my mind that these are part of the trials of life, and that they must be borne patiently. I will go on trying patiently in spite of all discouragements. The chief difficulty is that there are so many different things to try for at the same time. I mean that I have to control my temper and my eagerness in giving my own opinions, while at the same time I have to be very interested in other people's opinions, however mistaken they seem to me, and I am expected to seem very sympathetic and affectionate. These things may not sound as if they were in opposition to one another but they are with me, for if I control my temper I have to control everything in me, and if I get interested in what other people are saying, I find I am giving my own opinions too freely. So a fault always slips out with a virtue. But I ought to learn patience from you, for you are so endlessly patient with me and my grumbles.

The boys and I are going this evening to see *Henry VIII* at the Lyceum. I cannot see Irving as Cardinal Wolsey.

44 Elm Park Gardens, May 3

The play last night was very amusing, but not on account of the splendid acting. The first thing that strikes me in an English theatre after the French is the frightful affectation and vulgarity of all the actors. I daresay if I knew French as perfectly as I know English I should hear the difference of accent, but still in their gestures and movements they are so infinitely superior. At the Français they act the most splendid gentlemen, and you feel as you watch them that no one could seem more refined or well bred than they are. They had one play called *Henri III et sa Cour*, and I am sure no kind of court ever came up to them. They were all so dignified and you felt as you watched them that you were in the presence of great gentlemen. Now, last night there was not one actor or actress that either spoke or looked like an educated person, much less a nobleman. The vulgarity of it was awful. Ellen Terry was not acting, which was a bore, as I wished to see her. Katharine of Aragon's part was taken by a most ghastly creature, awfully fat and even more vulgar and repulsive than the others. We had a box close to the stage which was too near, for you saw the paint on their faces, and their wigs, which was very ghastly. The painting is done so much worse than in Paris for there, however near the stage you were, you would hardly see that they were painted at all. Cardinal Wolsey's part suited Irving in some ways, as he had no opportunity of ranting, but he made as many dreadful faces as he could, and stalked about the stage

in an absurd way. He talks as if it was such an awful effort to
get his words out that it is quite painful to sit and hear him.
I long to give him a good shake. He is not dignified or
impressive in any way, and his affectation is dreadful. The
scene with the Dukes of Norfolk and Suffolk after his
disgrace when they tell him to deliver up the Great Seal, and
which I think is a splendid scene, and Wolsey appears so
grand and dignified by the side of his enemies, is made as
poor as it can be. Irving is finer in that scene than in the
others, but only because the other actors were so utterly
contemptible. They shouted and danced about and looked
like drunken cabmen, shaking their fists at Wolsey. Irving
sat quite quiet and made faces. I do not think there was one
good actor. They all try and talk like Irving and consequently
are all ridiculous. I think it is a very fine play, and the
language in some parts is magnificent; but it is made as
absurd and vulgar as possible. Wolsey's character seems to
rise as his fortunes fall, and I think the last scene in which
he appears is splendid. The more his enemies delight in his
disgrace and heap insults upon him, the higher he seems to rise
above them. And I think his speech to Cromwell is beautiful.

Neville and I went to the Academy this morning, and with
the exception of three or four pictures I never saw such an
exhibition of horrors. They all deserve to be burned. There
are one or two of Millais which are rather good, but Sir
Frederick Leighton's are too awful for words. There is one
of some female, holding up her arm, which is supposed to be
foreshortened, and Con says it looks just like a fat French
asparagus. It really does. There is one of Watts which is
called "And she shall be called Woman." I do not know
whether it is most awful or ridiculous. I never saw such a
muddle of limbs. There is another dreadful one of Sir F.
Leighton's, "When the Sea gave up its Dead," and I heard
someone say behind me, "Well, it looks to me as if he had
put a lot of paint on and then scraped it off again."

Booton Rectory, May 4

Your description of *Henry VIII* at the Lyceum is precisely
what I witnessed, except that perhaps there was nothing quite

so bad, because nothing so pretentious, as Irving's fearful grimaces, his laboured attempts at a voice, not having got one, but only a miserable substitute of muffled sounds, and his abortive efforts at a dignified stalking tread when nature has been so unkind to his legs that he is not equal to the common walk of men in general.

In this same letter he wrote:
"I have a feel that you did your part by the boys this vacation more thoroughly than ever, more to their content consequently, and more to your own. The service is seldom quite equal. Sisters, as a rule, do more for brothers than brothers for sisters. Love is a boon in all its grades, but most to be valued when it is of the kind that never fails. You are exceedingly fortunate in Vic and Neville, and school lessons are a trifle compared to the benefit of another description which they will imbibe from their intercourse with you."

44 *Elm Park Gardens, May 5*

I am glad that you have the feeling that I have been of some use to the boys these holidays, for I trust your feels. I am certainly of no use to anyone else, but I think we get on very happily. I am often dreadfully irritated with them, but it is a kind of understood thing between us that tempers are more in fun than in earnest. Anyway they do not seem much impressed by mine. It is wonderful how much happier the holidays are, that is to say how much better the boys behave. We have hardly had any squabbles, and Mother now scolds me when they are naughty, or because they do not read, and as I pass the scoldings on in a very mild form, they are not much troubled by them. When they have headaches or are rather cross, Mother doses them with homeopathy, and I dose them with peppermint lozenges and eau de cologne bandages, which they greatly prefer. Mother has come to the conclusion that they are better left to themselves, or rather left to me, and though occasionally she still orders Neville to eat this and not to eat that, they are left pretty much alone. Vic, who never eats much, Mother presses to eat, and Neville,

who has got a good appetite and enjoys his food is forbidden
to eat at intervals, as Mother says he is stuffing. But on the
whole things have improved very much.

44 *Elm Park Gardens, May* 12

Mother is going down to Windsor on Monday to see the
Queen, and she is going to take Vic and me with her. It will
not be a delightful expedition, but my comfort is that it will
save me going to a drawing-room later on, for if I am
presented to the Queen now, I shall not have to be presented
again. This will be a great blessing, and I shall have Vic at
Windsor to keep me company. There is a certain amount of
interest in seeing the Queen at Windsor, while there is none
in seeing her at a drawing-room. She is the only one of the
Royal Family for whom I have any respect. From all I have
heard of her, in spite of her age and ugliness, she yet looks
and behaves like a queen, instead of like a dreadfully vulgar
shop-keeper, which all the others I have seen behave like.

My brother Victor and I accompanied my mother when
she went down to Windsor and we were both presented to
the Queen. There were some difficult moments, as my
brother's shoes squeaked dreadfully and he got violent
hiccups just before we were ushered into the presence, and
it was difficult not to laugh. The Queen, although she was so
tiny, gave an impression of tremendous dignity. She kissed
me, but we had a certain difficulty in coming together, as
when I stood up she could not reach me, and when I curtsied
I was too low.

44 *Elm Park Gardens, May* 26

Mother is in a low state about things in general. The
weather is glorious, but very hot, and in London there is no
air. Mother is miserable, abuses London, the heat, everything. The heat is rather too great, but for all that it is
delicious.

Then she is worried about Neville. He has got to have a
plate for his teeth, and he came up last Saturday from Dover [1]

---

[1] Where he was at a private school.

to have it fitted, and is to come up once or twice again. The journey by himself makes him very nervous, and when he was here he screamed very much at night, which he often does, only as a rule I go to him instead of Mother and so it is not noticed. Then he probably caught a chill, and when he got back to Dover he had a feverish attack, which the Matron, who is evidently very fussy, ascribes to nerves. Mother says she is afraid he is delicate, and he ought not to come up to London again, and she does not know what to do. He really is not a bit delicate, and his nervousness, will wear off if he is only treated in the right way. I have been looking forward to his coming up to London, as I thought the journey alone would be a good thing for him, and I believe it would if he is not fussed over. His feverish attack was probably a chill and nothing more, only the Matron is an old goose. Both she and Mother think the best cure for nervousness is starvation. If Neville screams at night he is allowed to take nothing next day but quinine and bromide. It is really the very way to make him worse. The stronger he gets the less nervous he will be and he should be fed up instead of starved. If you once let your nerves get the better of you they will become very troublesome, but if you keep a tight hand over them and never give in to them they soon cease to trouble. I always made a rule for myself that if I was very nervous about anything, I would do that thing till I ceased to mind it. As if medicine was any use at all. Neville suffers a good deal from eczema, and Mother says this upsets his nerves and gives him a feverish chill. One of his legs is dreadfully bad with it, and every night when he is at home I bandage it up for him with some ointment, and it is no worse now than it has been often before, only when Mother sees it, she makes a great fuss.

Neville is very anxious to have a tutor from his school next holidays, and he writes to Mother that he will give his £2 towards paying for him, and he would not make much difference in the food, as he eats very little. I tell you this because it is rather touching of Neville, and it shows so the kind of objections which he knew Mother would make.

44 Elm Park Gardens, June 6

Old Dr. Perry [1] came here on Saturday, and brought Mother an old notebook of Father's from Bonn. It is most heartbreakingly sad, and poor Mummie was quite upset by it. There is a kind of hopeless despair about his views of life and everything he says of childhood is very true, for I think a child's life is, as a rule, a life of despair and misery. But I do not believe anyone who says that all life is miserable or even that misery has the greatest share of life. In this book of father's he divides life into four different stages, and talks of the bitterness of the *Waters of Marah*, and it is all very curious, for it seems so like the beginning of the ideas which created *Marah*. [2] But what seems in both so false to me is to place before you a life which is passed in seeking for pleasure in things which must necessarily bring satiety and disgust, a life without any grand or noble aim, without anything which lifts it above earth and earthly things, and then to say, "Life is a disappointment, there is no reality, no happiness to be found in it, and all lives are alike. There is no reality in anything."

Of course there is no real happiness to be found in things which pass away and leave you without anything to lean upon. If you seek for happiness in sin, of course you will not find it; and there is no sadness in that, the sadness would be if you could find happiness in sin. And why should you make the lives of others dark and miserable, by telling them there is no happiness and no reality in life? I think it is cruel and wicked to start people in life and tell them there is nothing but disappointment and satiety and wretchedness to be found in the world. I feel that if I read a book like *Marah* and believed it and believed that there was no truth, no love, no reality in anything, I should kill myself at once. Even as it is, when I can distinguish clearly the true from the false, I feel as if a cloud was over me while I read it, and I can understand the despair which ends in suicide. If there was nothing else I disliked in *Marah* I think I could not enjoy it for this reason. Take a poem like this one:

[1] My father's tutor at Bonn.
[2] My father's last book of poems.

I have searched the Universe, beneath, above
And everywhere with this importunate lyre
Have wandered desperately seeking Love,
But everywhere have only found Desire.

I have prob'd the spheres above, the spheres beneath,
Their dim abysms have echoed to my shout
Invoking Truth. But time, space, life and death
And joy, and sorrow only answered Doubt.

and compare it to one page of the Bible, and in a minute you can see it is false. If people would but take that blessed Book first and build their lives upon it, they would not be moved by anything that anyone could say, for they would know for themselves that life was real, and love and happiness were real, and if they would but seek for happiness in real things they would find it. But it is cruel to tell you that all your hopes and ambitions are vain, for all things are empty and false. Solomon said, "Vanity, vanity, all is vanity," but he said that of things which are but vanity. He had tried the pleasures of earth and found they were pleasures which could not last, and he rightly said they were but vanity, but he also said, "Let us hear the conclusion of the whole matter. Fear God and keep His commandments, for this is the whole duty of Man." Solomon knew that the only way to be happy on earth was to fear God and keep His commandments, and he had not the sure and certain hope of the resurrection to eternal life through our Saviour Jesus Christ which we have got, and it is this hope which gives the reality and the joy of life. If you seek to do the will of God, to walk in His laws and keep His commandments, who will dare to say that life is but vanity and disappointment? You have the proof in your own heart that such a statement is false. God has shown us the way to live, the way to be happy, the way to die, and yet men are always seeking new paths of their own, and as is only natural, they find at last that their paths have only led them into disappointment, care and misery. The true path to happiness is shown us in the Bible, and we know from experience that if we walk in that

path we are happy, and the people and the books that try
to prove that life is vanity, happiness and truth a delusion,
are all false, for they have been trying to walk in their own
paths, and it is only in God's path that we can find happiness.
It makes me miserable to think that Father wrote *Marah*,
but I comfort myself with thinking what he was and what his
life was, and how grand it was in spite of everything. I only
feel sad to think that anyone should read him through *Marah*,
and sad that another book should have been sent into the
world to put despair and doubt into people's hearts. How
can I ever thank you enough for having shown me all things
clearly, and for having taught me the only way to happiness.
You have taught me to understand the Bible and to take it
for my guide through life, and I know I cannot go very wrong
because you have taught me to see, and you have shown me
the road to Heaven, and helped me along that road further
than you can have any idea of, and I will never, never turn
back from that road. Bless you for having taught me to see
all things clearly.

Booton Rectory, June 7

Johnson said life was made up of little things, and they
interest us more than the history of empires. The details in
your letters are their charm to me.

Your letter this morning I have enjoyed more than any
that has come before. It is deeply affecting, and made my
eyes moist, and calls up endless thanksgiving and fills me
with happiness. You are wondering perhaps why, and it is
probably in unconscious ways that you reveal the changes
which go on in you. They were very marked in your last
visit, and I see plainly that they continue. I always tell you
that there is an infinity in good things. However far we
advance there is still a boundless region beyond, and the
delight is to press forwards, and forwards. We never weary
in that journey, unless when we halt or go backwards.
Blessings on you.

44 Elm Park Gardens, June 10

I am so tremendously interested in the *Rise of the Dutch
Republic* which I am reading. It is like a thrilling novel with

the charm of being true, only it is difficult to believe that it is true. It really is almost impossible to believe that men should have been capable of such ghastly atrocities, and more impossible yet that they could have dared to commit them in the name of Religion. But it is so wonderful how in the midst of all that crime and misery, there should rise up a man like the Prince of Orange. I feel such a tremendous admiration for him that I have a lump in my throat as I read about him. I think he is a magnificent character. As it is impossible to believe that human beings can sink to such depths of wickedness as Philip of Spain and Alva, so it is almost equally impossible to believe they can rise as high as William of Orange. There is something so touching in his greatness that I cannot even think of him without emotion. Every day I think I feel more the miserable littleness of people who think they are showing their superiority by throwing away Religion, and laughing at the belief which all the wisest and greatest men have clung to as their hope and joy. It would be impossible to find a grander, nobler character than William of Orange, and what would he have been without his trust in God? The greater a man is the more he feels how helpless and how weak he is by himself, and it is the belief in the Almighty God that alone gives him the strength he needs. Perhaps the greatest height to which wickedness has ever gone is Napoleon, and what a mean, miserable man he seems compared with Orange. I feel that simply to share the same faith which saints and heroes have clung to lifts one far, far above the littleness of those who think to show their greatness by casting that faith away, even if the faith itself was not a glorious faith.

Betty was furious with me at one time, because she said I was so cold, that I had no enthusiasm about anything, simply because I said I thought ambition was wrong and contemptible, by which I meant worldly ambition. The real fact is I am more ambitious, for my ambition is higher. I would not lower myself to be always striving and working for money, and titles, or anything that this world can give. I should feel degraded if I did so. My ambition is for a higher life, a higher world, an honour which will be everlasting. My ambition is to hear the Great Lord say to me, "Well done, good and faithful servant." You know that I can be en-thusiastic over some things, but I do not waste my enthusiasm on things which are not worth it. I am so happy that I can let my enthusiasm out to you, knowing that you can sympathize with it, because you share it. The delight of saying every-thing out to you is greater than I am able to express. It used to trouble me that no one seemed to feel about religion as I did, and I used to wonder if I was ridiculous to think of it as I did, but now I have got you, and I know we think alike about all things, and I am so happy.

Booton Rectory, June 14

The favourite motto of William the Silent is in English, "For the king, the law, and the people." He meant that the prosperity of a nation depended on loyalty to the king, on obedience to the law, and on care for the welfare of the people. I have probably told you that Guizot, the French statesman and historian, said to me that he thought William the Silent and Washington were the two greatest characters in history, by which I understood him to mean that no two rulers of men, placed in a position of power, had so entirely sunk their own interests in the interests of their country. You have turned your History to admirable account. Nothing you could have read would have been of greater benefit to you.

I was speaking yesterday of the mad ambition of some people to be the handsomest person going, with the miser-able sequel of soon becoming a faded beauty vainly struggling to retain her youthful charms. This morning I happened to open a book by old Fuller, a quaint divine of the seventeenth century, and read that when we are vexed not to be hand-somer we should be thankful that we are not as unhandsome as we might be, and in particular that we are not deficient in any member, nor have one too many. It never occurred to me to be thankful for the last blessing, and for the first time I felt that to have only one arm or leg would be felicity compared to the misery of having, say, two noses. We should be ashamed to show our face in company. These are out of the way calamities that occur too seldom to come into our reckoning. But it is a genuine cause for gratitude, as I often call to mind, that we escape a number of afflictions that are thickly scattered among mankind. Fuller mentions the one use of deformity, that it has been the mother of invention. He declares it is a lie that Ann Boleyn contrived the ruff to conceal a wen on her neck, but seems to believe that Ericthonius, an early Greek, who had the body of a man and the tail of a serpent (which Fuller supposes to mean that he had bad legs), devised the chariot, as an alternative to riding on horse-back, that he might drive about and hide his extremities. To avoid exposing deformities to the public is modest reserve, and not vanity, and Ann Boleyn might be excused for wearing a ruff to cover her wen if she had happened to have one.

44 *Elm Park Gardens, June* 15

I went to dinner last night with Lady Rayleigh at Carlton Gardens. There was only Betty and Gerald and Lord Warkworth,[1] and I cannot conceive why she asked me. Of course Gerald and Lady Rayleigh talked in one corner of the room and Betty and Lord Warkworth in another and I tried to look as interested as I could, when I felt dreadfully bored, and wished the whole time I was home again. Every time I go out anywhere I feel more idiotic, and I come home and vow I will never go out again. I am very silly, but I suppose some day I shall grow less shy. I try to think of all the wise things you tell me, but they have no effect upon me until I am home again and then I am furious with myself for having been such an idiot. If only every one was not a Soul.[2] I hate the Souls and everything to do with them. How angry Betty would be with me, and I think rightly, only I can't help it. You see I am in a temper and had better stop. First to show

[1] Eldest son of Lord Percy, grandson of the Duke of Northumberland, and nephew of Lady Frances Balfour.
[2] This name was given to a little group of intellectuals, but I do not know if they had adopted the name themselves, or if it had been bestowed on them by others. Arthur Balfour was one of the leading lights of this coterie, which also included Mr. Asquith, Miss Margot Tennant, Frances Balfour, as well as Betty and Gerald, among others.

my repentance I will tell you that I love you, far more than
I hate the Souls. It is not necessary to tell you so, but I am
extra happy to think I need not go out tonight.

Booton Rectory, June 23

You told me of your dinner at Lady Rayleigh's with Lord
Warkworth, but with a tantalizing omission that I have
been daily meaning to ask you to repair. What did you
think of him? Is he a Soul? Or are the Souls a female society
only? Is he good-looking? Are his manners pleasant? Is he
an agreeable talker? Is he clever? Is he well informed? Did
he draw to you or you to him? Is he a man to fall in love
with, assuming that he comes out well on better knowledge?
Betty, the first time she met him, thought highly of him. My
definite questions make answers easy. You know what you
have to say. Speculatively I married him to somebody months
ago, and want to find out if he will suit.

44 Elm Park Gardens, June 24

I will now answer your questions about Lord Warkworth.
First, I had not much opportunity of forming any opinion
about him, as not a word passed between us. During dinner
I talked to Lady Rayleigh's little boy, and afterwards, as I
told you, Betty and Lord Warkworth retired into one corner
and Gerald and Evelyn sat in another, and as my companion
had gone to bed, I struggled to listen to both conversations
and heard neither properly. Lord Warkworth is not yet a
Soul, though I am sure Frances will do her best to make him
one of them. He has one good quality to prevent his becoming
a Soul, which is that though he is very clever he is also very
humble and no Soul is humble. He may, however, become
corrupted. Up till now he has been kept very strictly by his
parents, and Frances who has taken him under her wing will
hardly allow him out anywhere. He is treated just like a
child. He is madly fond of plays and everything connected
with the stage, and is at present writing a play in the old
Greek style, which makes his family furious because it is
so improper and Frances furious because it is so dull. Lord

Hugh Cecil, who is his great friend, says it is neither
improper nor dull. He is considered one of the rising young
men, and Frances talks of no one else. So I was prepared to
dislike him, but did not. He is not good looking and has a
rather stupid face and yet there is something very fascinating
about it. He is very short and looks about sixteen. He has a
very pleasant voice and manner and I feel I should like to see
more of him. You see, I have not fallen in love with him,
but neither do I think him a beast. I should like to know him,
if no one else was there to look on, by which I mean that I
should not dare to speak to him with Betty and Frances
listening with all their ears to find out if our conversation
was as soully and intellectual as it ought to be. When people
are as much made of as he is, I feel I have only a right to
look at them from a distance. I am afraid I only like stupid
people, as they generally like me, with some exceptions. I
certainly felt rather fascinated by him, and wished I could
be as soully as Betty. She is very taken with him and is to
read his play when it is finished. I should like to meet him
in a room where there was not one Soul, and then I might
dare to speak to him, but when Frances and Betty are anywhere near I can never open my lips. It is such a relief to meet
someone who will talk about the weather after you have
heard a conversation of Souls. How can I go up to Lord
Warkworth the first time I see him and begin a conversation
about dramatic construction? I know nothing about dramatic
construction or any other such deep subject. We talk of far
more interesting subjects when we are together, don't we?
I think I might dare to talk about dramatic construction if I
was sitting by your side and holding your hand. I wish
people would be content to be what they are without always
wishing to be so much cleverer than anyone else. How
thankful I am to be too stupid to be a Soul. I can laugh at
them from a safe distance. I sometimes wonder if anyone
who is not a fool will ever fall in love with me, but then I
comfort myself in that as I do in everything by the thought
that you manage to love me, and perhaps I shall find another
wonderful person one day. Have I satisfied your curiosity
about Lord Warkworth and are you pleased with my account

of him, or not? Do you think he will be a suitable husband
for your somebody?

I love Betty's face of despair when she introduces some
charming young man to me, and asks afterwards my opinion
of him and I generally answer, "I think he is a beast." She
gets very angry with me at times.

44 *Elm Park Gardens, June* 27

I hoped I had convinced you that your letters were as full
to me as they could possibly be, and that I do not wish them
to change in any way. If I am satisfied you may be. I have
not a want or wish which your letters do not satisfy. I only
remind you from time to time that you have a pupil who is
anxious to learn all that you can teach. The lessons are
about a subject which is dear to us both, and each lesson
draws us nearer to each other. I long to know and you like
to teach, and it is only time that is wanting. You are not to
put me before anything else. I remind you of your promise
to teach me what you know lest you should think I had
ceased to care.

It always makes me angry when people quote from the
Book of Revelation. No one can pretend to understand it,
and they twist it into the most awful and absurd meanings.
I think it is a beautiful book. Some passages are not to be
equalled by any other part of the Bible. If people would but
be content to let it remain in its beauty, without giving it a
meaning of their own.

I am glad I have given you a favourable impression of
Lord Warkworth. I will be sure and tell you when I next
meet him. Betty is an angel and nothing can spoil her
angelic nature, but when she is among Souls she becomes a
Soul for the time being, and so spoils herself. If Souls could
but have their thin coat of paint scraped off, what poor
wooden blocks they would be. Don't tell Betty so.

Booton Rectory, June 28

A large body of people draw towards the subjects which
admit of endless speculation because nothing is or can be

definitely known, as if a traveller should like to rove perpetually in misty regions where not an object could be seen except the visionary creations of his fancy. This is the charm of antiquarian studies to many. The Book of Revelation has had enormous attractions for the class of divines whose glory is to know the unknowable. The parts which belong to the future, and which the future alone can explain, are more precious to them the darker they seem. They can enlighten them, and they speak with a peculiar species of dogmatism as if their crude presumptuous theories had been communicated to them by heaven. In every direction we soon get a closed door which the united powers of mankind cannot force open, and it is a waste of mind when we expend it on barren problems, and neglect the wisdom which belongs to our condition. I echo back what you say to me to show you how entirely I agree with you.

Chapter Eight

I MUST here say something about the Blunt family, who now began to play a large part in my life. Wilfrid Blunt first became intimate with my father in 1866 when he was an attaché and my father was First Secretary at the British Embassy in Lisbon. They had a great bond in poetry, and Blunt was able greatly to assist my sister Betty in re-editing my father's poems after his death. Blunt came of a Sussex family and owned two estates in that county. At Crabbet Park he started the famous stud of Arab horses now carried on by his daughter, Lady Wentworth. He had inherited the property from an elder brother who had died young from tuberculosis. Blunt himself had suffered from the same disease, and for this reason he always passed the winters out of England, generally in Egypt, where he had bought an estate near Cairo.

Blunt was not only a poet and a landowner, but took an active part in politics, always supporting movements which were directed against his own country. In Ireland he joined the Home Rule movement, supported Parnell, and was imprisoned for sedition in Kilmainham Gaol. In Egypt he was also a trouble-maker, supporting Araby Pasha in his revolt against the British Administration.

His family were Roman Catholics, but Blunt himself, though brought up as a Catholic, told me that in later life he had become a Moslem. He was a man of great charm and artistic gifts (he had himself designed the house at Crabbet), but his morals were not of the best. Lady Anne, his wife, was the grand-daughter of Lord Byron by his daughter Ada, who married Lord Lovelace. She was a very kind and loveable person. She was very small, with a nut-brown face and bright beady eyes and always reminded me of a robin. She was an

Arabic scholar, having learnt that language in order to make a study of everything relating to the Arab horse. She was a passionate lover of horses and it was reported that she went to bed fully equipped for riding—top boots and all—in order that she might be ready to ride in the early hours of the morning. When ill she called in a vet instead of a doctor. She played the violin and practised diligently, but never played anything but scales.

Their only child, Judith, became my greatest friend and later my sister-in-law, for she married my brother Neville.

My next letter was from Crabbet, where I had gone on a visit.

Crabbet Park, Three Bridges, Sussex, June 29

I like Lady Anne, for she is so extremely kind and so dreadfully snubbed by her husband. Mr. Blunt and I sharpen our wits upon each other. I tell him plainly my opinion of him, which is that he is a goose and a hypocrite. He takes it all in good part, and returns me compliments much of the same nature. He came down to dinner last night in a most gorgeous Eastern costume with a turban on his head, and a most beautiful cloak of scarlet and gold. Of course we only chaff each other in fun, but when Mother is present she gets quite distressed and tries to make peace as if we were really quarrelling, and I invariably get a scolding when he has gone for having been so impudent. He asked me this afternoon if I would go out fishing, and though I hate all sports which mean killing some harmless animal, I thought it seemed so ungracious to refuse everything they asked me to do, and I made sure I should catch nothing and so consented to go. I was unlucky, however, and caught one trout. Fishing is not quite as cruel as shooting, but all the same I hate doing it, though I cannot help getting awfully excited over it.

Crabbet Park, June 30

I had a delicious ride yesterday, with a few little exceptions. I am always very shy of getting on to a horse, for I never manage to mount properly. When someone is helping me I always jump long before the other person is ready, and

then when I have come to the ground again they push me.
When at last I jump at the right moment I nearly tumble
over to the other side of the horse. Yesterday this difficulty
was removed by having a chair to mount with. I had begged
to have a very quiet horse, so they gave me one which would
hardly move, although I kicked and whipped it the whole
time. Mr. Blunt rode on in front without saying a word.
I rode in the middle and Lady Anne behind. Lady Anne,
who is very fussy, kept telling me to sit straight, and to
go faster, and to do this and that. We rode through
delicious woods, only the paths were so narrow and the
branches so low, I thought every moment I should be caught
by the hair like Absalom. I knew I was always doing the
wrong thing and spoiling their precious Arabs. There were
numberless small gates which Mr. Blunt pushed open and I
was expected to dash through before they swung to again,
but as I could not get my horse to move out of a very slow
walk this was no easy matter. Lady Anne found fault with
me a good deal, but tried to make up a little when we came
home, by saying, "You look so nice it is a pleasure to see
you." What I should really have enjoyed would have been a
good gallop all over the park instead of a slow walk through
the woods. In spite of their numberless horses I should say
they got as little pleasure from them as possible. As is the
case with most luxuries, they are made slaves to their horses
instead of the other way round. Though they ride every day,
from the fuss that is made about the horses you would suppose
that it was a very unusual thing to go for a ride. Lady Anne
fusses dreadfully over everything. Judith is very much sub-
dued this year, and she has a bad cold now, which makes
her very sorry for herself. I am very happy, for it is all so
easy, and I do not feel in the least shy. I enjoy myself and I
enjoy the comic things in the Blunts. They certainly are all
rather mad, but immensely kind.

Crabbet Park, July 1

I had a delicious ride yesterday alone with Lady Anne
through the most lovely woods where each turn seemed to
bring us to something more beautiful than before. The
9

country all round here is very lovely. Lady Anne is much nicer by herself than with other people and she was charming to me yesterday, and begged I would often come back here and have some really good riding, and she said I might have some lessons from their coachman, who is a splendid riding master, and learn to ride different horses and get quite accustomed to them. She said she had a feeling that I should get on very well with horses if I was more accustomed to them and I should soon learn to ride anything. It was very kind of her, and I really should enjoy having some good rides and learning more about riding, for I am very fond of it, only I have had so little practice. She was altogether very nice to me, and I had been rather dreading a ride alone with her, for she was in such a bad temper all day. I think Mr. Blunt had been scolding her in the morning, and then he went off to London, and she visited her displeasure on poor Judith. At luncheon it was most dreadful, for Judith happened not to hear something Lady Anne said to her, for which she was fearfully blown up. I pity Judith very much for the position she holds between her parents. Mr. Blunt is always scolding Lady Anne for not letting Judith go out more and bringing her more into the world, and though Lady Anne dare not scold Judith while he is there, directly she is left alone she scolds her as a kind of revenge for the scolding she has herself received from Mr. Blunt. They both simply worship Judith and yet quarrel about her. I do pity Lady Anne for the way she is snubbed, but I think that like all snubbed people she does the very things to make it worse. She is so very touchy about little things instead of giving in quietly to what he wants. They do not actually quarrel, for they hardly ever speak to one another.

I think there is nothing so foolish or so unkind as to scold people before strangers. It is fearfully unkind to the person who is being scolded, and it makes the onlookers feel very uncomfortable. I think to begin with it is wrong to scold people at all unless you have a very good reason for it, and then you ought never to do it if anyone else is present. What seems such an extraordinary thing to me is the way parents are always scolding their children for their want of respect

to themselves. It is generally some little trifling thing which
no one would notice if the parents themselves did not call
attention to it. I do not understand how anyone can bring
themselves to own they are offended. Can you understand
saying to anyone in the world, "You did not listen when I
spoke to you just now, you are very rude indeed, and I am
very offended with you." I simply could not bring myself
to be so ridiculous. I think the last thing you ought to do
with your children is to be always telling them to treat
you with respect. No parent ought to *ask* their children
for either love or respect. Teach them to be respectful to
other people, and they will learn of their own accord to give
you all the respect and love you can wish for. I think the
rule you have so often given me ought to be kept in every
relation of life. Be what you ought to be in yourself and you
will always find people to love and respect you. I always
feel that if I married a man who snubbed me, I would never
accuse him of it, or reproach him with it in any way. I am
convinced that almost every man who had any good in him
would come back to you in time, if you were not always
nagging at him and reproaching him. However hurt or
offended I might be with anyone, my pride alone would
prevent my showing it. I could not be always asking people
for love and respect as some people do.

Booton Rectory, July 1

I had your letter describing your visit this morning, all
greatly to my mind, except that I cannot approve of your
conduct to the trout. The celebrated Lord Erskine was a man
extremely pitiful to animals, and when he was Lord Chancellor the Lord Mayor presented him with a sturgeon that
had been caught in the Thames. This big rarity reached him
alive, and he had it immediately put into a water tank and
kept till night, when he conveyed it in a cart under cover of
darkness back to the Thames. The secrecy was to keep the
Lord Mayor in ignorance of the shocking use which had
been made of his present. Lord Erskine in your place would
have been clumsy enough to drop the caught trout into the
stream.

44 Elm Park Gardens, July 4

We had a most amusing day at Dover on Saturday. The
weather was glorious and very hot. Even at the sea there was
hardly a breath of wind. Neville was very pleased to have
us, and yet very ashamed and afraid we should disgrace him.
Being very hungry I asked him if I might eat a hearty lunch,
to which he answered, "You may eat moderately, but whatever you do, don't eat too much." I begged him to tell me
when I had eaten enough, and he said, "You may have two
helpings of everything if you like, but mind you don't have
more." I thought this very generous of him. Con said she
was sure to get the giggles as she always did on these
occasions. Poor Neville was in a terror at this, and begged
that she would on no account do that, as he did not know
what he should do. Happily we got a corner of the table,
and I sat behind a big flower pot, so our doings were not so
much seen. Neville very kindly told me what to eat and how
much, and after I had drunk two glasses of claret cup, he
said to me, "Knowing your habits I should advise you to
drink no more." This sounds bad for me, doesn't it? What
he meant by my habits I don't quite know. As he had hurt his
ankle with a cricket ball he was not allowed to run and so
sat by us all day until it was his turn to play, and then he
very grandly batted and got someone to run for him. He is
Captain of the Eleven now and very proud of himself,
and tells me he is very severe with the boys and rows them
awfully when they miss a catch, which he says makes them
more careful another time. Con was very anxious to sit on
the grass in the shade, but Neville would not hear of this
and made us sit up on a bench as everyone else was doing.
It is wonderful how polite boys are at school. Neville flew
about during teatime handing cakes and strawberries to
everyone but himself and treated us with the greatest respect
while his schoolmaster's eye was on him. He drove back
to the station with us and several other boys and their
people. This particular match is called the Fathers' Match,
and is a great day, for generally a great number of parents
come down, and all the fathers who know anything about
cricket are made to play. This year on account of the

elections [1] only three fathers were available, and Neville remarked, "We are going to try and make the best of them."
Only one father came to the station with us, but he received
three tremendous cheers, looking extremely ridiculous as he
bowed out of the window. Our day was not over by any means
yet. The Continental train by which everyone left had no
third-class carriages, and as the fare is very expensive, Con
and I determined to wait for half an hour longer and come
by a train which they told us was very quick. It was the
slowest train I have ever been in, or seemed to be. In our
carriage was an unfortunate woman with four little children,
one quite a baby, all looking fearfully ill, and one poor little
girl was sick all the way up to London. I took a great dislike
to the woman at first, for she was so fearfully cross to the
children, but I ended by admiring her for the wonderful way
she managed them all. We arrived in London about nine
o'clock. The poor woman besides four children had as many
huge parcels, which she was struggling to carry. Con with
her usual kindness insisted on taking the largest bundle and
I took another. As we were very late we thought the best
way at last was to pay a porter and get him to help the woman
with her children and bundles. We then got into a hansom,
the driver of which was quite drunk. He crawled along until
he saw a carriage in front of him and then dashed into it.
Con and I, being frightfully nervous, screamed to the man to
stop, jumped out and paid him, Con remarking in a stern
voice, "It's impossible to go along at this pace." We happily
got into another cab which though dreadfully slow landed us
safely home about half past nine. We longed to make much
of our adventures, but thought it best to suppress the poor
woman and her children, as it would only have given Mother
a fresh dislike to third-class carriages.

44 *Elm Park Gardens, July 5*
I am getting quite excited over the elections, though I
cannot bring myself to read all the speeches. I occasionally
look at Gladstone's and Arthur Balfour's. Gladstone's seem

[1] The General Election, in which Lord Salisbury was defeated by Gladstone

to me debased and unprincipled to a degree which is hardly credible. He does not even go through the pretence of having any principles, but tells the most awful and wicked lies, and tries to stir up all the differences between all classes simply to get in himself. I cannot imagine how any man with a single right feeling in him is not revolted. Besides this I think Gladstone's speeches are very dull and very bad. They seem to me endless words and arguments patched up together, with no sense or force about them. I should say they were wretched stuff from beginning to end, even if there were nothing worse, which there is. Arthur Balfour's speeches I think are very good. Very clear, very amusing, and very well put together. I also read Lord Salisbury's manifesto, which I thought splendid. It is especially grand by the side of Gladstone's wicked lies. I am getting quite political, ain't I? Thursday, the day of Gerald's election,[1] will be awfully exciting. We hope to hear about midnight the result. Have you seen in the *Daily Graphic* the picture of Lord Salisbury and Gladstone climbing up two ladders. I think it is most delicious, and as Con says, they seem to have caught the characteristics of each so well. Con laughs each time she looks at it.

I think I might get quite interested in the history of my own day, although it is so dull, if I knew anything at all about it, but I feel that it would take me a lifetime to learn all that I need to learn before being able properly to understand what is happening now, and as each day something fresh is happening, there never seems time to pick up the past.

It is raining hard and I am happy in the thought of staying in and being lazy. Mother is wild to go out for a walk. It really seems like a kind of madness with her. In heat and cold and rain her one object is to go out for a walk. My object is generally to stay in unless it is warm enough to sit out of doors. Mother never seems to get enough walking to satisfy her. I always get too much. People are always complaining of the changeable weather, but it would be dreadful if it were always the same, I think.

[1] Gerald was standing for one o the divisions of Leeds, and was elected.

44 *Elm Park Gardens, July 6*

Mother had a most delicious letter from Betty this morning, who seems bursting with excitement. Certainly elections are more amusing than I thought they were, and I am quite warming up to be interested in them. I think I am of a very excitable nature, or should be if I allowed my feelings to carry me away. If I were a man and in a position to let forth my opinions and my feelings, I should soon get into trouble, for if I once got loose I should never be able to stop myself. I think there is no lesson so necessary as to learn to control your feelings and keep a tight hand over them, especially if your feelings are inclined to run away with you. I have at last succeeded to a certain extent in controlling mine, and the consequence is I am supposed to be hard and unfeeling. When I allowed my feelings to get the better of me, I was told I was going mad, and since I have got the better of them I am supposed to be quite without feeling. I am not bringing up my old grievances, for they have ceased to trouble me and the things that maddened me before only amuse me now. I really think I am getting on slowly, though I have not nearly succeeded in pleasing myself yet; the vexing things though do not irritate me in nearly the same degree as they did. Mother still continues to tell me I am masterful and independent, but as I know that fact so well by this time I have ceased to mind very much. The thing which distresses me more than anything that Mother says is that I know I make Con angry with me, and she thinks that I am very domineering, and the way I give my opinions irritates her dreadfully. I do not think she understands me much, and certainly no two people could be more different than she and I. I do not know how it is, but I never seem able to agree with anyone. I have got into a bad habit of contradicting and often I do it more for fun than anything else, but I know it has got to be a bad habit and I am trying hard to overcome it. I am learning gradually to be less positive, but Con thinks I contradict on purpose, which is not at all the case. I know my manner is often very positive, although I have no intention of being so. I am sorry when I vex Con, but after all I can do no more than try and conquer

my faults, and if it takes very long to do, other people must
have patience with me. I mention all these things to you
because they happen to come into my mind, and because I
know you like to hear how I am getting on. I don't get on
very quick and I don't try nearly as hard as I ought to do,
but still I think I am gradually improving. I go to sleep
sometimes, but when I wake I try extra hard to make up. I
think I have just woke up and I am going to try as I have
never tried before. All things take such a long time to learn
and I am so dreadfully impatient.

The rules made by boys for themselves are very absurd.
I told Neville he was even more severe than Victor. Their
rules are very laughable, and I get so much amusement out
of them that they do not seem annoying. Mother treats them
so seriously and is always angry with me when I laugh at
them when I go to Eton, but it is really impossible to help
laughing. Con says as the boys suffer such tortures lest their
people should disgrace them, she does not believe they can
enjoy having them down, but I am sure they do. Con gets
very angry at the absurdity of their rules, but I think it is
silly to do anything but laugh at them. Con dislikes boys as
a rule and everything to do with them. I, on the contrary,
have a particular liking for them. I think Con is too much of
an old maid to like boys, she is so fidgetty when they make
a noise and make a mess of everything. There is one thing
where I think even Betty makes a great mistake with the
boys, and Mother certainly does, and that is expecting them
to like books and serious talks better than games and their
own interests. Betty is always disappointed when Vic goes to
see her that he will talk of cricket and shooting, instead of
discussing the last new book with her. I am sure one of the
first things necessary with boys is to enter into their interests
if you wish them to enter into yours. If you listen patiently
while they tell you long stories of their doings, they get to
listen patiently when you talk to them of yours. Mother is
distressed because our boys talk of nothing but games, but
my only surprise is that they allow me to lecture them and
read to them as much as they do.

Booton Rectory, July 7

Nature has made most things charming in their place,
boys among the rest, when they are true boys and not prigs.
I relish them when they are lovers of tarts and ginger beer,
and cricket, shooting, fishing, and the like, and I remember
how dear such things were to me in my own juvenile time,
and half live it over again when I witness it in the coming
race, and wish that I myself had not outgrown the fun. Cut
out that chapter in a man's life, and for want of the recollec-
tions he would be maimed in mind, and had better be one-
armed, one-legged, or one-eyed. Old men of ten and fifteen
are a horror to me.

Nobody tries systematically to improve without advancing
day by day, and the slow growth, long invisible, will be
apparent to everybody, say, in a twelvemonth. A bad
character sticks to us after we have ceased to deserve it.
Each deviation from perfection is noted as if it were still a
habit, and besides the outward manner may remain when the
inward disposition has changed. The one point which
signifies is that we should not grow weary of well-doing, or
of striving after it, and in the end we shall seem to be what
we actually are. It appears strange that we should hug our
defects when we must all be aware that it is immensely for
our interest to get rid of them.

44 Elm Park Gardens, July 7

Today is Gerald's election and I do not know how we shall
all live through the day, our excitement is so great. I am
really getting excited enough over the elections to please
even Frances. I rush downstairs in the morning to see if
Lord Salisbury is still the highest on the ladder. Every fresh
bit I read of Gladstone's speeches makes me hate him more.
I almost choke with rage at the cool way in which he tells
the most awful lies. Most politicians, however ambitious
and selfish they may be, at least pretend to care a little for the
good of the country, but Gladstone takes no trouble whatever
to hide his utter selfishness. Betty says she expresses her
hatred for him freely, to Frances' great indignation. It is
sufficient to abuse a person for Frances immediately to stand

up for him as the noblest and best of human beings. Betty
said a sickening feeling came over her the other day of the
possibility of Gerald's losing. It would be even worse, she
said, than losing a game of golf. What a dreadful day this
will be for them, and how sick they will get with excitement.
Fancy what that waiting time must be like while the votes
are being counted.

We are all going to Hatfield for two days next Tuesday.
Frances is going to be there too, and perhaps Betty and
Gerald, so it will be very nice. Mother did not at all wish
to go at first, as she has refused to go anywhere yet and so
thought she might offend her friends if they heard she had
been at Hatfield. Also going out anywhere makes her so
miserable. She thought, however, it was better to accept, as
Lady Salisbury has been so very kind, and she was rather
offended before when Mother refused to go or let me go. I
have made up my mind never to think of visits until I am
actually there, as either I look forward to them, in which
case I am always disappointed, or else I dread them, so that
I am perfectly miserable. I always rather enjoy my visits
even when I am too shy to be at my ease, and anyhow I
console myself with thinking that each visit makes me less
shy.

Booton Rectory, July 8

A cause is desperate when a man can only support it by
falsehoods. The election has obliged Gladstone to state his
case in the best form he can, and the result is that his speeches
are not only dishonest but drivel. Poorer stuff for a man in
his position I never read. His partisans cheer, and they
would equally stamp and roar if he called out, "Open
Sesame" and sat down again. You will observe the philo-
sophic calm of my language, the consequence of living in
retirement, far from the "madding crowd," which is Gray's
expression.

Even going out cannot be all pleasure. But to go to Hatfield with your whole family will be as near perfection as a
state visit can be. The shyness is the drop of bitter, and is of
small account, for it does not amount to more than discomfort. It is neither grief nor pain. And you are pretty sure to

have intervals of happy ease, and besides you can console yourself with the reflection that you are employed in the primary duty of making friends and acquaintances, and you need grudge nothing which contributes to that end. In your place, I should carry hope with me wherever I went, and I myself have it for you wherever you go. Mind in your nervousness you do not snap. Unless you watch, the old manner will come up when you are flustered. The soft, gentle voice alone represents truly the plenitude of your love. Could you carry your heart on your sleeve you would have a whole flock of birds pecking at it. You will be nearer your best the more you appear as you really are.

44 Elm Park Gardens, July 9

Betty and Frances both dined here with us last night. Betty is looking splendidly well in spite of fatigues and excitement. She gave us a most wonderful description of all their time at Leeds, and to hear her tell it was far better than to have seen it all. Her account made me thrill with excitement. She must tell it you all herself, for I should only spoil it by repeating her words. I think I should have been in tears the whole time from excitement and emotion. It seems such impossible joy to think it is really over.

Some days everything seems to go well, and everyone is in a good humour, and my spirits go up even higher than usual. Today is one of these good days. To begin with I had your letter, which was dear enough to make anyone's heart leap for joy. Mine did and does still. Then it is a lovely day and everyone seems so cheerful and pleased with themselves. I feel as if I had not written you a proper letter for days, and I have not over much time today, for Vic and I were at the cricket match [1] all the morning and as Mother has gone out for the day I have him still on my hands. I must tell you all about the match, which I have enjoyed very much. Vic arrived yesterday in full Eton glory with light blue ribbons stuck all over him, and even had a light blue edge to his handkerchief. He and I went off together, which was great fun, as having a brother is almost better than being alone,

[1] Eton *v.* Harrow at Lord's.

and we had no third person to spoil our enjoyment. He, of course, sneered and turned up his nose at every Harrow boy we passed and was much offended at being offered dark blue cornflowers to put in his buttonhole. At Neville's cricket match we were not allowed to applaud at all, but it was much more amusing at Lord's, for we clapped and shouted loudly when Eton did anything at all remarkable. The different people looking on were very amusing, and there was some foreigner who sat behind us and asked exceedingly ignorant questions all the time in broken English. Harrow, who had gone in first, was all out by luncheon time for 214 runs, and Vic and I then went to the Lockers' coach and had lunch, and we stayed with them all the afternoon. It was nearly impossible to see from where their coach was placed, but we had great fun all together.

In the evening Vic went to the theatre with the Lockers, and I think enjoyed himself as much as he possibly could. Today we have passed much the same day, only came back here to lunch with Godfrey,[1] as the match was all over by one o'clock. Eton played very badly and got beaten by 65 runs, but on the whole it was a very good match and most exciting. So you see I have been enjoying myself, which you will like to hear.

Vic and Godfrey seem thicker friends than ever. Vic says Godfrey thinks we are horribly cold to him and do not treat their friendship half seriously enough. The Lockers have been most tremendously kind and I do not think we have been nearly cordial enough to them. We cannot ask them for visits as they do us, for we have no house except this one, but I think we ought to be as cordial to them as we can. The other morning Mr. Locker came round to ask if Con or I would go to the play with them last night, and Mother having refused on account of Betty's being here, added, "And they would not in the least care to go." "Oh, wouldn't they?" said poor Mr. Locker in a very crushed voice. What Mother meant was they will not be disappointed, but as she put it, it sounded so dreadfully rude. One thing which is rather dreadful is the way in which Mr. Locker tips Vic. He gives

---

[1] Godfrey Locker, Victor's friend and contemporary at Eton.

him £1 each time he sees him, and of course Mother is not
rich enough to tip Godfrey very often, and it seems so horrid
of us to be always receiving and never giving anything. Of
course it is absurd, I think, to expect giving to be always
equal on both sides, and in our position now we cannot be
always giving, but I think Mother might be more cordial,
only of course as Vic has made a friend, she must oppose
him, because he chose his friend for himself instead of getting
her to choose it for him. And Godfrey is especially a friend
whom she ought to like, as he makes Vic read and think, and
does not care about cricket or any kind of sport. Mother says
she has no interest in common with the boys and gets so
dreadfully bored with their interests, and yet she expects
them to be interested in hers.

Booton Rectory, July 10

I have a splendid history this morning from Betty of the
Leeds election. The experience to her would of itself be
worth the money they have spent. Better to be rich in mind
than in purse. Your account of the cricket match comes close
upon the election in the extent of the excitement it appears
to create. There is a gap in your narrative. You omit the
description of Vic's feelings when the beggarly Harrow chaps
beat the kingly Etonians. Will Vic change schools, Gladstone
fashion, and go over to the winners? He need not hesitate
because he has denounced them hitherto as murderers,
robbers, seditious, and the like. Gladstone's example will
bear him out. It is enough that in the cricket match they
seemed the strongest.

44 Elm Park Gardens, July 11

You wish me to be happy and so you will like to hear I
am and that my Sunday was full of blessing to me. Some days
I am suddenly seized with the feeling of what a beast I am
and I feel as if all my faults were increasing and none of my
virtues, and I get a kind of loathing of myself, until I feel
perfectly miserable. I felt this very much yesterday, which
may make you wonder why I say I was happy, but I will
explain to you. I was chiefly miserable because I felt I had
been so hard and unjust to Mother. I get so to forget all her

grand qualities and virtues, and feel and see only the
irritations and the faults, and then yesterday Betty was
talking to me of her, and pointing out the fearful loneliness
and misery of her life, and I suddenly felt such a fearful pang
at the thought of my hardness to her. My chief fault is that
I have not sufficiently realized how much she feels little
things like being poor, and having to live in a small house
and have few servants. I do not in the least feel these things
myself, as I do not see that they in any way add to my
happiness, and this makes me hard on Mother. Not missing
any luxuries myself, I do not see why she should, but I realize
now to the full how different it is for her, and I feel so vexed
with myself when I think that I did not see it all before. All
her life she has been accustomed to luxuries, and naturally
now she is getting older and needs them more, she feels
dreadfully having to rough it. She loves being in a position
in which she can give to other people, and as a great lady
she feels in her element. Of course it is natural she should
feel the difference of her position now from what it was in
Paris. I am sure this is one reason why she wishes so to go
to the country, as there she can make far more show with a
little money than she can in London. It made me miserable
yesterday to think of all this, and also I felt unhappy to think
of my manner, and that I always gave people the idea that I
was cross when I most wished to seem amiable. You tell me
not to snap at Hatfield, but you know I never snap intentionally, and when I think I have got an amiable smile on my
face I am told I look so fearfully cross. Of course it is in some
way my fault and I will do my best to change it, but as I
cannot see my own face what I think is an amiable expression
looks quite differently to other people. Do I look cross when
I am looking at you? If so, I shall give up trying to look
otherwise, for certainly if I cannot look amiable when I am
with you, nobody else can hope to see me anything but
furiously cross. It is dreadful to have a face which you must
always be thinking about for fear it should be expressing
feelings which you have not got. I love to tell you all this,
and to tell you all my faults, though they are too evident to
need much telling, but when I have suddenly realized my

faults, as I did yesterday more strongly than ever before, and have determined to try and be altogether different, I feel so crimson with shame at the thought of what I was and probably still am to a great degree, that I can hardly bring myself to tell you of my faults, lest you should hate me as I hate myself. But when this fit passes off, I feel how great the change is in me, and then I think I must try and make it clear to you, lest you think I am still the beast I was. There are many, many changes that go on in me before there is the slightest outward change, and I want you to know my inward changes, and to know that I realize how wrong I have been, and that I am determined with all my might to try and do better. I felt rather miserable altogether yesterday and yet I felt it was a day full of blessing, and today I am as happy as possible. First I am happy because though I feel I have been horrid to Mother, yet I know this last week I have behaved to her much better than before. I have tried to be more loving and I have succeeded. I am also happy because I have not been in a real temper for some time, though yesterday I felt dreadfully cross because we were late for church, only I managed to control it more or less. Thirdly, I am happy to have been miserable yesterday, by which I mean I am glad to have realized my faults more fully, that I may fight against them more earnestly. Yesterday I was miserable at the thought of how little I had done, today I am happy at the thought of how much I may do, and above all I am happy with your dear letter.

It will be a tremendously exciting time at Hatfield with all the last elections going on. Lord Cranborne's is today, and Betty says if he does not get in she will not go to Hatfield. It would indeed be dreadful. Betty and Con say their election fever has greatly diminished since last Thursday; my excitement still continues, though not to the same extent, but I still boil over with rage at Gladstone's speeches. Lady Lathom,[1] who was here yesterday, says she hears he is so fearfully excited that they dare not let him see the papers, or tell him how the elections are really going, but pretend he has got all the majority he wants, which is some

[1] My mother's first cousin, born Alice Villiers.

hundreds. What a sell it will be for him when he is obliged to be told the truth.

Booton Rectory, July 11

Tomorrow is the day you move to Hatfield, is it not? There you will increase your knowledge of elections and the politics of your time, which are the politics that concern us most. Listen with both ears, use your tongue to ask questions, particularly when you can get hold of Lord Salisbury by the button, give yourself up to the excitement of the hour (if I were there I should hardly keep my limbs together through the vehemence of my feelings) and be sure and write me a full account of the doings and sayings and effervescencies of each day. My prospect is bounded by an agricultural hedge. Think what animation it must be to me when you throw open a door that gives me a glimpse into the Hatfield world.

Hatfield House, Hatfield, Herts, July 13

My excitement is growing to such a pitch, I can hardly sit still to write. Rage and misery are the uppermost feelings however in everyone's mind at the present moment, as the news has come of Lord Cranborne's defeat. I must begin my story at the beginning though. Miss Alderson,[1] Lord Rowton, and Alice Balfour are the only people here besides ourselves. This is what they call having no one in the house, but with the family and ourselves it seems a huge party. The Salisburys seem dreadfully upset, especially Lord Salisbury. He looks most fearfully depressed, it makes one miserable to see him. Lady Gwenny [2] is away with Lord Cranborne, which is sad, but they all come back this evening, which will be yet sadder after his defeat. We arrived about teatime, and as there was only Lady Salisbury and Miss Alderson present I did not feel shy. The worst part of the day is the evening, but I lived through it and was almost happy. Poor Mother is fearfully nervous and upset and I thought she would faint before dinner. Although dreadfully

---

[1] Lady Salisbury's sister.
[2] Lady Gwendolen Cecil, Lord Salisbury's daughter.

trying I think it is good for her. Betty and Conny both pretended to be very shy, so I felt happier. Mother gave me a
lecture before dinner about talking. I can assure you I should
be agreeable enough to please you or anybody if advice
could make me so. I get it from all quarters. Mother makes
me so dreadfully shy, for she keeps calling attention to the
fact that I am just out, and that this is my first visit, which
she has said every time I have been anywhere for the last
year. However, it has been said to Betty and Con in their
turn, and I must put up with it in mine. At dinner last night
I sat between Eustace Balfour [1] and one of the curates who
is half a Spaniard. Frances sat on his other side and Betty
was next to Eustace, so I felt pretty comfortable. Betty says
she will write and report to you every word of my conversation with the curate, so I will not go to the trouble of writing
it now. I occasionally caught sight of Frances from the other
side looking the unfortunate man up and down as if he was
not fit to sit by her side. She also darted furious glances at
me because I did not talk as freely as she wished me to do.
Betty looked perfectly lovely and it was all I could do not
to get up and hug her. Con also looked very pretty, and much
the oldest of us all. For some time after dinner I sat and
talked to Betty, who lectured me severely on my behaviour
to the curate. I told her he ought to have begun the conversation as I did not. He ought to have had pity on me, as he
was not shy and I was. When the gentlemen came in Betty
talked to someone else, and Frances then came and gave me
a bit of her mind in a very loud whisper, when she discovered
the curate was standing close to her! She was very much taken
aback, though I do not think he heard what she said, and I
was very glad, as she had no business to lecture me in public.
As I said to her, with three relations treasuring up every
word I utter, and with three lectures to come at the end of
the evening, she could not expect me to be agreeable. I
cannot repeat any conversation to you, as though I listened
hard and was much interested I caught nothing worth
repeating. The chief topic was of course the elections.
Everyone trying to seem indifferent to our losses, and

[1] The youngest Balfour brother, husband of Lady Frances.

delighted at the idea of Gladstone getting in, but they all
failed hopelessly and everyone was as gloomy as possible.

A dreadful thing has happened this morning, at least
rather dreadful for me, which will amuse you very much. I
gave Betty your yesterday's letter to read, as she wished to
see the bits about her, and as I was going out I told her to be
sure and put your letter back in my room, which is next to
Mother's. Instead of which she went and put it into Miss
Alderson's, which is also next Mother's on the other side.
Miss Alderson took the letter to Conny and said, "I think
you or your sister have left a letter in my room. I cannot
think how it came there, but it seems quite a private letter
from Mr. Elwin." So evidently she had opened it and
probably read it, as I believe she is rather given to that
kind of thing. The dreadful thing for me is that it was the
letter in which you said I was to try to keep my ears open
and use my tongue to ask questions, especially when I could
get Lord Salisbury by the button. Of course there is nothing
really to matter, and it is awfully funny and makes me feel
very uncomfortable. I was extremely fond of Miss Alderson
before and thought she was a dear, and now I feel to hate her.
I did pitch into Betty, though it was not really her fault.

Today has been one of the most exciting and sickening
days I have ever spent. All the morning I passed in the
garden with the children eating fruit. The excitement began
just before lunch. There were five Americans coming to
lunch, and we were all ordered to remain calm and indifferent
before them should we hear of Jim Cranborne's defeat.
About half an hour before lunch the telegrams began to
arrive. Every time the door opened there was nearly a
scream from excitement. Nigs [1] and Miss Alderson were
waiting on the steps and we were all assembled in the
drawing-room. Telegram after telegram arrived but no news
of Lord Cranborne. Lord Salisbury made constant excuses
for going out on to the steps. He was far more nervous than
she was. The Americans arrived and we proceeded to lunch,
and were halfway through before the telegram arrived. Nigs
had opened it outside, and Alice Balfour brought it in and

[1] Lord Edward Cecil.

gave it to Lord Salisbury. He read it and simply said, "Bad news from Darwen, we have lost it by 200." Lady Salisbury at the other end of the table saw something was wrong, but as she was listening to a story she could not ask the news for some minutes. When at last the telegram was passed to her, she read it out and said in the calmest voice, "Oh, that is a great bore." And Linky,[1] who was sitting next her, said, "Very tiresome!" They were wonderful, though you could see how much they both felt it, he especially. There was a sickening silence for a few minutes. I very nearly burst into tears. Several batches of telegrams arrived after that, most of them losses, but nothing seemed to matter after that. What Lord Salisbury feels most is the ingratitude of the country. I long to throw myself on the ground and kiss his feet, I feel such an admiration for him. I feel that this election has so stirred me up, and especially this day, that I shall take an interest in politics ever after. I never realized before the overwhelming interest of them. Con says Lady Salisbury had a good breakdown afterwards, which must have done her good, for she behaved in a marvellous way. I feel now as if every other interest in life was miserably insignificant compared to politics. I am almost too excited to be shy and everyone is much too excited to notice me. I am glad to see I can wake up when there is a sufficient reason for it. I have enjoyed myself immensely up to the present time. Whether I have been agreeable or not I do not know. You must ask someone else that question. It is too much for you to tell me you will love me in proportion as I have made myself agreeable. With my only treasure at stake I shall be much too nervous to be amiable. I feel I must have more to tell you, but I shall have to wait till I get home to give you fuller details. I think this house is perfectly lovely and really luxurious. All the same, nothing would induce me to live here. It was rather funny last night when we went to the drawing-room. Lord Salisbury seized up a candle and lit the fire. Lady Salisbury rushed to the window and threw it wide open. When Lord Salisbury perceived this, though, he soon shut it again. I was very glad, for it was bitterly cold.

Lord Hugh Cecil.

Booton Rectory, July 14

You have transferred to your letter the excitement around you. I am pleased that you have caught the fever and turned politician. You will have to live with the people of your own generation, and must share their interests, or be left on one side. The frenzied feelings of the present hour will subside, and you will retain a healthy concern in what is going on around you, just sufficient to make you companionable in mixed society. Special alliances from deeper sympathies can only be few. You cannot divine how or when the chief alliance of all will come about, but it is clear as a rule that the more amiable and winning and conversable you are—not in an artificial, acted, make-believe fashion, but in a gentle, natural, easy way—the greater will be the opportunity of knowing and being known.

44 Elm Park Gardens, July 15

I thought my Hatfield letter was as dull as it could be and would not amuse you in the least. I longed to be able to write to you like Betty, that you might realize the intense excitement we were going through. Now you assure me I succeeded in my object, and that you were satisfied, I shall be happier in telling you the rest of my story. We could not possibly have been there at a more interesting time or at a better time in every way. Though Jim Cranborne's defeat was very tragic, yet there was something very dramatic and very touching about it. Betty says after all it is rather absurd to be so miserable. They could not have seemed much more miserable had he been dead. It was of course a great disappointment and a dreadful snub to Lord Salisbury. I must tell you about the evening when the defeated party turned up. They were expected about nine o'clock, so we began dinner without them. I went in with Linky and sat between him and Gerald, nearly opposite to Lord Salisbury, and I can assure you I did not feel altogether at my ease. Linky did his duty bravely and talked to me on various subjects. I did my best to answer him, but the conversation did not flow very freely. I felt so paralysed I could hardly open my lips. I get so stupidly nervous I can hardly help crying. A discussion began between Linky and some of the others about Rudyard Kipling, and Betty scolded me severely afterwards for not having joined in, but I could no more have joined in than I could fly. I know it is utterly silly but I cannot help it. I told Betty she was probably just as bad at her first dinner party, but she says she talked beautifully, so I can only say she is, and always was, a model in all things and I am not. Do not think I don't try to be agreeable, for of course I am just as anxious to make friends and be amiable as you could wish me to be. I do try hard, though it is real agony to me, and I am miserable afterwards from the feeling that if anything I have made myself disliked instead of liked. All the same I am sure I get less shy, and I should have been almost content with myself if Betty had not scolded me. It really seems silly to scold people because they are not as agreeable as they might be. Is it likely I should keep silent if I were not too shy to talk? People do not sufficiently realize what real pain shyness is, or they would not add to it by scolding. I never knew how old Betty was getting till she said she had talked beautifully at her first dinner party. It is so long ago she has forgotten her shyness. Bless her, she only tries to help me, but I wish she would not scold. Now I must tell you something more amusing. I have bored you with my shyness that you may know I tried my best.

Linky talked to me a little about the elections and I showed my ignorance, until he gave that subject up in despair. Having told me the Hatfield election was on Friday, I immediately asked if St. Albans was on Tuesday, when of course Hatfield is in the St. Albans division. They were all in a fever of excitement about Lord Cranborne's arrival, and every time a servant opened the door the whole table turned. At length they really did arrive, Gwenny, Alice Cranborne and Lord Robert's wife coming in first. Gwenny looked most awfully ill and white. They rushed off to change their dresses, and the door opened again and Lord Cranborne and Lord Robert entered. Lord Cranborne stood in the doorway first as if he could not summon up courage to come in, but Lady Salisbury called out to him, and he just came and passed through, shaking his father's hand on the way. They all tried to seem in high spirits, and Lady Salisbury exclaimed, "Oh, they are all right. Bless 'em." After dinner we all proceeded to the drawing-room to hear their news, Gwenny in a very excited voice telling it all to Lord Salisbury, who sat with tears in his eyes the whole evening. They say it was the Catholic vote that lost them the seat, as there are 1,600 Roman Catholics in Darwen and they all voted against him. Alice Cranborne said it was awful driving through the Irish roughs, who actually spat upon her and threw bits of orange peel. Just fancy how dreadful. At first she heard Lord Cranborne was in, then they saw a yellow flag go up, and the mob began to cheer. They reassured themselves, though, with the thought that it was only because of Gladstone being in, and then they saw the face of one of the workers getting from white to green and from green to yellow and then knew it was all up with them. Alice pretends this was much better than knowing the truth at once, as they drank large tumblers of champagne when they heard the good news, which supported them when they heard of their defeat. I think, though, it must have been an awful moment. The worst, they say, was leaving the workers, who were all sobbing; even the men were in tears, begging that he would stand again and they promised to return him another time. They say their distress was heart-breaking.

I think it made it much better at Hatfield having them all there, and Lady Salisbury said she did not care in the least, but stood in the middle of the room exclaiming in a loud voice, "Damn the Catholics! Damn the Catholics!" Frances and Eustace say she took a drop too much to keep her up and that towards the end of the evening she could hardly walk straight. Lord Salisbury and Gwenny looked the most miserable, both so utterly crushed. I think he feels too terribly the ingratitude of the country, for which he has done everything a man could do. Linky told Frances, which is very funny, that when Lord Salisbury opened the telegram announcing Jim's defeat, he first turned sick, and thought he should faint, and afterwards got the giggles at the sight of the Lytton family all wondering what they should say next.

Yesterday morning at breakfast Miss Alderson said,
"Emily leaves her love letters about in my room." Betty
said, "I think it was very indiscreet of you to open it." "Oh,"
she said, "I wanted to know what it was, and when I saw
'My dear Emmie' and saw it was from Mr. Elwin I shut it
up. Of course I read no more." This she said in a tone which
meant, I think, that she had read it all. I felt very cross about
it at first, but now I think it is so awfully comic.

Booton Rectory, July 18

Your Hatfield narrative is first-rate. Imagine us to have as
faithful a chronicle of the domestic or private scenes which
ensued with all the kings and prime ministers of England
at every national crisis from William the Conqueror onwards,
and our national history would be lively reading. The
Woman in White and the *Moonstone* would pale before it. Vic
and Neville would listen in holiday hours, and prefer historical
studies to play. I hope artists would be found to illustrate it
properly. The pictures alone, were they all of the Hatfield
type, would be more dramatic than a play.

I am of Betty's mind that the disaster was wrongly esti-
mated. Rightly considered it was a disappointment, and
nothing more, and a vexation that will quickly pass and leave
no scar. The blightings of heart are the real sorrows. The
rest are no more than the withered leaves of autumn; they
drop and the green leaves succeed. If Lord Cranborne is
anxious for a political career another seat will be found for
him before he is many years older. Neither do I consider that
this defeat is a "snub" to his father in any sense to cause
pain. It is not the verdict of enlightened men, calmly judging
his policy, but the verdict of a mob of ignorant voters (I
speak of the majority) solely governed by party passion or
imagined self-interest. You might as well accept the yelping
of a pack of hounds for an estimate of your character, mental
and moral. I grant the ingratitude, but who would reckon
upon gratitude from a mob? Hounds, as is well known, will
eat up the man who feeds them if he trips and falls and they
can take him at a disadvantage, and the voter does likewise.
His vote is not governed by past favours. He votes for the

plunder he trusts will come. He sees that Gladstone and Harcourt will pander to any iniquity for place, and he rightly infers that they are the proper instruments for him. Lord Salisbury is a great man, the greatest statesman in the kingdom, and the blackguards of Darwen are not competent to take the measure of his shoe. I should not dream of hanging down my head because there was a small number too many in the wrong side among the dregs of a big constituency. Does my language sound violent? To my own apprehension I speak the language of sober sense.

44 *Elm Park Gardens, July* 19

Why is it that people ever expect gratitude from human beings, when everything ought to tell them they will not get it, or very rarely? It seems to me that anyone with however little experience can see that, and yet men like Lord Salisbury and Father, who you would think were wiser, are surprised and distressed because they do not get it. Father's life was to a great degree embittered by ingratitude, and yet considering that it is the complaint of almost every great man, and every little man too, it seems strange to me that he should have expected it. Some people would say it showed a bitter feeling to say so, but it seems to me it is simply a question of observation. You cannot be blind to the fact that no one ever does receive what they think is due to them. It seems to me that you ought never to undertake any great work without a determination to give all that you have to it, your life if necessary, without asking or expecting one word of recognition or gratitude in return. On the contrary, to expect abuse. It is only what you get, whether you expect it or not, and so it seems to me that it would be far better to make up your mind to it at the beginning, than to go on hoping for a gratitude which all your experience and observation ought to teach you is very rarely given to those who deserve it, and then be bitterly disappointed. Here as in everything else you can also feel the deep joy and blessing of religion. If you had to work on all your life, with the uncertain gratitude of men as your only reward, life would be dreary and miserable in the extreme, but if you think that your reward is certain in the future, and that it is a reward far greater than you could ever deserve, what does it matter whether you get the gratitude of men or not? You can have the blessed consciousness at all times that you are pleasing God, and working for His honour and glory, and no act, however small and insignificant, will pass unrecognized by Him. If it was not a matter of experience that gratitude is the rarest thing in the world, this fact alone should prevent people from expecting it. What gratitude does God receive from us, what gratitude did the Blessed Lord receive? His life ought to be proof enough of what we ought to expect as our reward on earth, and it seems to me that thought ought also to reconcile us to any ingratitude we may receive, for what can we ever do for others compared to what He did, and what ingratitude can we receive in comparison to the ingratitude He received? It really seems wonderful that anyone should go on expecting praise or gratitude with the Saviour's life before their eyes. Why is it that people are so extraordinarily blind to what seems so evident to the merest child?

When I have written a long paragraph like this and read it over afterwards I feel how you must laugh at the tone in which I write it. I talk to you as if you were a child and I was teaching you a fact you did not already know. The reason is that when I get interested in anything I am writing to you, I forget in a way to whom I am writing, and simply put down my thoughts as they come into my head without thinking. It does not matter though, for you know I do not mean to teach you. I only wish to tell you my thoughts, that you may be able to see whether they fit in with yours. I think as a rule I may take for granted they do.

I was showing Betty one of your letters the other day, and the only remark she made was, "Tell him with my love accidentally is spelt with two c's." It is something new for Betty to turn spelling mistress. Let us hope she has taught herself first.

Herbert Stephen [1] dined here last night and was as funny as ever. Mother was telling him she had heard no one dared

---

[1] Eldest son of Sir James Stephen, the eminent Judge.

tell Gladstone what his majority really was, but let him suppose it as big as he wished. "Oh," said Herbert Stephen in his solemn voice, "the story I heard was that someone tried to break the news to Gladstone and began, 'I am very much afraid that through some mischance the majority will not be quite as big as we hoped, in fact that it will be considerably reduced, indeed I fear it will not be much more than 1,000 or 1,500.' At first Gladstone refused to believe it, but when at last they succeeded in convincing him, he retired to bed in a temper." I think it will be great fun watching what he will do, as I suppose he is not capable of doing much harm, with such a small majority. My interest in politics still lasts and I hope will continue to do so.

No doubt it is a good thing to continue to ask questions about a subject I do not understand, when I am sitting next someone at a dinner party who can explain it to me, but it depends what the subject is. I should be like Lady Pembroke if I were to say to my neighbour, "Now, tell me all about politics." What maddens me is to think that all the years I spent in the schoolroom I did not even learn what Paisy was capable of teaching me. I read over perpetually the Saxon Period and the Norman Conquest while I might have been learning something about the history of my own time. I certainly think the Norman Conquest was far more interesting than anything that has happened lately, but still it is not of much use to me now.

Booton Rectory, July 20

There used to be a story in the jest books of a dispute between two clerks who belonged to two rival commercial houses as to which firm did the largest business. Says one, "Our ink alone costs a thousand a year." "That is nothing," said the other, "we save more than that by not dotting our i's and crossing our t's." I am not sparing of letters to save the ink, but to a man writing in a hurry abbreviation saves time. Let Betty point out what benefit there is in the second c of accidental. The word is just as easily read and understood without it as with it. Besides the omission might be accidental and not intentional, and I plead both these causes

as my justification. They are contradictory, and so frequently
are legal pleas. But you put forth the second in case the first
fails.

44 Elm Park Gardens, July 22

I am going to a garden party at Syon House [1] this afternoon with Betty. Mother has given her orders to introduce
me to everyone she knows. I know more Souls already than
I want to know.

You asked me if anyone mentioned deficiencies when
talking of me at Hatfield. Frances told Betty the way I bit
my fingers was quite dreadful and I must really be stopped.
I looked as if I was so absorbed biting my nails that I could
not talk. When I am fearfully shy, biting my nails is my only
comfort. This will make you vexed with me, but before
getting your scolding, I tell you I am very penitent and will
do my best to reform. I have made many resolutions not to
bite my fingers but they have all failed. I here make another.
It amused me, though, for Frances to scold me about it, for her
fingers are always covered with blood from biting, and they
look far nastier than mine. I want you to scold me, but I am
sorry to need it. You can hardly realize the need I feel, when
I am nervous or cross, to bite something. Fingers are the
first things that come to me. I should scream sometimes if
I did not bite. But I promise you to make another great
effort to give it up.

44 Elm Park Gardens, July 23

I enjoyed myself at the garden party very much, and was
not shy, as I had no one to talk to. The only thing I hated,
but which I suppose I must go through, was being introduced to everybody. Betty did her duty admirably. To
everyone she met it was, "How do you do! May I introduce
you to my youngest sister?" The first person we came
across was Sir George Russell, Frances' great friend. Betty
seized hold of him and took him off into the garden, telling
Con and me to follow her. We did not wish to interrupt her
tête-à-tête and did not quite see the fun of trudging after
her, so then Con began introducing me to her friends. All

[1] Belonging to the Duke of Northumberland.

cousins or bores, but far preferable to Souls. Betty was
indignant afterwards, and said we ought to have kept near
her and made an audience for Sir G. Russell, who was so
amusing. We then proceeded to tea, and afterwards Betty
introduced me right and left, but soon coming across a fellow
Soul she plunged into intellectual conversation. Con and I
were carried off by another Soul, Willie Peel [1], whom I daresay
you have heard Betty mention, to see the house. This was the
only part that bored me, for the house did not interest me a
bit and I was very tired and longed to sit down. The conversation between Willie Peel and Con was rather amusing,
though very high-flown and artistic. Con always amazes me
by the way she gives forth upon architecture, painting,
sculpture, as if she had studied art all her life. It also makes
me laugh very much, and she indulges freely in the most
awful lies and appeals to me to confirm them. Willie Peel
would examine so very carefully the walls and pictures and
furniture as if they were unique, and it was dreadfully tiresome. One awful portrait of some ancient lady he declared to
be a Van Dyke. "Yes," said Conny, "it is rather Van Dyke's
style of painting, and yet it seems to me the flesh is not
quite so rich as Van Dyke's, it looks rather shallow." Willie
Peel, who was rather inclined to be superior, soon came
down and was most respectful, though occasionally he looked
very surprised at the knowledge Con displayed. When we
were looking at one landscape she remarked, "I think that
might be a Claude, it is so like his atmosphere." In the midst
of Van Dykes and Claudes and no end of gorgeous things,
on one sofa Con discovered a ghastly cushion such as you
buy at a bazaar, with little bits of red flannel stuck about to
represent geranium leaves. It was very funny. Con kept
darting after distant cousins, to Betty's great indignation,
but Con said she made a special point of being polite to
cousins when Betty was anywhere near, as she is always so
very rude to them.

Booton Rectory, July 24

Your garden party is richly amusing in the description.
They are benevolent institutions, diffusing pleasures far and

[1] Eldest son of Lord Peel, the Speaker.

wide. I who was not invited, and who would have been
refused admittance if I had applied, partake of its sweets at
this distance, and thank your host and hostess for the grati-
fication. I hope many who saw you in the crowd may have
received as much satisfaction as you have conveyed to me.
Each party to which you go will be the parent of new parties,
and new benefits, and I trust you to improve the shining hour.

You enjoy the garden party because you are a spectator,
not an actor, and need talk to no one. A more exquisite
pleasure is behind. The day will come when your delight will
be to talk to somebody, and will never weary of it. Hours
will melt down to minutes in that fascinating society. You
will be sorry that the colloquy should cease, and restless till
it begins again. Then you will estimate parties by the
presence or absence of a single person. He not there the
sun will be blotted out of your heaven. You are not yet at
your zenith. You have that rapturous stage of existence to
which to look forward, and it may begin any day. And there
is something higher yet when love has been proved and is
unfathomable even to itself in its depth, and the effervescence
is succeeded by a matchless serenity. That stage will come
too, and in the meanwhile you can hug the joys of the
present home, which is the best preparation for the home to
come.

I hardly suppose you deliberately bite your nails for the
pleasure of it, or for the relief it affords you, as a man drinks
too much wine, preferring sensual allurements to sobriety.
When it came to the point of asking yourself, "Shall I
indulge myself in a bite or forbear?" I presume you would
have self-control enough to stop. I cannot but think, though
you seem to say otherwise, that the habit being confirmed
you mostly in your nervous states give way to it unconsciously, and undoubtedly it is difficult not to do the deed
before you are aware of what you are doing. In your idle
moments could you not contrive to have something in each
hand—a fan, say, in one, a handkerchief in the other? Employment for your mouth can take its turn with that for your
hand. At dinner dawdle over the delicacy in your plate, and
when you are not eating force yourself to talk. I throw out

small hints. Improve upon them. Above all resolve to conquer. No wonder the fingers of Lady Frances are bloody. She has eaten her pasturage bare, and must bite the soil in which it grows.

44 Elm Park Gardens, July 25

Your letter is dearer than usual, and I am a great deal happier in consequence. I always wonder so on Sunday what your letter will be, and all my feelings during the week turn upon it. This week I ought to be extra happy, and I think I shall be. I am in high spirits today, or rather I am deeply and tranquilly happy, which is better, and I am much looking forward to our Cromer time. Your fear is, you say, lest you should seem a bore. I can promise you that there is one person who will not be bored by you. It seems strange, but it is true. How can you talk of being a bore? I can only think you are fishing for compliments, and I will not fill your net for you. If you think you are a bore you can at least feel satisfied in knowing that there is one person who delights in being bored.

I am glad my letters do not seem to you dreadfully selfish, as I was afraid they might. I know I am selfish, that is I am very thoughtless, and I do not realize until after I have said or done a thing how selfish I must seem, and then I am ashamed of myself. It is not intentional selfishness, but I forget until it is too late what I am doing. I suppose as I grow older I shall learn to think more of other people. I would do anything in the world to add to the happiness of those I love, and yet from mere thoughtlessness I often say and do things which afterwards I would give anything not to have said or done. I distress myself when I think of these things, as I distressed myself about what I had written to you, but then I think it is no use whatever lamenting over what is past: there is the future in which to do better.

I have been for a little walk with Mother this morning, and I am afraid I was very cross to her, but I felt so awfully irritated, for at every step she told me to hold up, not to roll, but to walk gracefully. They are such silly little things to be cross about, and yet they make me feel quite frantic. Mother has a way of holding my arm and rubbing it when she is going to find fault, which irritates me more than anything. Then today I felt extra cross, because I have got a bad cold, which is what I have constantly, and Mother was pressing all her remedies on me, and telling me I was so weak, I really ought to have some quinine, and I must take care of myself. She was very kind, and I feel so ungrateful, but it did annoy me fearfully. I know I cannot help feeling irritated, but I am afraid I was very sulky and I ought to have controlled it. However, it is past and I must try harder next time. Mother has been wonderfully less irritating this last week or so, and I have tried my hardest not to irritate her. We were talking this morning about the way Lady Frances treats her children, and I said that though I thought she bullied them they were quite devoted to her. "Yes," said Mother, "children who are bullied always love their parents more than the children who have been petted." I am sure she meant this as a hint to me, for she went on to say, "When I tell Neville to do a thing you must not contradict me, for he is still young enough to be ruled." It makes me sad that Mother should think we do not love her sufficiently, only this chiefly comes from the fact that she cannot rule us now as she used to do, and also I comfort myself with the thought that we do all love her with as much love as we have to give. I know that I do, and I am the one she thinks cares least for her. I know she is chiefly vexed with me, because I have reached an age when she knows she cannot rule me. I do not for a moment think she loves me less, only she has fits of being vexed with me.

Mother says that I am to tell you that John Morley came to see her on Saturday, and brought all his letters from Father. He seems to have been nice, but it tried Mother very much seeing him. Mother asked him a little about political questions and he said he thought Gladstone was very old for the House of Commons. He raved of Lord Rosebery and said he was certain of the Foreign Office, no one else could take it.

Mother also wished me to ask you about Mr. Locker's poetry, which she thinks she ought to read before going to Cromer. She wishes to know what he has written, and what you think of his poetry. Con and I both tell her it is quite ridiculous to think of reading it, on purpose to tell him she has done so.

I feel that I am beginning to realize more and more how everything in our life has changed, or rather, I have never realized it before, and only do so now in flashes. When I go out and the thought comes across me of how happy we should all have been together, when we came to settle in England, and how different it is now, a sick feeling seizes hold of me, and there seems to be no pleasure in anything. This thought only comes, though, in flashes, for which I am grateful. At other times the thought of the sorrow only seems to add a softening influence to my pleasures. I feel that to dwell on the past would be more than I could bear, or than anyone could bear, or rather to dwell on the present. I like to think of the happiness that has been, and the happiness that will be some day, and not on the sorrow now. I cannot explain myself, but you will know what I mean. I feel as if I could not be really miserable for very long, and live. I cannot help always turning to the happy side of everything, and there is a happy side to every trial, however great. To be happy does not mean that you forget the object of your sorrow, only I would always rather remember everything as happy. It is not always possible, but I think it is best always to try. I do not know why I have said this, but it came into my head.

Booton Rectory, July 26

I had been a long while pretty intimate with Locker before I knew that he had written poetry, insomuch that when somebody asked me whether my friend was the poet, I boldly answered "No," adding that I had never heard of a poet Locker, and that though my Locker was not a poet he was something better. There the subject dropped, and I thought no more about it. It was after a considerable interval that I discovered my error, and after another considerable interval I chanced to light upon some lines he had written. I had not gone in search of them. I believe his pieces are short and not numerous, and all of them, or nearly all, of the

kind which are called "Society Verses." A few of the few I
have read are happily turned, and his three little lines on the
dog Tray (which you have heard me quote) are to my
thinking a felicitous embodiment in language of the relations
which subsist between two beings who have a thorough love
for each other. It could not be told more vividly, more completely, more tersely, and more simply. Neat and simple
English is a characteristic of his verses throughout. Not that
I can speak positively. My knowledge is limited. None is
needed. He himself is a hater of poetry, speaking generally,
and, unless when he is wishing to drop asleep, he reads only
prose.

Gladstone is old for anything that requires prolonged
mental and bodily exertion. His election speeches were a
conclusive proof of failing power. He had every motive to do
his best and doubtless did, and that best was bad. A physician
told Warwick a couple of days ago that in his fits of passion
his pulse quickens very slightly, and however worried, he
sleeps at night like a baby, his system being, as I infer,
lethargic, and soporific from age. He has spared no pains
to secure for himself a troubled last act, but nature is kinder
to him than he is to himself, and will not altogether allow the
saying to come true that as he makes his bed so he must lie
upon it. Lassitude overtakes him, and his mind, as it were,
goes out with his candle.

44 *Elm Park Gardens, July* 27

I want to tell you of a conversation I had yesterday with
Betty which made me very angry, and yet I cannot help
laughing about it, it was so ridiculous. She first began by
saying that the Saturday or Monday she was at Cromer, she
wished us all to go over and lunch at Blickling,[1] all con-
sisting of you and she, Con, the Lockers and me. "The
Lockers will so enjoy driving us all over if they come too."
She knows how to make use of her friends! She then went on
to say, and this is the part that makes me angry: "And when
you are there, you are not to be demonstrative with his Rev.

---

[1] Lady Lothian's house quite near Booton. We were to be at Cromer for
the summer holidays.

11

You must not sit by him and hold his hand. It is just the same as if an engaged couple were demonstrative in public, it makes people very uncomfortable and is very bad manners." My first inclination was to burst out laughing at the utter absurdity of it, my next feeling was one of rage, and I am afraid that is the strongest feeling in me still. My rage is not directed against Betty, but against Frances. If Betty is to be spoilt by anything, Frances will spoil her. It is not the real Betty that talks as she did to me, but it is the Betty that Frances would like her to be. Frances, for some reason or other, seems to think she has got a right to lecture me and scold me as if I was one of her own children. I never see Betty now but that she begins to lecture me about some thing which Frances disapproves of in me. When Frances lectures me herself, I only feel amused, and it does not annoy me in the least, but it does make me angry when Betty takes seriously every remark Frances chooses to make, and gives me a long lecture upon it. It is just the same with the children. Frances hates children and never loses an opportunity of abusing Ruth and Nellie.[1] No two children could behave better in every way than Betty's do, and yet she is continually distressing herself about what Frances says of them. It is now the same with me. If Betty chooses to let Frances rule her life, I do not. I am very fond of Frances, as you know, and she has always been very kind to me, but that is no reason why she should always be scolding me. I had looked forward to going out with Betty, as I thought she, at any rate, would allow me my liberty, and she is ten times worse than the fussiest mother. She not only tells me how to behave when I go out, listens to all I say while I am out, and scolds me for it afterwards, but now she is teaching me how I am to behave to you. I do not mean to say unkind things about Betty, for my only feeling towards her is one of the most intense love and gratitude, but I feel vexed that she should so completely have forgotten what she was at my age, and that she should treat me now in the way that most maddened her. It is trying enough to be ruled by Mother, but I will not be ruled by everybody.

[1] Betty's children.

Betty told me yesterday that she had written to you about not being demonstrative with me before people, which is why I have mentioned this. An awful fear came over me for a minute, though I know you could never really think such a thing of me, lest you should think I had said anything to Betty to make her write such nonsense to you. The day you tell me you are ashamed of holding my hand with anyone in the room, I will leave off doing so, but till then when I can get near enough to you to hold your hand I shall. Betty could not have said anything to make me resolve more firmly than anything to show my feelings on every possible occasion. I shall not now be bothered with scruples that Betty is wishing to hold your hand when I have got it. I am not often scolded for being too demonstrative, and it is rather funny that Betty should be the person to scold me. I told Con, who was properly indignant, and agreed that Betty was too ridiculous, and she is going to give her a piece of her mind the next time she has an occasion. My next feeling is one of indignation against Frances, as you can see plainly enough by my language. I may be wrong and ridiculous, but I will not have her interfering with me at every turn. I think I shall give her a piece of my mind soon. After all, I cannot help laughing at the absurdity of the whole thing, which I am sure you must do, and laugh at me into the bargain. I do think though that when you see Betty next time you might tell her to be more reasonable, when she takes me out, and not ask Frances her opinion of me. I daresay I am self-willed, but I do not see what right Frances has to lecture me. You tell me today that it is very easy to be good in a letter. I do not know to what you refer, but I know it is also very easy to show temper in a letter. Don't you think I have shown mine pretty well? I hope to show you my love as successfully.

Now I must tell you about our dinner [1] last night. I went to it feeling very cross, and not expecting to enjoy it at all, so as usual I enjoyed it immensely. Mr. Longman, [2] Mr. Bernard Holland, Mr. Finlay, [3] Frances and Eustace, Con and

---

[1] At Betty's house in Addison Road.   [2] The publisher.
[3] Later, Sir Robert Finlay.

myself were the guests. Mr. Longman is not particularly brilliant. I sat next him at dinner, and his first remark to me was, "Perhaps you are not aware that I am a deaf man, and I am sorry to say you have got my worst side." This did not make me more cheerful, but he was very kind and tried every subject of conversation in turn, and we got on pretty well, though when I began to speak in a loud tone that he might hear me there seemed to be a pause in the conversation. I can tell you nothing about Mr. Bernard Holland, except that he admires Con very much. Mother says he looks like a nice labouring man. I agree about the labouring man but am not quite sure about the nice. He always begins very Souly conversation, and yet in quite a different way from the Souls, who I think would hate him as a base imitator. The dinner was agreeable but not brilliant. Much amusement was caused by Betty having spelt cauliflower on her menus "cawliflower." Evidently after some thought, as there were several tries before she got it right, as she thought. As usual in a colony [1] dinner, Gerald and Eustace quarrelled, and Betty had to soothe Eustace at her end of the table. After dinner we went to sit in the garden, which was very nice, though not too warm. The moment I love best at a dinner party is when the gentlemen are left in the dining-room. Con and I congratulated each other at having got through dinner more or less successfully. While we were talking to each other, I heard Frances say to Betty, "I wonder which she talked to most." Then Betty inquired of me, "Which did you talk to most, Bernard Holland or Longman?" As I informed her, I was not going to report my conversation to her or anyone. It is wonderful how much easier it is to talk in the dark. Altogether I got on quite well and was much amused. The dinner was as a special honour to Mr. Longman, who seemed entirely out of it all. I think it is a great mistake to introduce one unfortunate stranger into a colony dinner party. He was too deaf to hear general conversation, and nobody spoke to him. After he had sat in the garden some time and was nearly frozen, he asked to go indoors, where Betty accompanied him. I am very anxious to hear from Betty what Frances has

[1] This refers to friends who lived in or near Addison Road.

to remark about my behaviour last night. It is like having
three mothers instead of one.

Neville has come up from school today, and while I am
writing to you he is telling me of his feats at cricket. I
confess I have been attending more to you than to him, but
I have just caught this sentence: "The courage of despair
goaded me to victory."

I next write from Cromer, where we were spending the
summer holidays:

Marlborough House, Cromer, July 30
Mother wishes me to tell you that Victor has done very
well in his trials, and his reports are excellent. Mr. Donaldson
says he wishes he had thirty-five more like him. Mother says
she has brought here a life of Napoleon, which means that
she will soon suggest reading it in the evening. We have to
endure a yet worse infliction, which is that Vic is made to
read poetry aloud to us. He has a very sing-songy voice and
is furious if we do not listen attentively. Last night he was
reading Neville some of Hood's comic ballads and they were
giggling over them together, when Mother asked Vic to
read them out to her, and Neville then was scolded for
daring to laugh. Mother said today I might read to them in
the evening whatever book they liked and she would listen,
which is a great concession. Neville and I have been out to
buy some exciting novel. Unfortunately they had every book
in the shop except the books we wanted.

Cromer, August 2
The boys spend their afternoons with the Lockers, which
makes them happy, and I spend mine writing to you, so you
do not need to be told that I am happy. Neville and I, being
the brave members of the family, bathe in the morning; Con
and Vic are afraid of the cold. All things considered everyone
is remarkably good tempered, but a day never passes without
some storms. Everyone was very cross yesterday, I especially.
The boys were particularly irritating, and in the evening I
foolishly got into quite a rage. I was sitting alone when

Mother came in and scolded me for having opened the window. I sulkily got up and shut it with a bang, which made Mother remark: "Why, what is the matter? You seem quite in a rage." I told her I was in a rage, not with her but with the boys, upon which she said: "Oh, you must not be cross with them, you will make them so much worse tempered." She said this in a calm voice, which only enraged me worse than ever. Nothing is so maddening when one is in a temper as for someone else to say: "Why are you in a rage?" or else: "You must control yourself and not be cross." I was in a really bad temper last night, and longed to hit somebody or something. My greatest longing, though, when I am angry is to bite somebody and my poor nails suffer in consequence. You have no idea how soothing it is to one's temper. I am very angry with myself now for being so silly, but at times the boys are perfectly maddening. However, it is my fault for getting cross, and there is no excuse for me.

The Lockers are most immensely kind to us, and ask us to their house some time every day. A letter generally arrives at breakfast time from some member of the family. The first morning Godfrey sent Vic a basket of roses, which was rather an odd present from one boy to another.

Cromer, August 20

Our dinner at the Lockers' last night was very amusing. I sat next dear Mr. Locker and Sir Mount Stewart Grant Duff [1] (what an awful name to possess). Mr. Locker said to me at the beginning of dinner, "Your other neighbour is a very well-informed and clever man, but he is subject to long fits of taciturnity, so you must wake him up." This I did not feel at all inclined to do. Nothing makes me so shy as to be told that the person sitting next to me is well-informed, as that means I ought to get something out of him, which I never do. Happily Sir M.S.G.D. was very much taken up with Miss Davy, who sat on his other side, and so I talked to Mr. Locker, which was much nicer. Mrs. Locker said she had asked the Hoares and Gurneys and Buxtons, or rather some of them, to come in after dinner, upon which there

---

[1] Former Governor of Madras.

were loud groans from Mr. Locker and Godfrey. Several
people did turn up after dinner, amongst them Mr. Hoare [2]
and his two daughters. One of the Miss Hoares is evidently
considered a beauty, and thinks so herself.

Con was set down to play. It always kills me to watch the
expression of people's faces while she is playing. Last night
Lady Grant Duff went to sleep in one corner and kept
trying to rouse herself, and suddenly waking up with a
start. I heard many deep sighs and yawns from someone else
who was sitting next to me. Mr. Gurney, another of the
guests, perched on his stool, twirled his eye-glasses, and
tried to look sentimental. When Con had finished he exclaimed, "Charming talent. Wonderful play. Most delightful
indeed." I very nearly got the giggles, he was so funny.
Then Mr. Hoare came and sat upon the stool and talked to
me. This great heavy man on a small stool was a most
comic sight. He rattled away, telling endless stories, and
talking as if the whole Government of England, if not of the
world, lay upon his shoulders. All I had to do was to listen,
which I enjoyed.

[2] Father of Sir Samuel Hoare, who is now Lord Templewood.

Chapter Nine

In October my mother and Conny went off to the Cape, where my Uncle Henry, later Lord Loch, was High Commissioner, and I was left in charge of my sister Betty. I was given the chance to go to the Cape with them, but did not want to be so far away from his Rev, which shows that he influenced my life in more ways than one. After their departure I paid a visit to Booton and then joined Betty at Whittingehame, near Edinburgh, the home of Arthur Balfour.

My mother had always insisted on seeing my letters from his Rev, though fortunately not mine to him. This had always annoyed me, and I was thankful to have my letters to myself after she went away. I do not think that he wrote very differently, though perhaps he put in a few more endearments which I called sugar.

From Whittingehame I write to his Rev:

Whittingehame, October 24

Now I must tell you all I have to tell, or I shall not have time. On arriving at East Linton I found the beloved Betty waiting for me, and the sight of her made me quite happy at once. She made the cold day seem warm. On the way she told me the latest Whittinghame news. When I arrived at the house Alice Balfour came into the hall to greet me, and behind the glass door at the further end I saw two little faces. It was a joy to see Betty's two children, Ruth and Nellie. Frances also came out to see me and shook hands in an offhand sort of way. I think she did not kiss me as a Balfour was present! At lunch I first saw Arthur. He came in when we were all assembled. I saw Betty and Frances look at me, expecting I should sink into the ground with shyness. He is certainly very pleasant and not at all alarming in himself, except that he never tries to talk to people who do not talk to him. I am shy of him chiefly because I know I am expected to be. He is of course the centre of everything here, and it is a tremendous privilege to sit next him or talk to him, a privilege which I willingly give up to other people.

The happiest times of the day to me are breakfast time, when the children come down and Arthur does not, and after tea, which is also given up to the children. The morning is also happy, as I sit in Betty's room and write to you. On Saturday night Arthur took me into dinner. I nearly burst out laughing, partly from shyness and partly because I knew Betty was pitying me so. I did not say much during dinner, and during the evening I got so sleepy, not having been to bed the night before, that I was not conscious what I said or did. We all go into the hall to get our candles before going to bed, and as Betty did not say goodnight to anyone nor did I, as I thought nothing was so wrong as to be polite in a Balfour household. For this, however, I was much scolded and told that as a guest I ought to say goodnight. Last night I took care to shake hands warmly. Betty has been very good to me and only says I ought to smile more and speak louder when I am spoken to. I will try my best to be pleasant and I can do no more for anyone.

Betty is more angelic than ever. She is charming to everyone and has been specially so to me. I love to be with her and there is nothing else to make this place pleasant. To sit in the same room with her and to hear her voice and see her bewitching smile is enough to make one happy. She is a darling all round, and each time I see her I am surprised at her goodness. No one could help loving her.

Whittingehame, October 25

Betty only scolds me very mildly, though I know she is cross with me for not talking. Last night at dinner the conversation was about people I did not know and had never heard of, nearly the whole time. Though I did not the least understand what was being said or the point of any joke, I looked as interested as if it was the subject I cared most for in the world and laughed immoderately at all the jokes. This part Betty says I did very well, but afterwards, the conversation having gradually come round to Americans, Arthur turned to me and asked if I felt towards Americans like brothers. I answered that I did not, and the conversation went on. Here Betty says I ought to have enlarged upon Americans and my ideas about them. I daresay I might, but I did not, so it cannot be helped. All the same I am angry with myself. Having failed I can only try to do better another time. If I have been very long silent, I dare not speak even if I have something to say, because everyone gives a sort of start of surprise when they hear my voice. I shall get over this gradually. I was rather amused last night, for as the Folkestones [1] had gone, and there was only one visitor left, a cousin of the Balfours, Johnnie Campbell by name, Frances said, "Don't go through the absurd ceremony of taking anyone into dinner, but let us go in anyhow," and she and Betty rushed into the dining-room. I was following when Arthur said, "There is no reason why you should be treated like this because the others are unsociable. Take my arm." So, to my horror, he took me in and I was forced to sit down beside him. Alice looked across at me with a smile, as much as to say, "I know you are very shy but it is good for you and such a privilege to sit next Arthur." Frances was in a very disagreeable mood yesterday and several characteristic scenes occurred. In the afternoon I went for a ride with Betty, and the family assembled to see us off. Alice said to me, "You must not ride that pony hard, as he is not accustomed to the weight of a heavy woman." "Absurd," said Frances. "That pony's back is broad enough to carry anyone." Then in the evening Alice was talking with Arthur about some changes that were to be made in one of the bedrooms and said she should change the name of the room when the new paper was put up. Frances had been reading but looked up when she saw the chance of being disagreeable and said, "Can you believe that anyone except a perfect fool would change the name of a room because they changed the paper? I for one shall call it by its old name as long as I live." It was quite

[1] Lady Folkestone was a cousin of both the Lyttons and the Balfours.

unnecessary for her to say this and was said simply and solely
to annoy Alice. I try to be as nice to Alice as I can, but I have
not yet had much opportunity of speaking to her. I smile at
her when I can do nothing else. Last night Betty played
backgammon with Johnnie Campbell, and Arthur played
billiards with Frances. I sat in an armchair and read Marbot,
and thought of somebody, can you guess who? I was very
happy, which shows the person I thought of was a nice
person. There are many nice people in the world I might
have thought of, but this particular person was something
more than nice. He was the dearest, wisest, best person that
ever lived and ever will live. I leave you to guess that
person's name, and it ought not to be very difficult.

Booton Rectory, October 24

I yesterday had the imprudence to preach on the duty of
Compassion. A greedy public determined to put me to the
test and see whether I practised what I preached (cold
weather, no blankets, etc.) and this morning, sore against
my will, I was dragged forth into a neighbouring parish to
investigate cases which I trusted would turn out impositions.
You will perhaps remember that in De Quincey's description
of the nights he spent in the deserted house with the servant
girl he breaks out into the exclamation, prompted by his own
nightly misery, "O ancient women, daughters of toil and
suffering, amongst all the hardships and bitter inheritances
of flesh that ye are called upon to face, not one, not even
hunger, seems in my eyes, comparable to that of nightly
cold."

Yet it is amazing how some women, not ancient, and
having the warmer blood of youth to help a little, endure it
without a murmur. A few years ago I heard that a woman
hard by had been confined with twins, and was lying on a
bedstead without a bed below or a covering above her,
though it was the depth of winter, and the thermometer
many degrees below freezing point, and so I found her,
with a nightgown and nothing else besides, cuddling her
infants, heroically calm and uncomplaining.

De Quincey's Ann (bless her) afterwards brought to my

mind what Bewick, the famous wood-engraver, says in his autobiography, of her class of persons as they appeared to him as he went from Newcastle to London in 1776: "One of the first things that struck me, and that constantly hurt my feelings, was the seeing such a number of fine looking women engaged in the wretched business of street walking. Of these I often enquired as to the cause of their becoming so lost to themselves, and to the world. Their usual reply was that they had been basely seduced, and then basely betrayed. This I believed, and was grieved to think that they were thus, perhaps, prevented from becoming the best of mothers to an offspring of lovely and healthy children. I often told them so, and this ended in their tears, and if they were in poverty, I contributed my mite to relieve them."

This was my experience. The better woman was rarely dead in them. Once in the outskirts of Cambridge, I was walking with some brother undergraduate, and we came across a female acquaintance of his belonging to the tribe, and he stopped to talk to her. He spoke to her neither brutally nor tenderly, but I remember that, touched by some expression in her face, I said something kind to her, and when we passed on she presently turned back, and without uttering a word, or lingering more than a moment, she put her face to mine and kissed me. To this hour I have never received a kiss that went more to my heart than the kiss of this poor girl. She, depend upon it, was another Ann.

Whittingehame, October 26

I keep thinking of De Quincey's story of Ann, each time with fresh pleasure. It is a wonderful story, and makes one love De Quincey for the qualities he must have had in him to draw forth the lovely qualities in Ann. One longs to know the end of poor Ann, and yet it is better not known, and one can be happy about her in that thought. It does seem wonderful that in the midst of such surroundings should grow up a love as pure and noble and beautiful as existed between those two. I never before have been so struck with the sense of the beauty that is to be found in everything, no matter how bad it might seem on the surface. It seems to have thrown a new light upon life to me, and I feel I can never think again as I did before. The whole world seems to me to be lifted up and beautified by that story. I have always had a sort of yearning for those poor women, for they seem to me to need more pity than anyone else in the world, and they are treated with greater cruelty and injustice. Men, who have helped to make them what they are, treat them like beasts and nothing more, and women will not hold out a finger to help them. It makes my blood boil sometimes to see the cruel things that happen and no one takes any notice of them. I remember in Paris we had a housemaid who was a most charming and delightful girl, and she had a child by one of the footmen in the house. Of course the poor girl was sent away, and she went to a wretched lodging in London, where her child was born and she died, which was the best thing that could happen to her, poor thing. In the meanwhile the man married her sister and went off to America, where he settled. Of course things like that happen every day, only I always remember the story, because it seems to me so dreadful that the sister of this poor girl should have married the very man who wronged her, when she probably would have thought it a degradation to help her sister in any way. And if the poor girl had lived, her character would have been gone for ever. All the blame is laid upon the unfortunate woman, when the man is generally the only guilty one. It seems such a monstrous injustice. I wonder people can remain quiet and see it happen every day. I feel I could do everything in the world to help a poor girl in that situation, and she is more to be pitied and helped than most people, and very often more to be loved.

How shocked Mother would be if she thought I knew the story I have just told you! That is one thing in which parents are deceived. Mother would have thought it dreadful to tell me about that poor housemaid, but I probably heard a good many more details than she knew herself. Parents are certainly wonderfully blind.

Yesterday I had a game of golf with Alice, Betty and Johnnie Campbell. I always thought the game dull to watch, but it is still more dull to play. To see Betty play is a very delicious sight. She tries to be so very serious over it, and puts on the regular golfing expression, swings her club in quite a professional way, and after a huge effort only succeeds in knocking up a large bit of turf and never touches the ball. I being a beginner hardly ever hit the ball, and never sent it where it ought to go. After we had dawdled round the house in this way for about half an hour, Betty and I decided we preferred a short sharp walk to golf. I have always heard of Scotch air as life-giving. The only effect it has had upon me at present is to give me a bad cold. The air is certainly colder than anywhere else, if that is a merit.

Arthur has gone away today and will not be back until we leave. You can guess whether my feelings are those of joy or sorrow. He has been very nice to me and I think he is a very charming man. He has a pleasant voice and smile, and I like him, for he seems evidently devoted to Betty, which shows his good taste.

Betty and I are beginning to read the *Confessions of St. Augustine*. Frances told Betty it was not a book for girls to read, but Betty replied that having read *Tristram Shandy* I might read anything. We began it last night and both think it is magnificent. The language is so fine and shows such a depth of thought. Did St. Augustine write the book when he was a very old man? Was he not the great Father of the Church? I suppose he was a very wonderful man?

It never struck me before that in the account of the Creation there was no evening to the Sabbath Day. It is a very fine idea and I think St. Augustine has expressed it in a beautiful way.

Booton Rectory, October 27

You probably remember the passage in *Hamlet*:

"O, villain, villain, smiling, damned villain!
    My tables—meet it is I set it down,
    That one may smile, and smile, and be a villain."

I fear that this is what you are coming to. You have begun to practise artificial smiles that belie your feelings, and with your power of face will soon become an artificial hypocrite. I laugh over your dilemmas and Betty's lectures. I repeat be

natural. Keep up an amiable and social intention, and circumstances will do the rest. You will win your way and be more
esteemed for not having forced it. Let nothing induce you to
depart from the deference you owe to Miss Balfour.

Arthur B's manner to you seems pleasant. I should be glad
if your shyness with him wore away soon. There is no
occasion for it, and he would take to you, I think, if you were
at your ease with him, and he would know you exactly as
you are.

One love has never driven out another with me. All the
people I ever loved, dead or living, I love still, and when
they rise up before me I bless them for their goodness to me.
But though the old love does not die away, the life changes,
and the new duties do not permit the love to be manifested
outwardly to the same extent exactly in the same form as
before. That is all I mean when I speak of the life which is
coming to you, we trust. Unless I coveted it for you my
love would be vastly less than it is. Being what it is I have
your welfare always in view.

Whittingehame, October 27

Frances is very vexed with me for having caught a cold,
and looks upon it as an insult to Scotch air! She consoles
herself by ordering me her remedies and insists on my
staying indoors. She has been very kind to me, as she always
is, but I do not intend to be ruled.

Rather a funny thing has happened. I told you Johnnie
Campbell was staying here. He is a cousin of the Balfours
and no relation to Frances, a Guardsman and rather a nice
creature. He invited himself, to Frances's disgust, and she
has been hoping every day that he would go. Betty said to
him in a very pointed way, "When *must* you go?" Last
night, to everyone's horror, he asked Alice if he might stay
here till November 5, as he had nowhere else to go. Alice
replied that she had no means of amusing him, but he said
he was quite happy and was glad of the opportunity of reading
a little. We expected Frances would kick him out of the
house when she heard this, but happily she is so struck with
the comic side of it that she is hardly angry. She contents

herself with proposing expeditions for him which will get
him out of the house, but he has not taken to the idea. It is
very funny, for last night Frances said grandly, "He must
go tomorrow, and we really cannot put up with a night of
him alone, as it is impossible to talk to him, and we cannot
talk over his head the whole time, so ask someone in to meet
him." Accordingly the clergyman and his wife were asked,
and now Frances fears she will have to put up with Johnnie
C. for nearly a fortnight. I think it is very cool of him to
stay so long, but still I am very amused to watch what will
happen. Betty's new fear is that I shall fall in love with him.
It is all very funny. The unfortunate man is called by Frances
"That creature." He is not a bad sort of man, but certainly
not attractive.

Booton Rectory, October 28

"*Augustine's Confessions* not a book for a girl to read!"
Perhaps girls are not fit company for saints and angels. That
is the only sense in which to pretend that the *Confessions*
should be a closed volume to them. It is one of the loftiest
books ever written. The Bible does not proceed on the
principle that holiness consists in ignorance of sin. It takes
for granted that sin will and must be known, sets it forth in
its enormity, and teaches you to resist and conquer it. St.
Augustine sets forth his own sin. And so you love it? No, you
revere him for his triumph over it, and feel that human
grandeur consists in following his humble but majestic foot-
steps. His mind was over-subtle and metaphysical, which
sometimes detracts from the interest, but he was a great
thinker nevertheless, mighty in intellect and almost a St.
Paul in saintliness, zeal, and valour. He died at seventy-six,
and his *Confessions* was a late work, one of his latest, the
product of his entire experience, boyhood, youth, manhood,
and old age.

Whittingehame, October 29

It was foolish of me to feel happy because Arthur had left.
There was absolutely no reason why he should make me feel
shy more than anyone else, only he did, and I felt more at
ease after he left. Still, after a few days I should probably

have got over my shyness with him and it would have been all right. Now I have lost my opportunity as he has gone. He was very pleasant to me and told Betty he quite understood my shyness, that nothing was as alarming as a family party where everyone had their own interests and you were an outsider. I feel sorry now that he has left. I expect the visits I am to pay afterwards will be the most alarming, but I will do as you tell me and be natural. It is not possible for me to talk at once in the way Betty does, but it will come by degrees, and I will try hard to be as pleasant as I can and not trouble my head about anything else. I don't think I ever try to be anything more than I am, for as I told you, I do not know what to be, but I am too much inclined to think how stupid I am and how stupid people will think me, and that of course makes me shy and nervous. Now I have made up my mind not to think of myself at all. I am what I am and I can be nothing else, and therefore there is nothing for it but just to be as pleasant as I can. I will try and not think of what is to happen to me, but just let myself drift wherever I am carried. One has to learn even to be natural, but I can see at once that is the happiest as well as the best thing to do.

I am enjoying myself here very much and wish I was not going so soon. I hate moving about so much. Just when I have got accustomed to a place and am getting over my shyness, I go off somewhere else.

After this visit to Whittingehame we returned to London, and I write from Betty's house where I was staying:

67 Addison Road, November 7

I have begun a correspondence with Blunt. That is to say, he wrote to me first and I felt it my duty to return him some good advice. I told him in my last letter that when he was tired of flattery and wanted truth he had better come to me and I would be sure and give it him, so this morning I had a letter from him saying he was tired of flattery and felt himself much in need of a little serious spiritual advice and therefore he would call here this afternoon. Betty tells me to send his letters to you, as you would be amused by them, but

12

I assured her you only cared to hear about Judith. And you are quite right, for she is the only person worth hearing about. I cannot help liking Blunt very much, though I certainly do not respect or admire him, simply because I know he likes me. Did you hear what he told Margot Tennant [1] about me? It is the strongest proof of his bad taste. I ought not to repeat it to you, but I do. He said I had the greatest personal charm of any member of my family. Don't you despise him now, if you did not before? Did I tell you Aunt T.[2] thought I flirted with him so desperately that it was quite serious. She did not say this in words, but her whole manner to me changed, and she became so affectionate and interested in me.

67 *Addison Road, November* 8

Mr. Blunt paid us a long visit yesterday afternoon, and while Betty supplied him with tea, I gave him wholesome advice. She was amused and rather shocked at the way I talked to him, especially when I asked if no one had offered him the poet-laureateship, and when he gave Betty a copy of his new poems, I said he had told me his dogs devoured all the rubbish he wrote. When she repeated it to Gerald afterwards, he said in a very shocked voice, "I call that flirtation." I call it truth. Blunt said he had never written anything wicked enough to give to me, but when he did he would dedicate it to me. He told us a good deal about the new paper the Souls are bringing out. It is to be called *Tomorrow*, a journal written by women for men. Margot is editor. Did Betty tell you that when she was asked to write for it, she replied that she never wrote except for money. In *Truth* some proverbs were suggested for mottoes to the paper. The funniest one was, "Girls will be boys." Betty repeated this to Blunt yesterday, only missed the point by saying "Women will be men." We then got to talking of poetry, and he said Rossetti's sonnets were the finest in the language, and again expressed his opinion that in poetry as well as painting the meaning was quite a minor detail, he never cared to understand poetry. I asked him if this was

[1] Later Mrs. Asquith and then Lady Oxford.
[2] Mrs. Earle.

what he aimed at in his own poetry. We next got on to Milton, and he said all that Milton had written was far better expressed in the Old Testament if you wanted to read it, and *Paradise Lost* was nothing but bombastic nonsense. Betty asked him if he shared Sir James Stephen's view that if Milton wished to express the thoughts he had written in *Paradise Lost* he might have done it in a prose pamphlet. Blunt never in the least saw the fun of this, but said quite seriously he would rather not have had even the prose pamphlet. And he calls himself a poet!

We had a very comic scene at breakfast this morning. You must know that Gerald is always laughing at me for being so fat. Well, Betty said she had written to you to say she was uneasy about my health and continued colds. At this Gerald burst into a roar of laughter and exclaimed, "Upon my word, I never heard anything so ridiculous." At this Betty said, "Gerald, you know nothing whatever about health. You are all as blind as a bat, and if a person was dying of consumption before your eyes, you would never notice it." "Do you mean to tell me, dear, that Emmie is dying of consumption? Why, just look at her." "I never said anything of the kind," replied Betty. "I talk sensibly. Emmie is always having colds and gets very easily tired, and she cannot walk fast and is altogether weak." Gerald looked at me and said, "I quite understand why she can't walk fast, but as for the rest, it's all rubbish. If she does have continual colds I am sure she has enough strength to fall back upon and to spare. Why, just look at her." I was so intensely amused that I nearly rolled off my chair with laughter. Gerald's looks at me were so very comic. He talks about me as if I was a sort of world's wonder for my size. Certainly if he judges everyone by himself I am fat.

                    67 *Addison Road, November 9*
We had a most amusing luncheon yesterday, and so characteristic of Betty. She was expecting a Mrs. Hamilton to luncheon, but as there was a dense fog, thought she would probably never turn up. We waited for her till 2.30, and as she never appeared, went in to lunch. When he saw what

Betty had provided for us to eat, Gerald said, "Thank goodness she has not come, or she would have been starved." There was a dish of tiny little veal cutlets and bacon, and four very small pheasant rissoles. Gerald pronounced it very shabby. At that moment the bell rang, and Betty hastily ordered up the remains of a cold pie. All that remained of it was one small slice. Presently in walked a lovely lady dressed in the richest furs, and evidently thinking she had done Betty a great kindness in coming so far to see her. Betty herself was so taken up with her shabby luncheon she could hardly say a word, but happily Mrs. Hamilton was quite able to keep up the conversation by herself. Betty presently rushed out of the room, the reason of which appeared afterwards. Betty ate absolutely nothing herself, as she thought the only way was to seem as if she had finished, and the little left on the table was the remains of the feast. Mrs. Hamilton took one veal cutlet and left the greater part of it untasted. When we had finished the pudding, which consisted of a few stewed figs, which did not nearly go round, Betty rang and asked in as unconcerned a voice as she could manage to put out, "Are the pancakes ready?"—trying not to betray that she had only rushed out to order them a few minutes ago. The maid answered in very loud tones, "Cook is afraid she cannot get pancakes done in time, but she will try and make a sweet omelette." And long after we had finished, the sweet omelette appeared and was not eaten by anyone. It was really most comic, and, after Mrs. Hamilton had gone, Betty laughed over it as much as anyone. Gerald was very solemn and rather vexed, and told Betty she really must not be so mean. She pretended to be equally ashamed, but could not hide her amusement.

67 Addison Road, November 12

In spite of the fog we managed to get to our dinner at Mr. Blunt's and it was a very amusing evening. There was one other guest, a Mr. Lane Fox. He is rather a curious man, and has travelled a great deal in India, believes in all sorts of spiritual beings, amongst others Mahatmas. He is rather like an Indian himself, to look at. He was very silent

himself at dinner, and I do not like to chaff Mr. Blunt if there
are any strangers present, though he always expects it and
tries to lead me on. After dinner we talked chiefly of con-
juring tricks, or magic, as Blunt says he firmly believes it
to be, and I told him some home truths which amused and
rather shocked Gerald. I do not feel that there is any depth
in Blunt's character and very little worthy of respect, and
yet I cannot help liking him. I suppose it is that I know he
is fond of me, and I always like people who like me. I know
that Blunt takes a real pleasure in having me with him and in
talking to me, and directly I know that, I feel quite an
affection for him, simply because he likes me. I suppose this
is a natural feeling.

Blunt says the laureateship has been offered both to Swinburne and William Morris, and both have refused. The
Prince of Wales told Arthur Balfour that it was to be held
in abeyance, as no one suitable could be found to fill the post.

Booton Rectory, November 14

You are profiting greatly by society. Conversation not
utterly frivolous is an education. You have started with a
sense of beauties and excellencies in many departments
which is precisely what is wanted to enable you to profit by
the opportunities which are opening to you. Hatfield is a
grand and luxurious school for you. Lady Cranborne must
be the grand-daughter of Sir William Napier's daughter,
Lady Arran. You might question her on the subject.

It is a relief to me to be told that no tenth-rate versifier is
to be appointed Laureate. Now that the office has been held
in succession by Southey, Wordsworth, and Tennyson, it
ought not to be degraded by sinking lower than a second-
rate poet, and it would have tasked the powers of Swinburne
and Morris to have sustained it at that level. I have not
read much of either, and least of Morris. I am in the case of
Bob Lowe,[1] who said to me, "My sister wants me to read
Morris's poems, but I won't." My reply would have been,
"I can't," which is what he meant, for he had made trial
of them.

[1] Lord Sherbrooke.

After a day or two in London Betty and I went to Hatfield on a visit.

Hatfield House, November 15

I have not much time and so will not waste it in talking nonsense. Betty and I arranged to meet yesterday at King's Cross, but of course, as always happens, we did not, and I came on here by myself. I determined to be brave and drive up to the house alone, but when I arrived at the station, felt I could not face it, and would wait till the last train rather than go up alone. Happily for me, Betty arrived by another train ten minutes after, and how we managed to miss each other, I cannot think. We arrived just in time to dress for dinner. Our party consists of Lord and Lady Granby,[1] the Pagets,[2] the Windsors,[3] Lady Galloway, Henry Cust, Sir Philip Curry, the Speaker [4] and Miss Peel, and I think that is all. Lord Granby I have hardly seen, but the little I have seen has not impressed me favourably. Lady Granby is a beauty of the Burne-Jones type. She is now getting rather old and shrivelled, but she still looks very beautiful at times. Sir Augustus Paget I love. He is so kind and fatherly and altogether charming. Lady Paget I do not much care for; she treats me in such a horribly patronizing way which, though she may have the right to do, annoys me frightfully. Lady Windsor is the Pagets' daughter and considered to be a great beauty. I think she is particularly ugly, and not to be compared to her mother for looks. I like Lord W. because he talked to me last night at dinner. Lady Galloway I like very much, as she has always been nice to me. I cannot tell you much about her, but I expect as you know everybody you will know all these far better than I do. Harry Cust is supposed to be a most fascinating young man. Betty says she could fall in love with him at any moment if he tried to make her, so let us hope he will not try. He is a great flirt, and I think an odious person. He is frightfully patronizing, which seems to me one of the greatest faults a young man

---

[1] Son of the Duke of Rutland and his wife.
[2] Sir Augustus and Lady Paget.
[3] Lord Windsor (later 1st Earl of Plymouth) and his wife.
[4] Lord Peel.

can have. I long to box his ears. My evening yesterday
passed off most successfully. I did not feel shy and managed
to talk quite tolerably, only I feel that all my energies have
been exhausted on that one evening, and the thought that
there are still four evenings to be lived through makes me
groan. I get positively to hate all the people in the house,
and it certainly would be a test if you fell in love with somebody staying in a country house with you. If you did not get
to hate them in those few days you would certainly love them
through life.

Last night I sat between Pom Macdonald [1] and Lord
Windsor, who both talked to me in turn, for which I was
most grateful. I talked about the Labour Commission as if I
understood it all thoroughly, though I was afraid every
minute that I should say something to betray my ignorance.
I am determined to show my ignorance and ask questions
when I can get them answered, but Betty says this is a
shocking plan. You cannot think how tiring it is to make
conversation. To talk for a week to people whom you do not
care about on subjects which do not interest you requires a
tremendous effort. People suppose you have finished lessons
when you come out, but I think the hardest lessons are just
then beginning. However, there is always the hope that
some day the reward will come in the shape of somebody who
is not altogether disagreeable. Poor Betty had a dreadful
sick headache yesterday and was obliged to go to bed after
dinner, leaving me alone amongst those awful people. I nearly
got up and followed her, but thought it would be too silly.
Lord Cranborne came and talked to me and I was not really
a bit shy or uncomfortable. Only the joy of getting to one's
own room is almost inexpressible. This is all I have to tell
you of Hatfield.

Hatfield House, November 16

Now to tell you something of myself. The day is a great
deal worse than the night. For one thing it is so much longer,
and in the light of the day my shyness increases. On the

---

[1] The Hon. Schomberg McDonnell, son of the Earl of Antrim, private
secretary to Lord Salisbury.

whole, though, I have got on pretty well. I have tried very, very hard to be natural and not think of myself at all, and it does make an enormous difference to my happiness. I feel it is the only way to get on, and though of course it will not altogether take away my shyness, it makes it very much better. Betty and I spent most of our morning yesterday in peace upstairs, but for half an hour before lunch we had a short walk with Lady Gwenny. I would give anything to become intimate with her, and I do really love her. I enjoy hearing her talk on any subject which excites her, for her eyes seem to start out of her head and her whole face quivers with excitement. In the afternoon we drove over to Panshanger, but unfortunately everyone was out. I was quite happy during the drive, for I sat next Miss Peel, whom I like very much, and we got on very well. I was also quite happy at dinner between Pom Macdonald and Lord Cranborne, and succeeded with much difficulty in making conversation for a whole meal. I cannot understand why people find so much pleasure in talking. It is so far more enjoyable to be silent. I feel that when I have escaped from here, I will not say a word to anyone unless I am obliged. I certainly do enjoy talking to *some* people, but then I talk because I have something to say and not merely for the sake of talking. I was very shy in the evening yesterday, for I kept getting into corners where I knew I was not wanted, and was too shy to get out again. However, I console myself with the thought that I am very much less shy already than I was a little time ago, and that is a great thing, only when I come up to my room at night I feel as if I must cry, not because I am the least unhappy, but simply from shyness and the feeling of relief I have at getting to my own room. I cannot help hating all the people I have been with for the same reason, that they have made me shy. Betty is angelically good to me, very sympathetic, and she neither watches nor listens to me, but she is very angry when I say I hate the other people. She told me last night when I said it that it was most unchristian, and that though she had been shy she had never hated the person of whom she was shy. What I feel exactly is this, and though it may be very stupid I still feel it. All the people here are in a set, they all know and like each other, they are all of a different age from what I am, and I am the one outsider, which is a very disagreeable position. I long for another girl to be here, or someone who would be an outsider with me. Then I feel that no one talks to me because they want to talk to me, but because they think they ought. This you may say is silly and self-conscious, but I feel it and cannot help it. Everyone talks to me in a patronizing way. I would not miss coming for anything, for it is all an education, it is the means by which to make friends, and there is always a certain amount of amusement to be got out of it. But it is absolutely no pleasure to me to talk to anyone, on the contrary it is a gigantic effort. Of course this is quite different in a house where I have my own friends. At Crabbet, for instance, I am never shy, because there I am not an outsider, and if anyone talks to me they do not talk in a patronizing way. Then I enjoy myself. I say there are three sorts of conversation: a conversation about nothing, an outside made-up talk; a conversation upon more intellectual subjects such as discussions about books, politics, and more abstract subjects; and the close and intimate conversation you have with a friend. The last seems to me quite unfit for general conversation for I could not say anything intimately to anyone at a dinner party. The second I say I am not capable of, though Betty says that is ridiculous; anyhow I am too shy to enter into any discussion, so the only conversation I feel capable of is about nothing at all. This, if it is a laboured conversation with someone you do not care about and who does not care about you, is a frightful effort and gives you no pleasure whatever. But supposing you are talking to a person whom you like very much and you know likes you and cares to hear you talk and to talk to you, whatever is said has some interest in it and is a means of drawing you together. This stage I have not yet reached, but when I do I shall begin to be happy in society. No doubt when I come across my somebody, I shall think there is no other way of being happy than by talking to that one person.

After dinner Lady Granby sang. Gwenny said she had been singing all day a song beginning: "Come back to me.

Beloved, or I die," and she thought that at the end the beloved would be heartily glad of the fact, the song was so doleful. So when Lady Granby again sang this song, it was difficult not to laugh, and I saw Gwenny stuffing her handkerchief into her mouth and becoming red in the face in her efforts to control her laughter. After that we played a game which was a great relief to me. Gerald played amongst others, and it was too comic to watch his excitement. His lips trembled and became perfectly white, and if he had not happily won, I believe there would have been an explosion.

Hatfield House, November 17

Betty and I thought it right to put in an appearance downstairs before lunch, and we all collected round the fire and worked and gossiped quite like a mothers' meeting. I had rather an awful time at lunch. Betty and I were both near the end of the table, and we both had a vacant place on one side. Lord Salisbury was not yet down, and we both trembled for fear he should seat himself beside us. Like a sensible man he sat next Betty. I think I should have sunk under the table if he had come by me. It was a pouring wet day, but Lady Salisbury arranged an expedition to St. Albans to inspect the Cathedral, and nine of the guests were packed off in three shut carriages. I was amongst the number and was happily sent in a carriage with Gwenny and Lady Robert.

We drove home in the same order, and I think in our carriage we all went to sleep. This I told to Betty, and she with her usual tact said to Gwenny at tea, "Emily says you all went to sleep and it was so nice." After tea we played a game, and Lady Granby, at the other end of the room, sang, "Come back to me, Beloved, or I die." I think she is almost the loveliest woman I have ever seen and I can hardly take my eyes off her. She is besides quite charming, simple, natural and unaffected, which is wonderful considering she is a fashionable beauty. She is devoted to her children and her house, and is very simple in all her tastes. It is quite a new thing for me to admire a generally admired person, especially of the Burne-Jones type, but she has a beautiful shaped head, a lovely neck and shoulders, and a most perfect figure. My dinner last night was very alarming and yet very funny. I sat between Lord Cranborne, whom I think perfectly charming, and Linky, who was here for one night and who makes me feel terribly shy. The conversation was so funny I must tell it you in the order it came. Headaches, pretty women, dogs, music, poetry, painting, sculpture, waxworks, and finally tortures. Doesn't it sound ridiculous? I first listened to Lord Cranborne and Lady Galloway and occasionally joined in, till we got down to poetry. There Lord C. turned to me and said, "I expect you are an authority on this subject." I said no, I hardly ever read poetry, to which he replied, "Nor do I, but I talk of it just the same." He then said he thought it a great mistake when people could only admire music from a technical point of view, or a picture because it was so well painted. Linky, on my other side, said, "Is there an art discussion going on?" and then we discussed pictures and sculpture, and I grew quite bold and gave my views on art in general as if I had studied it for years. You would have laughed to hear me. Linky said his opinion of the Greeks was much lowered by the fact that they never made an intellectual woman, that the statues of Venus one and all looked idiotic. From Greek sculpture we got down to waxworks, and this led us to Mme Tussaud's Chamber of Horrors, and then we each described horrible tortures, which you would think was hardly a lively subject. After dinner everyone played games, and some few happy people like myself watched the game without joining in it. So the evening passed off successfully. Breakfast is almost the worst meal of the day, for there are little tables spread about and you may get caught by some alarming person. Con says she was once in an awful situation, having begun a table by herself when Lord Salisbury came in and felt obliged to sit by her, and they talked about *jam*. Con says this was the most awful moment of her life.

Booton Rectory, November 17

Your description of your position in the Hatfield party is true to the letter. You have to work your way into acquaintanceship, and in the nature of things must be an outsider at starting. The right course, to my thinking, is to school your mind as far as possible into accepting the inevitable, to respond amicably to advances, to allow your genuine self to speak for you without pretending to be what you are not, and to have full faith that bit by bit events will work in your favour, and furnish you with a court of your own. To say my opinion more briefly, I think you should go on as you have begun. Severe as the discipline is, you are getting on capitally. You were happy in your walk with Lady Gwen and Betty, happy at dinner between Lord Cranborne and Pom Macdonald, not unhappy in the evening listening to the conversation between Betty and Lady Gwen, and in a high state of mirthfulness when Lady Granby sang, "Come back to me, Beloved, or I die." This is pretty tolerable for a doleful day. Your state was enviable compared to that of Lady Granby, whose beloved has deserted her and won't come back.

Hatfield House, November 18

There was a general feeling of depression here yesterday. Betty and I both felt so miserable we should have sat down to cry if we had not happily thought of *Tristram Shandy*, and between Mr. Shandy and Trim we were more or less comforted. Lady Salisbury thought the evening before had been so dull, which it was not, that she had a band display during yesterday evening. They began with dance music, which, however, made us all so wildly wretched that it was soon put a stop to. Nothing makes me feel so unhappy as dance music. I enjoyed my evening, though, for I sat and talked to Lady Cranborne, who is most charming to me. Today everyone has left except ourselves, and I am shyer than ever with a family party. I really have enjoyed myself here far more than I expected, in spite of my shyness, and I feel it has been a gain to me in many ways. Several comic things have happened which I have forgotten to report to you. Lady Paget is very amusing, as she is full of the most mad and ridiculous health theories. To begin with, she is a vegetarian, which is not so out of the way, and a great believer in homeopathy. Her chief cures, though, are to sit wrapped in wet blankets and to walk about bare-foot. Poor

Sir Augustus is obliged to submit to all this, and he must look a pitiful sight wrapped up in a wet blanket. At the Embassy in Vienna one day a secretary was going upstairs to see Sir Augustus, but was stopped halfway by a servant, who said, "You must not go up, because Sir Augustus and Lady Paget are paddling about on the landing." They had upset a jug or two of cold water on the floor and were paddling about in this. Can you conceive a more comic sight? When Sir Augustus is suffering from ague, his wife makes passes over him, which he is not supposed to know, and when he comes down cured next morning, Lady Paget supposes it to be the result of her magical signs, while Sir Augustus puts it down to Eno's Fruit Salts.

Aunt T. has been to see *King Lear* at the Lyceum, and writing about it to Betty today, she says she owes Shakespeare a grudge for having written that play, as he is such a Bible to the English people, fathers are now never willing to help their children. Isn't it rather funny? Everyone says Irving is shocking as Lear, as I am sure he must be. He begins raving mad and rants and raves through the whole play.

Hatfield House, November 19

I have filled my letters with accounts of myself and never said a word about Betty or anyone else. She can tell her own story when we come to Booton. But what she will not tell is how much she is loved here. Lady Cranborne said Lord Salisbury adored her and liked talking to her better than anyone else. Lady Salisbury plainly does the same, and it is the case with everyone else. Lady Cranborne said she had such a sunny nature, that she was so wonderfully sympathetic. And last night Fluffy [1] was loud in praises of her looks. Whatever subject of conversation was started, Fluffy still went back to Betty's looks, exclaiming, "She does look lovely tonight." Betty said to me the other night, "I *should* like to be a fashionable beauty." I assured her she was as lovely as and lovelier than most of the beauties in the house. Besides, their faces were mindless, and Betty's is not. Her

---

[1] Lady William Cecil.

chief beauty is her lovely expression, and that is worth all the insipid beauties put together. I feel quite low at leaving her today, she has been so good to me. I am afraid I shall have a good many feelings of regret when Mother comes home. For one thing I shall again have to show all your letters, which means you cannot put so much sugar in them as you do now. And for another thing it is so delightful living with Betty that I shall feel miserable when I leave her. And lastly I am now free to do what I like and go where I like, and I do not feel inclined to have a yoke upon my neck again. However, I must be thankful for three months of liberty and make the best of the bondage when I am obliged to submit to it. I feel now how easy it is to live peacefully and happily. During all the time I have been with Betty she has not said a single cross or unkind word to me, but all has been as peaceful as possible, and I think I should learn soon to be good tempered too.

Lady Salisbury says she has got three nice young men coming today, and she is very disappointed that I should go away.[1] I expect you will be disappointed too, for I have had no nice young man to tell you about this time.

Lady Cranborne told us a story yesterday of the gardener here who had a new house built for him, and Lord Salisbury asked him one day if he liked it. He replied, "I like it very well, but I should have preferred something more in the style of your Lordship's mansion."

Hatfield House, November 20

As I was obliged to stay yesterday [2] I thought I would make good use of my time. I sat between two young men at dinner and got so intimate with one that before the end of the meal he offered to send me a poem. Are not your ears burning with curiosity to know who he was and if today I am engaged to him? You will think I have gone about it as rapidly as even you could wish. Now that I have raised your curiosity to such a pitch, I am going to disappoint it by telling you that the young man was a cousin, and the poem

---

[1] I was going on another visit.
[2] I had missed the train.

he is to send me is not upon love but upon shyness. Isn't
that a great come-down? I must give you a fuller account of
my evening. The guests staying in the house are Mrs. and
Miss Stuart Wortley. They are both very nice. Eric Barring-
ton and his wife. They are both the essence of everything
cousinly and priggish and tiresome. I suppose most people
think their relations tiresome, but I am sure mine are a
specially awful lot. I could tell a cousin anywhere, for prig
and bore is written in every line of their face. The young
cousin whom I have made friends with is Arthur Stanley,
Lord Derby's son. His mother is sister to Lady Lathom and
Lady Ampthill, only very much nicer than either of them.
They are all a delightful family and I used to be very fond
of the daughter. They are now in Canada. Arthur gave me
news of his whole family and we soon became friends. The
other young man was George Talbot. I met him once before
at Terling [1] and did not care very much for him, but I am
coming round and now I think he is very pleasant. He is a
lawyer (are gentlemen lawyers or barristers, I am always in
a muddle about the differences?), very shy, very serious, very
good. Betty likes him immensely. Last night there was a
funny party to dinner, as some country neighbours were
got in to increase the party. Gerald sat between two of
these good ladies, and it was delightful to watch his face
with a polite smile to cover his intense boredom. I love to
see him caught by these sort of people. One very stout, very
smart lady, with snow white hair, came with all the family
diamonds. When she entered the room, she exclaimed: "My
daughter told me not to put on my diamonds. She said
'Mamma, put on your butterflies instead, no one will be
wearing diamonds'—but I thought, you never know whom
you may meet, and I shall make myself look as nice as I
possibly can, so I put them on, and now I see my daughter
was right, for you have none of you got on diamonds." She
was assured it was only because no one possessed them, but
it was so delightful of her to enter into the whole history of
the discussion with her daughter on the subject. Her husband
sat next Lady Cranborne, and Lady Salisbury, who was two

[1] The home of Lord and Lady Rayleigh.

chairs off, said in a loud whisper to Alice, "He's quite blind, so you must hold his arm when he eats." The unfortunate man heard this and said, "I am very short-sighted, but it is not quite as bad as all that."

Alice Cranborne was talking again last night about Betty, and said she would rather be like her than almost anyone, that she was so genial, so sympathetic, so unselfish, and that to hear her laugh from the other end of the room did one's heart good, it was so natural and hearty. She also admired the way she talked of Frances. She said, "Betty is so undoubtedly the cleverest of the two, and yet she always talks as if Frances did everything best." Lady Cranborne was also very complimentary about me to Betty, but what she said I leave for someone else to tell you.

After Hatfield, I made a round of visits with Betty. Only one is worth recording. It was to Mells, the home of the Horners. Mrs. Horner was a leading "Soul" and on this occasion there was a select company of fellow "Souls." I write on December 5th:

Mells Park

We came here by a train which took three hours and only arrived at seven o'clock. By the same train came D. D. Lyttleton [1] and Mr. Asquith. We drove up to the house, a drive of about four miles in two carriages. The snow was on the ground and the moon shone brightly. Quite a fairy-tale beginning! Betty arrived before me, so I was obliged to enter alone, but Mrs. Horner came forward in a charming way and we all sat down to tea, though it was 8 o'clock. I was quite prepared to detest Mrs. Horner, and I have ended by loving her. She is a perfect hostess, so kind, so natural, so amusing, and altogether delightful. Mr. Horner I also love. He is rather a nice simple creature, only unfortunately rather deaf. There are four children, two girls and two boys. They are very precocious, and already play intellectual games. Having described the family I will proceed to the guests. D.D., the Sydney Herberts, [2] the Whites, [3] the

---

[1] Mrs. Alfred Lyttleton.   [2] Son of the Earl of Pembroke.

[3] The American Ambassador.

Ribblesdales,[1] Dol Liddell, Asquith, and for three days Mr. Quentin Hogg.[2] I am desperately in love with D.D. and think her one of the most fascinating people I have ever seen. Sydney Herbert, who is supposed to be splendidly handsome, looks to my mind a great fool, but I rather like him all the same. Lady Beatrice Herbert is Nellie Cecil's sister, and very like her, only much taller. She is a model wife and mother, with very strict and old-fashioned ideas about the bringing up of girls, a great Philistine, withal a great dear, and perfectly charming to me. Her chief fault is continual back-biting. Into my ear she poured all her household troubles, and all the sins of her different friends, which amused me from a person 'with her views. I was quite fascinated with Lady Ribblesdale. She is so genial, so beamingly good-natured, and so very nice to me. Asquith's appearance is very much against him, and I do not feel at all attracted by him, but apart from this he is very natural, easy and agreeable and you can see he is an able man. He is not quite a gentleman, which is very much against him. Quentin Hogg is a brother-in-law of Mrs. Horner's and a very interesting man. He founded the Polytechnic, whatever that may be (Betty said to someone: "Now do explain to me what the Polytechnic really is?" "Why, I suppose it is *the* Polytechnic," was the answer. "Oh," said Betty, "it is *the* Polytechnic, is it?" and she got no further.), and has worked all his life in the East End. He is very interesting on his own subjects. I think I have now told you about everyone. I cannot elaborately describe every day, so will give you my general impressions.

On Tuesday we drove over to Downside, a place some miles distant where is a Roman Catholic monastery. The monks are building a church there quite in the old style, bit by bit, regardless of money or time. It is about half done and they have been at it thirteen years. A monk showed us over it. He clung to Mr. Asquith, who was the only male member of the party, and kept his eyes from falling on a female form lest he should be led into temptation.

[1] Lord Ribblesdale.
[2] Founder of the Polytechnic.

13

Our drive home was very amusing. Asquith entreated Mrs. Horner and D.D. to quote some of their poetry, so at last they began. They were all love poems and atrociously bad. Asquith pulled them to pieces in every possible way— the meaning is obscure, the metre halting, the metaphors absurd, etc., and so on in the same style. They were most good-natured and seemed to enjoy the criticisms as much as we did. This was kept up for some time, when at last D.D. betrayed herself by quoting something by Beaumont and Fletcher which Asquith recognized, and then it turned out that all this time they had been deceiving us, and their pretended poems were all quotations from Swinburne, M. Arnold, Emerson, and other well-known writers. You may imagine we felt small, as none of us had suspected their trick for an instant, and it was specially comic as Asquith is supposed to know almost every line M. Arnold ever wrote and he was cutting him to pieces right and left. They did it splendidly and it was great fun.

Saturday the Herberts left and a horrid small party of intimate friends remained. They had terrible intellectual games that evening, but dear Mr. Horner carried me off to play piquet with him and before we stopped it was one o'clock. Doesn't it sound dissipated to say I sat up till one in the morning playing cards?

Although not recorded in a letter, a further experience of that visit has been indelibly impressed upon my mind, as at the time it caused me so much distress. On Sunday evening our game of piquet was abandoned, as it was not considered right to play cards on a Sunday, and to my consternation I was roped into the intellectual games of the other members of the party. On this particular occasion Mrs. Horner went out of the room and each member of the company made some remark about her. These remarks were read aloud to her on her re-entry and she had to guess the author of each remark. Betty insisted that I should join in the game, and when I protested she said, "Say anything that comes into your head, it need not be true." Thus driven into a corner, I said with great emphasis, "I think she is an awful bore." Horrified silence! Happily Mrs. Horner guessed all the other remarks, so my unfortunate one was never repeated, but I got a scolding from Betty for my rudeness.

I should add here that there never lived anyone less of a bore than Mrs. Horner.

Booton Rectory, December 7

I speculate much on the course of events at Mells, and fancy pictures alternate states, and I wonder which prevails. Is time sweeping onwards with his swiftest wing, or heavily dragging along at a pace that is sad as well as slow? Dull days at a country-house party are the weariest that can be. Whatever they are to you they will furnish entertainment for me, and I hope for the first chapter tomorrow morning.

There are two ways of enjoying society, one by taking your share in it, the other by observing it. Lockhart [1] used to say that the last was the most amusing. It was a perpetual play in which nature performed the parts. The affectations and false pretences might be innumerable, but they were nature in the actors, who were deliberate hypocrites. However long you watch jealousies, rivalries, spite, disappointments, mortification, anger and all manner of by-play they will still be exhibited under new forms, and keep vigilant eyes entertained by fresh discoveries. In summing up the advantages you have derived from your short season, it is evident that you can relish society under both its aspects. You can find pleasure by mixing in it—the pleasure of companionship—and pleasure by looking on, which is a compound of pleasures, and as wide and varied as human nature itself. It is a special advantage for you that you have thus early discovered a source of amusement and instruction that will make many a dull party a festive lesson to you.

[1] Sir Walter Scott's son-in-law.

Chapter Ten

In January of this year my mother and Con returned from the Cape and we settled back in London for a few months, but my mother wished to make a home in the country, and after much family discussion a house was taken near Hertford. We moved into it in the middle of the summer.

I was much afraid that on her return home my mother would want once more to read my letters from his Rev, but I think Betty must have intervened on my behalf and told her that I must be allowed to keep my letters to myself.

The suggestion also came from Betty that I needed some occupation other than my daily letters to his Rev. I do not know what turned my mind to botany, but I took up the subject with great enthusiasm and went regularly to the Natural History Museum, where under a delightful teacher, Miss Annie Smith, I learnt not only about flowers in general, but also learnt to cut and draw sections under the microscope. I also went to a dancing class and learnt skirt dancing, which was then fashionable, from Mrs. Wordsworth, a well-known teacher.

I have no letters of mine for the next few months, but in May I take up my story again:

44 Elm Park Gardens, May 2
I spent three hours and a half at the Museum this morning and the time passed like five minutes. I had a most delightful lesson. Miss Smith was very pleased with my drawing, which pleased me. I cut some lovely sections today, and Miss Smith showed me how to stain them with different preparations and how to mount them permanently. Miss Smith praised my cutting and said it was wonderfully good for the first day, I had quite the knack of doing it. One section,

she said, was perfect, and she was quite excited over it. I like to tell you when she praises me, although I ought not.

Every day I feel the fascination of it grows, and it is a joy to wake up in the morning and feel it is there to go to. It adds a thousand times to my pleasure that you are interested in it. All that I learned before without the microscope seems dull compared to what I know now. Every day I feel more certain that it was this thing of all others to make my life happy. I always felt the need of an occupation but never hit upon the right one. The usual accomplishments that Mother wished me to learn, such as music and drawing, I felt to hate, and yet there seemed nothing else. Now I have got something which satisfies me altogether. I do not think I could ever have been happy without some occupation which would satisfy my deepest feelings, but botany does. The more I learn of the wonders of creation, the nearer it seems to bring me to the Creator, and so I am happy all round in it.

I dined last night with Lady Wentworth.[1] The other guests were Lady Dolly Neville, Sir Redvers [2] and Lady Buller, Sir Philip Curry, the Stuart Wortleys, Miss Talbot, Lord Morpeth and another couple whose names I do not know. I sat between Lord Morpeth and Mr. Wortley. Lord Morpeth is an odd-looking man, being only about twenty-five and with quite a young face and grey hair. He has got an eternal smile on his face, which annoys me, besides being, I think, very dull; so we did not get on very well and I am sure we were mutually annoyed with each other, but to everything he asked me, I said "I don't know," which was not encouraging. After dinner I talked to Lord Wharncliffe, who was also there. Lord Morpeth is Lord Carlisle's eldest son, and Mother is disappointed that I have not fallen in love with an eldest son when I had the opportunity.

Lady Dorothy Neville I am very fond of, and she looks so wonderfully young. The dinner was rather dull.

Sir Redvers Buller, whom I dare say Betty has told you about as she often meets him, looked, I thought, stupid and

---

[1] Lord Wentworth was a grandson of Lord Byron and brother of Lady Anne Blunt.
[2] A leading general.

bad-tempered. His wife looked dying of melancholia. Miss Talbot was rather big, with a fine manly voice, and not very attractive.

44 *Elm Park Gardens, May 3*

Con and I have been this morning to a lecture at Lady Cowper's on the *Uses of Poetry* by Churton Collins. There is to be a course of lectures, and as Con wished to be civil to Lady Cowper she went to this one and I accompanied her, hoping to pick up something comic that I might report to you. We both thought the subject of the lecture gave room for comedies, but unfortunately the lecture was more or less successful and, consequently, dull.

There were many fine ladies listening to the lecture and the solemnity of everyone was quite painful. The lecturer began by trying to define poetry or, rather, quoted other people's definitions, but as Con says, they were all so bad that whatever he had himself said afterwards would have seemed good by comparison. His own definition of poetry was—"Anyhow, it isn't prose," which fact I had arrived at myself. He said poetry was the embodiment of ideal truth and his object was to show what great truths it taught. But his lecture chiefly consisted in quotations, and though there was nothing specially interesting in it, there was nothing very ridiculous.

The most amusing incident was the entrance of Margot Tennant. She arrived in the middle of the lecture and the butler opened the door very gently so that she might quietly slip in, but Margot was determined to be noticed. She banged the door and marched up the room with a great noise, patted me on the back and seated herself beside me, and afterwards made remarks in a loud whisper. It was extra funny from the fact that everyone else was so silent and solemn.

Last night I went with Betty to a ball, which was highly comic. It was given at the Hotel Metropole by the Duke of Portland in aid of a Home of Rest for Horses. Lady Salisbury had given Mother four tickets, so Betty and I went with Phil Burne-Jones [1] and Theo Russell. [2] Amongst other

[1] Son of the painter.　　　　[2] My cousin, son of Lord Ampthill.

attractions we were offered palmistry, photography, and a
champagne supper. There was not a single soul in the room
that we any of us knew. The ballroom was large and Betty
said it took one back to the Assembly Rooms at Bath in
Miss Austen's day. There were the most wonderful collection of people I have ever seen, and their costumes were
more wonderful than themselves. The dresses are going
back to early Victorian fashion, and it really looked like the
old ballrooms of fifty years ago. The people were very smart
and there were a great many hideous and bright colours,
heliotrope prevailing of a shade that took the skin off one's
eyes. The people were all of a class which you would never
meet anywhere else. They seemed to be all strangers to each
other, and there was occasionally a couple seated on the
same sofa both looking miserable and not saying a word.

Mr. Phil and Betty amused themselves by making
fictitious likenesses to their acquaintances, and some were
very funny. We laughed until we nearly cried and were so
amused that we stayed until two o'clock.

When we were tired of dancing, we thought we would
try the palmistry. It was announced that Mrs. St. Hill had
generously offered her services—fee 7/6d. before twelve,
5/- after twelve. We went into a room which was just like
the waiting-room of a station, and there were a great many
odd-looking couples. Mrs. St. Hill was practising her art
behind a screen and we did not get a chance of going in before
twelve. Then we agreed it was too expensive, so we tried
the supper instead. It was in a gigantic room and the supper
was colossal. Masses of cold meats of every description
piled up into elaborate shapes. Mr. Phil suggested that it
was all horse ingeniously disguised under these various
forms. The supper did not succeed much better than the
palmistry, and we were unable to get very far in it, but
amused ourselves with watching our neighbours, who were
wonderfully comic, and we then returned to the ballroom
and danced wildly for some time. I have never enjoyed a
party more.

Mother and Con have started a most terrible new theory,
which is that to breathe very hard through the nose is as good

a form of exercise as you can have. So when they have nothing better to do, they both begin snorting valiantly for exercise, which is terrible to listen to.

Booton Rectory, May 4

I would not give a farthing to be told what poetry is. I am content to know it when I see it. Do not Churton Collins' audience ask him what prose is? They must, one would suppose, be equally inquisitive on that point, and when he informs them will they be wiser on the subject than they are now?

You are accumulating experiences. I can picture the fun the ball must have been to you. The company were probably a compound of affectation and nature. They meant to be artificial—that is, highly fashionable—but their lesson had been imperfectly learnt, and nature, stronger than their efforts, kept breaking through. As you knew nobody, and "danced wildly," how did you pick up partners, and what sort of folk did they turn out upon acquaintance? Lucky you to be mothered by Betty. My Lady would not have taken you to the ball, or if she had she would not have stayed, or staying would have frowned down wild dancing and up-roarious mirth. You would have had a dull, decorous evening, and gone weary to bed, feeling that you had lost a day.

44 Elm Park Gardens, May 6

I went to another ball last night and feel a wreck this morning after all my festivities this week. The ball was amusing, but not so good as the others because the room was too crowded to dance much and my partners were very dull. Betty had brought me lovely flowers to wear—it is delicious when she tries to be very motherly and asks how many times I danced and who were my partners. Then she thinks it right to find fault a little too, but she must do the thing thoroughly, so she told me my dress looked dirty, which offended me as it was quite new.

I sat out with one man whose name I have forgotten and he began talking to me about the National Gallery, which he said was the finest gallery in the world, though he had never seen another. What he admired in it he did not say, but when I asked him whether he knew Velasquez's "Admiral" and if he admired it, he replied: "Yes, I know it; I suppose it is splendidly painted and all that, but then the subject is so uninteresting. Who wants to know anything about an old Admiral?" I was so amused. He also said that to have given £72,000 for Raphael's "Madonna" was a great waste of money, as he saw nothing beautiful in the picture. He said it was a pity so few people went to the National Gallery, and I said I thought you ought to be educated in pictures before you appreciated them, and he, thinking of course that he had the necessary education, replied: "Oh, but I find the lower classes often know as much about pictures as we do." I longed to say, "They might know as much as you do without knowing anything."

It is a comfort to think men don't like party-going as much as women, because I have often thought that if I marry it would be so awful to keep up that eternal round of daily parties.

44 *Elm Park Gardens, May* 11

We had a very comic expedition yesterday to see the Procession.[1] The Lathoms had given us three places at Knightsbridge Barracks and Mother was asked to chaperone their three girls, as Lord and Lady Lathom were going inside the Imperial Institute. We were told to be at the Barracks by a quarter to ten, but Mother said this was absurdly early and she should not leave home until that hour. It was rather past that hour when we started, and Con, thinking it hard on the Lathoms to keep them waiting, said she had suddenly discovered she was very rich and was going to have a cab. Mother, of course, had an objection ready. The bus was far more convenient, far cheaper, in fact a cab was not to be thought of. However, we were eventually obliged to take one, as every bus was full. Con said she would pay and we were neither of us to interfere. The fare was 1/6d. and Con, having no change, gave 2/–. Mother was perfectly furious,

[1] The opening of the Imperial Institute by the Prince of Wales.

saying, "I do think it is too hard that when I slave from
morning till night to be economical, you should be so
reckless. You make me feel so ill and upset." The awful recklessness consisted in spending an unnecessary sixpence. It
was so very comic that Mother should be scolding Con for
her utter recklessness.

The Wilbrahams [1] had dared to take seats inside the
Barracks, unchaperoned. We sat there from 10 until 2, and
all for the mere purpose of seeing the Queen and a few other
Royalties drive by. It is astounding what human beings will
do, and the only thing about it which was good was the
luncheon, of which I ate largely. The Procession was poor
and the crowd very cold. One thing was rather comic. The
band played a few bars of God Save the Queen as each
carriage drove by. The first carriage contained Lord Suffield,
and as the band struck up he put his head out and made
violent signs of disapproval. The finest part of the Procession
were four Indian soldiers. They had splendid faces and rode
magnificently—it was all a frightful waste of time.

44 *Elm Park Gardens, May* 24
I think I have never told you that I am reading *Vanity
Fair* and think it delicious. As you said, it is written in such
a pleasant easy style, which is delightful to read. I suppose
it is very true to human nature of a certain kind. There is not
one lovable character. Did Thackeray always see people
from that point of view? Becky Sharp is a wonderful character,
there are some delightful touches in it.

His Rev replies, on May 26th:

Booton Rectory
Thackeray had a keen perception of what was beautiful in
those he knew, and did homage to their virtues. But his lot
was cast in the midst of a society in which selfishness, meanness, vanity and the like predominated, and it was easier to
him to make a pungent book out of the failings than out of the
goodness of mankind. There was nothing sour or malignant

------

[1] The family name of the Lathoms.

in his own nature. He was warm-hearted, generous and benevolent.

In general I dislike reflections that interrupt a story. But I am partial to Thackeray's moralizings. They seem to me very felicitous in themselves, and fitted to their place as he introduces them. In his later books, when he had written himself out, they are frequently redundant. I once told him that a reviewer had denounced them, and he said "Oh, they are part of the play."

Social ideas have undergone a great change even in the course of my life. People are accepted for gentlemen in many callings which in my boyhood would have deprived them of all title to the name. The addition of Esq. on the direction of a letter was confined to a class. Now it has descended till it has become unmeaning. Wealth goes a long way still in elevating a man, and poverty in degrading him, but little compared to what they did in my early time. The causes of the change are in part obvious to any one who has lived in both periods, and a man who worked out the subject would probably discover others that are not apparent at a glance.

44 *Elm Park Gardens, May* 27

We are very busy thinking of the furniture for our country house. I say we, but I mean Mother and Con. I am not allowed to know what they settle on, for which I am thankful. It is bad enough for two people to agree, impossible for three. Whatever they choose I am sure to think hideous, but no matter so long as I settle on my own room.

I am sure we shall like our country house directly we are settled in it, but at present I feel very sorry to be leaving London. There are so many resources here. However, I know I can be happy anywhere.

Your report on what Betty says about my temper has made me very happy. She is an angel herself and sees everyone in the light of her own angelic nature. I do honestly think my temper is better than it was, but that does not say it is good. I know that my own selfishness is unbounded and I never, by any chance, think of other people before myself.

Yesterday, poor Mother was unwell after a sleepless

night and is upset because our household is breaking up
preparatory to the move into the country. Then I went to
Betty and found her unwell and very depressed, and she told
me Con was sad, and then I felt such a horrid beast, I could
have killed myself. All the while, I go on enjoying myself
and never give a thought to other people's feelings. It is not
from unkindness but from thoughtlessness. When I am
happy myself, I forget to remember that others may not be as
happy as I am, and even when I notice it, I am not sympathetic. I see Mother is low and fretting over different things
which do not affect me, and I pay no attention to them, and
I find it very difficult to be sympathetic in the way that
people want. If I sympathize with them in the way I should
wish them to sympathize with me, which is by letting me
alone, that does not please them. I suppose sympathy for
others is a thing which comes as one grows older and has
more to bear. When one is beginning life, it is difficult to
understand the feelings of those who have lived their lives.

You are the only person who can understand everyone of
all ages and sympathize with each one as they want sympathy.
It would be no good to ask you how you did it, because if
you told me, I could not imitate you.

Booton Rectory, May 28

No one can feel the trials of another as we feel our own.
There is a wise reason for this, for if we had been constituted
so as to feel for others as we do for ourselves we should all
of us at all times be paralysed by the accumulation of sorrow,
and life could not go on. Yet for want of thought, people in
misery commonly expect sympathy beyond what nature
allows, and, as Johnson says, invariably are of opinion that
you do not feel enough. We must do our best to understand
their troubles and relieve them, and not expect to be more
than very partially successful.

44 *Elm Park Gardens, May* 30

Betty and I went to a dreadfully dull party at Lady
Brassey's last night. It was a musical party, which of all
dreadful things is the worst. Going upstairs, we met Lady

Ampthill [1] and Constance,[2] which was nice, and we got
together on a sofa in a distant room where we could not hear
the music, and I nearly fell asleep. Betty stayed with Lady A.,
and this is a report of her conversation, which must have been
killing:

Lady A.: Did you see the Flower Show at the Temple? It
was so beautiful, such lovely begonias.

Betty: I myself think those double flowers are always
hideous, but of course it was a wonderful show. I went with
Emily, who is a botanist, and she told me many amazing
things about flowers.

Lady A.: Oh, a botanist, is she? I suppose she doesn't go
in for it very thoroughly.

Betty: Oh, indeed she does. Very thoroughly indeed. She
does nothing else now.

Lady A.: But I believe Botany is very improper when you
go in for it thoroughly?

Betty: It is just the fun of it. Emily tells us such amazing
things about the sexes of the plants. All sciences are improper
when you go in for them thoroughly.

Lady A.: How about Astronomy?

Betty: I mean things of the earth, earthy.

Lady A.: I do not think there would be anything improper
about Geology.

Betty: I don't know, but there has been a lot written and
told about it. Darwin, you know, has written a lot about it,
and then there are footprints, we are told a lot about those.

Betty had no idea what had been written about Geology
or how it can be made improper, but she said Lady A. was
very much impressed.

44 *Elm Park Gardens, June* 1

Mother was in a very comic mood yesterday, and there
were some good scenes. I went to tea with Mrs. Norman
Grosvenor, who is a sister of Mrs. Talbot's, and always very
nice to me. This, to begin with, displeased Mother; that I

---

[1] My mother's first cousin.
[2] Her daughter.

should go and see anyone that gave me pleasure was a trial, but that I should be going alone and without her was a still greater grievance.

Mother walked with me yesterday a little way, and to amuse her I told her about my tea at the Stillmans' and that I had met Anstey [1] there. She asked me if he was amusing. I said I only spoke to him to persuade him to join our Club. Judith and I and some other distinguished people belong to a Club which goes by the name of the Pawsoff and Rude Club, the rules of which are that members may not shake hands, are to be as rude to each other as they can, the object of the Club being for the promotion of good manners, which consist, as explained by one member, in the true rudeness of a gentleman. Judith says it is to do away with conventionalities of all sorts and that members, instead of talking about the weather as they otherwise might, are at once at their ease and talk naturally. When there is a meeting at the Club it generally ends in the members fighting, which certainly shows they are at their ease.

I have been unanimously elected this year, it being considered that true rudeness came so naturally to me that I should be a distinguished member. Of course, it all sounds an idiotic society, as no doubt it is, but we all enjoy being rude to each other and it helps on friendships a great deal.

I have told you all about it to add that Mother takes it all quite seriously and thinks it an odious institution and says I am quite rude enough already. So when I told her Judith and I had been persuading Anstey to join our Club, she was furious and said: "Oh, that Club is so silly, I do hate it so and wish you would drop it!" I assured her it was a most excellent institution.

One thing I like so about Lady Anne is that she enters into all Judith's jokes and encourages her to enjoy herself in her own way. No doubt youth does seem idiotic to age, but so long as youth is happy in a harmless way, what can it signify? It is extraordinary to me how impossible it seems for one age to understand another. The age at which people enjoy themselves is all spoiled by the way elders interfere

1 Mr. Anstey Guthrie, the author of *Vice Versa*.

Wilfrid Blunt
From a painting by Maloney, Newbuildings Collection

Emily at Crabbet, aged 18, joking with Blunt

Edwin Lutyens

Edwin Lutyens
1897

Emily, in 1898, soon after her marriage

with their pleasures. I enjoy being silly, and what does it
matter to anyone else whether I am or not?

Mrs. Grosvenor was particularly nice to me. I think she
has taken a fancy to me and I consequently like her very
much. She asked me whether I would go with her one
evening to the Earl's Court Exhibition. I said I should
enjoy it. When I came home and reported this to Mother, there
was a most comic scene. Mother said she would not hear of
my going; the Earl's Court Exhibition was a terribly
vulgar place; Mrs. Grosvenor might have all sorts of horrid
people; it would get talked about; I should get such a bad
reputation; no one would dance with me—which amused me.

Every day I live I think the world is a more extraordinary
place. I suppose half the world and more find their pleasure
in making others unhappy. I pine so for freedom sometimes
I hardly know what to do, and yet I am so infinitely better
off than most people. But it is strange that people do submit
to be tyrannized over without revolting.

Booton Rectory, June 2

And did you persuade Anstey? He can have no sense of
humour if he refused. The Club may not be suited for a
permanent institution, but be capital fun for a change.
Diversions grow stale unless they are varied.

Where does your Club meet? And have you refreshments?
or are you simply bound by the rules to be uncivil to one
another when any two members chance to come together?
In the latter case people not acquainted with the society must
be astonished at the freedom you take when they chance to
overhear your conversation with a confederate.

I delight to hear of your friendships, and think with you
that your season has been an unusual success.

44 Elm Park Gardens, June 3

It is a holiday and the boys are up from Eton. After they
arrived this morning, Mother took Vic out and left Neville
to me. Being very greedy we went off to Gunters and ate
strawberry ices and sponge cake. I felt this would excite
Mother's wrath and so we agreed to say we had been studying

Natural History. However, that excuse did not pass and I was obliged to confess. The answer was characteristic: "Oh, Emily, I wish you would not. There is nothing so unwholesome as ices and it is bad for Neville, he is sure to be ill. I wish you would take me to Gunters one day."—It was rather a nice conclusion.

44 Elm Park Gardens, June 5

I am afraid my chapter on the drama of life will not be very exciting today, and I wonder you can ever find it interesting.

I suppose the history of one individual is in reality as interesting as the history of the world would be, for it is the same thing on a small scale, only there are few people who care about it.

Con and I were agreeing last night that we felt in our own lives to have lived the life of every other person in the world, and to have had all their experiences, by which I mean that I have had so many different sensations and feelings about different things that when I hear of other people being in odd situations, I know exactly what their feelings must be. I often talk about being in love in a way which makes people think I must myself be in love at the present moment, but the fact is I have been in love so often, though I am not at present, that I know what people feel when in that situation. Con said when she was last at Hatfield someone began talking about a book which had lately come out and said the feelings of a murderer were so vividly described in it that the writer must be a fearful criminal himself. Lord Cranborne disagreed with this and said he knew perfectly the feelings of the very worst criminals because he had them himself. We were also saying how strangely blind people were. If others see through me as easily as I appear to see through them, it would be a poor look-out for me. Con and I agreed we were both made up of a mass of deceit, which was perfectly visible to anyone who looked. Happily, the world as a general rule is blind. What a lot of nonsense I am writing!

Yesterday, Lady Anne lunched here by herself and, as usual, told us many stories of Arabs and horses, to which

Mother listened with ill-suppressed yawns and movements of impatience, and interrupted whenever she could.

Lady Anne and Judith took me in their carriage to tea with Mrs. Leslie Stephen. Mrs. Stephen was a Mrs. Duckworth and she has a large family by both husbands, which is very puzzling. Her present husband is a most haggard, melancholy man, and a greater contrast to Sir James [1] can hardly be imagined. Mrs. Stephen is supposed to be beautiful, and is languid and sugary. Her daughter Stella is very like her, and someone described her as looking like a ruminating cow, which is rather a good description.

We found ourselves among friends, as Miss Stillman was there and Gerald Duckworth,[2] one of the sons, is a newly elected member of our Club. To prove how well qualified he was, he came up to me and said: "I hear you are frightfully rude," and after that, you may guess, there was no stiffness between us.

An old General Beadle came in while we were there, who was the funniest old man I have ever met. He was very stout and very deaf and never by any chance heard any remark that was made to him. He began by saying he liked young ladies to come up to him in a fighting attitude, upon which Judith and Miss Stillman drew themselves up and glowered at him, and the old gentleman immediately collapsed. He made a great many extraordinary remarks and ended by saying as we left, "I feel like a nymph." He was assured he did not look like one. What he meant, no one could make out.

I am almost afraid of taking up a subject now, because I am obliged to go into it so thoroughly. I wished to read Kinglake's *History of the Crimean War* and so asked Max Earle [3] to lend me his copy, as he possesses a military library. He wrote back to say Kinglake was in nine volumes and so detailed that I should never get through it. He therefore sent a short account by Sir E. Hamley, and if I liked, he had some letters from an uncle who had been all through the Crimea. I said I should be very interested to see them, and

[1] Sir James Stephen, the judge, was his brother.
[2] Founder of the publishing firm of Duckworth.
[3] My first cousin, youngest son of Mrs. C. W. Earle.

yesterday arrived two large books of letters, three volumes of Kinglake, one by Hamley, and also the account by Russell, the *Times* correspondent. So, you see, I am well supplied with works on the Crimea.

Booton Rectory, June 6

In a general way it may be said that all men are in each man. But I cannot go quite so far as Lord Cranborne, who however is notoriously a scrupulously upright person. I can understand the commission of most crimes, though some of them are no temptation to myself in my particular circumstances. But there are also some to which nothing in my own nature corresponds. I cannot conceive, for instance, that in any condition I could be brought to commit a murder. Suppose I could frame the intention, I think I should relent before I could complete the deed. This is not saying much for one's self. Jeremy Taylor in a prayer intended for general use makes the petitioner call himself the chief of sinners, and it has been objected that it is an exaggeration, because many men must know that they are not. I, on the contrary, believe that the best men would use the petition in good faith. We know more evil of ourselves than we know of anybody else or at least think ourselves more guilty than others when we take into account our opportunities for learning what is right, and doing what is right. The very candour with which some people have told me of their misdoings gives me a consciousness of their superiority, and has raised them in my estimation. I have felt little by the side of them.

44 Elm Park Gardens, June 7

When I left the Museum yesterday, I went to tea with the Parrys.[1] They were particularly nice to me and asked me to go with Dolly to some private theatricals in a little theatre at the top of the Albert Hall. As it was to go alone with Dolly I felt that Mother would not like me to go, but promised to telegraph when I got home. By some lucky chance Mother allowed me and I had a very amusing evening. The

[1] Sir Hubert Parry, the composer, whose daughter Dolly was a great friend of mine.

theatre was quite small, but very full of people, who were the
most extraordinary types. It was an opera in two acts written
by a young lady by the name of Sopwith, who took the chief
part. She has three sisters, one of whom acted and the other
two formed the orchestra. From the sounds which came from
the piano, you would have thought they were sitting on it.
The music was a sort of mixture of all the popular arias. The
acting was very comic. One young man who was very
sentimental slapped himself so often in his efforts to find
his heart that he must have been quite sore by the end of
the performance. The audience were all friends and very
enthusiastic, and they sang and encored. There was a good
deal of skirt dancing, all very funny, very bad. I really like
Dolly Parry and she has been so very nice to me whenever I
have met her lately.

When I got home I found Mother had not realized I was
going alone with Dolly, but happily she was not vexed.

Dolly is a year younger than I am and says she acts as
chaperone to all her friends, and next year she is going to
take a young lady abroad. It is a new idea to become a lady
companion at seventeen. I think I shall take to it.

44 *Elm Park Gardens, June* 15

Yesterday I had a telegram from Betty, telling me to join
them at dinner at Mr. Cole's and to go to a play afterwards.
Mr. Cole is one of Gerald's oldest friends, who worships
Gerald. I went off to dinner, quite in the dark as to what I
was going to see. Mr. Cole was suffering from gout, which
prevented his going to the play, and I had been sent for in his
place. The play we went to see was Ibsen's *Doll's House,*
acted in Italian by a new actress, Eleanor Duse, about whom
everyone is talking very much. It seems an odd combination
acted in Italian, but it was intensely interesting. Of course,
I don't know a word of the language, which I think probably
made it seem less absurd, as Ibsen's language is the most
ridiculous part of his plays. It also, I think, made the acting
seem more natural, and Italian, like French, is a language
which lends itself to gesticulation. A most interesting thing,
though, was this actress, who really is a genius. She quite

refuses to paint or get herself up in any way, and she seems entirely wrapped up in the character she is acting. When she first comes on the stage, you don't think her pretty or graceful or striking, but after a little you cannot take your eyes from her face and she seems to grow quite beautiful and very fascinating, and her acting is marvellous, so quiet and dignified and so natural, and her power of expression is marvellous. Never for one moment do you feel she is acting a part, but only that she is the character she portrays, and she is carried away herself as much as you are. She seemed to hate appearing before the curtain, and there was a very funny scene after the last act when the curtain went up and she was nowhere to be found. The hero was rushing about the stage in search of her, tearing his hair. When she did appear, it was only for a second and she looked very cross.

Another comic but annoying thing was that the prompter spoke so loud he almost drowned the voices of the actors.

In spite of not understanding the language, I never for one moment felt bored.

44 Elm Park Gardens, June 22

The Garden Party yesterday at Holland House was very nice. The house and gardens are too lovely. Betty and I wandered into the different rooms and sat and read your letter, which was a delightful way of enjoying a garden party. We spent the rest of the time eating nectarines and strawberries. Mr. Phil Burne-Jones was with us and told Betty to sit down, when he would bring her what she wanted. Betty exclaimed, "No, certainly not, I want to come to the table and help myself." After two nectarines and a large plateful of strawberries and cream, she said to Mr. Phil, "Do you now understand why I prefer to help myself?"

Olive Schreiner has been lunching here, and she stayed such an eternal time that I shall be obliged to cut short my letter. I have tried my best to like her, but hopelessly failed. She speaks with a strong Cape accent which perhaps makes her seem rather vulgar, but I think she is decidedly common. Then she has very wild views about everything and only loves freedom and a desert and hates all conventionality. I thought she was very tiresome. Perhaps I shall come round, but at present the less I see of her the better I shall be pleased.

We moved to the new house, The Danes, near Hertford, at the end of June. I write on June 27th, still from Elm Park Gardens:

The house is turned topsy-turvy, and we run great dangers of breaking our necks every time we move, as every room and passage is blocked up with books and packages. The first step towards packing always seems to be dragging everything into the middle of the room and making as much dust and muddle as possible. The carpets are being taken up today, and we are choked by dust and half-deafened by the noise of everything going up and downstairs. Needless to tell you, I am in a vile temper and can hardly bring myself to be civil to a soul. I alternately cry and storm, which is not much help to other people who are, I expect, feeling the same as I am. But I grow more selfish every day and give no thought to anyone's feelings but my own. If I am happy it irritates me to see other people depressed, and when I am low myself I can only sit and think over my woes. I hate myself for it, but I do not change. It will be a relief to get to the country and be settled once more. The nuisance and discomfort of moving is enough to keep one fixed in one house for a lifetime.

I went to a ball last night at Lady Battersea's [1] with Lady Lathom. It is such a lovely house and so perfect for a ball that merely to be there was a pleasure. I did dance a good bit besides, and enjoyed myself thoroughly. It was one of the nicest balls I have been to, as there was plenty of room for dancing and a nice lot of rooms for sitting out, and all beautiful. The band was up in a gallery out of the way and there were very short pauses between the dances, which I thought was nice, as the tiresome part of a ball, to my mind, is talking to your partner when the dance is over, unless it is someone very nice, which does not happen often.

I saw a good many French people last night whom I used to see in Paris, so that it seemed like old times. They none

---

[1] Cyril Flower had been created Lord Battersea.

of them recognized me, but I suppose I have changed a good deal since those days. Margot was there in great form, but I thought she looked very ill.

I suppose Betty has told you about *Dodo*.[1] She was very angry with the description of Margot, which she said gave all her bad points and none of her good ones.

I am really longing to get to the country now, as I mean to do such a lot. I feel that I have spent the last month or two in London in such a frivolous way that it is quite disgraceful, but I will start to work earnestly in the country. I mean to become as great a botanist as I know how. I have got a large commonplace book which looks like some enormous ledger and I want to fill this with drawings and notes of my lessons.

His Rev was recovering from a sharp attack of influenza and his letters for the moment are brief. In reply to my mention of *Dodo* he writes:

"Want of time is not among my wants at present. I am not allowed to get up till evening, and I have only to receive a few reports from outside, and give directions when necessary. The hindrance to writing is that I have to lie flat on my back, and hold my paper as I will my hands get weary. I finished a few minutes since a not long but I believe dreary letter to Betty, and my arms feel much as if I had done a day's work in the hay-field. They ought to be ashamed of themselves. I am ashamed for them. Imagine what a recreation it would have been to me to read *Dodo* in this vacant period. How invigorated I should have felt at every mortal stab delivered to Margot by her too lenient biographer. I speak according to what I know to be the secret view of many who hold a different language. In reality I should not like to be the person to inflict this sort of wanton pain on a woman of fashion whose foibles do not concern the public. I would not earn money or procure readers for my trumpery book by such cruel methods. And if I were the son of the Archbishop of Canterbury I hope I should consider that my

[1] A recent novel by E. F. Benson, son of the Archbishop of Canterbury, which was a skit upon Margot Tennant.

genealogy, in my father's lifetime, ought to keep me from proceedings in contradiction to the spirit of his office and teaching. Indifferent as I might be to disgracing myself, I would not recklessly discredit him. This is my sober view of the business when I reflect on it seriously, which is not my constant mood."

44 Elm Park Gardens, July 3

Con came in on Friday evening very happy because she had made some money by selling worthless old jewellery. She took her things to a pawnbroker and asked what he would give her for them. He asked in return what she would take. She nearly said £2, but happily thought better of it and said nothing. After a long examination he said, "Will you take £9 for them?" She could hardly control her joy and walked out of the shop feeling rich for life. When Con told me her good fortune, I promptly scratched up some old bits of jewellery and am going to take them to the shop this afternoon and see what I can get. I will tell you the result tomorrow.

How horrified poor Mother would be at these transactions. Con immediately spent some of her money in buying a revolving bookcase for Mother, which is a thing she has long coveted.

I always feel intensely proud of myself if I manage to get anything cheaper than Con. The other day at a sale she bought a parasol for 3/6d. It was very pretty, but made of cotton. I went the next day to the same place and bought a blue silk parasol for 2/11d. The cheapness of some things you can pick up in London is perfectly marvellous.

Booton Rectory, July 4

Monday's post brought *Dodo* and I read it before going to bed. The author's knowledge of human nature is only skin-deep, and almost as limited in extent as in depth. There is some cleverness in the book, but to my thinking it is of a low order, and of a kind so little desirable that the writer would be a more respectable person without it.

I enjoy Con's dealings with the pawnbroker. They are more thrilling by far than *Dodo*. He seems to have been a reputable man, and being so he has probably paid her nearly half the value of her jewellery. I am impatient for the history of your negotiations. I fear this time you will not fare as well as Con. These by-incidents give a relish and a charm to life. We should most of us have a dreary time of it if we did nothing without the direct sanction of constituted authorities. In acting for ourselves we do them a service by relieving them of responsibilities.

44 Elm Park Gardens, July 4

No letter from you this morning, which I hope means pleasure and not business. Perhaps *Dodo* has arrived and you are engrossed in it and the charms of the book prevent your thinking of anything else. Betty and I are both indulging wickedly in novels. She is reading *Nicholas Nickleby* and can think of nothing else, and I am reading what a shopman called the other day when I asked for the book, Victor Hugo's *Miserables*, pronounced in English. I neglect all my duties and spend most of my day in bed pretending I need a rest, but in reality that I may read my book.

When I am reading a novel I enjoy it so much that I wonder why I am not always reading novels, but having finished my book I never think of reading another until the fit seizes me again, which is lucky or I should never do anything.

Betty and I felt proud of ourselves last night because we beat our record for lateness at the ball and stayed until 3 o'clock. I enjoyed myself very much. The room was lovely, the floor perfect and the band played good tunes. Partners I consider a secondary consideration. Con said she hated balls, not because she knew no one but because those she knew never danced with her. I don't mind that. I am introduced to a new set of partners every ball I go to, who hardly ever recognize me at the next ball or ask me to dance again, but this does not offend me. I feel extremely pleased and flattered when a partner does ask me to dance a second time, but I look upon the rest as necessary appendages to the dance and it does not matter to me whether it is one or the other, as I care for none of them. If I cared very much for any one, it would be a different thing. But as it is, I enjoy myself and think of nothing else.

Margot was very much to the fore last night and she looked almost prettier than I had ever seen her, and danced beautifully. She came up to Betty and said she had been dining at the Staels' [Russian Ambassador] to meet the Prince and Princess of Wales, and the Prince had come up to her and said, "How do you do, Miss Dodo?" He is the only man who would have had bad taste enough to do such a thing. Margot said, "If young Benson did but know the harm he had done me with that book—not that I mind what he says about my character, but I am so sick of hearing it, it is so stupid and so vulgar." Whatever Margot's faults may be, I think Mr. Benson deserves a good kicking.

My transactions yesterday with the pawnbroker were not very successful. I felt very shy when I entered the shop and there was an old man who eyed me up and down and then said, "Were you here last week?" I said, "No," and foolishly added, "It was my sister." "Your sister, was it?" he said. He then examined my things, which Con thought might have fetched £4. After some while he said, "I will give you a sovereign for them." I felt terribly crushed, but took the sovereign, feeling I was being horribly cheated. I shall leave these things for Con to do. I cannot look poor and interesting and knowing, as Con says she does.

Chapter Eleven

The Danes, July 6

I am in such a state of happiness I hardly know what to do with myself. Now I am in the country I wonder I could ever have endured London. The weather is divine, hot, with a delicious breeze. The country looking lovely beyond description and the house and village and everything seems even more perfect than I expected it to be.

We are already deep in village gossip, which seems all mad. Mother told me as a great bit of news yesterday when I arrived that the clergyman had been up to tell her that the charwoman we are employing, who is a delightful woman, has a very bad character in the village and has children without fathers. Mother added, "Mind you don't repeat this," as if I should be spreading abroad a matter of such intense interest. I remarked this, and Mother said, "Well, I don't want you to be gossiping with the servants, as Paisy used to do."

All the rooms here are perfection, but mine is the most perfect of all. It has three large windows and is beautifully light. I have a lovely view and can see the sunset. I have a nursery paper which the rest of the family think hideous and I like, plenty of cupboards and shelves, a kitchen table and kitchen chair, which is ideal. Altogether, I feel in the lap of luxury. We all mean to get up very early and go to a Service there is every morning at 8, and go to bed about 10. I feel young again already and equal to running, jumping and all sorts of things.

I was given a reception last night like a Royal guest or a "boy," as Con says. Mother kept apologizing for the untidiness, the best china was had out, dinner ordered specially for me, and everyone's room rifled to furnish mine.

Mother is spoiling me very much but is otherwise in an aggravating mood, that is, disagreeing with everything proposed. The servants are radiant. Mother persists in thinking them miserable.

The house is enormous compared to London. Mother will call it tiny.

These things all add to the comedy, and I try not to mind.

Characteristically, the boys' rooms have been furnished far more expensively than all of ours put together.

The Danes, Hertford, July 8

We heard yesterday that Mrs. Lambert, widow of the old family lawyer, was dead. She always told Father she was going to leave him something in her Will and we have always had expectations from her, so Mother tried in vain to look sad on hearing of her death. We treated her extremely badly, as we never went near her unless we wanted a present of some sort. Last time Father was in England he paid her several visits to tell her I was coming out, and a lovely jewel was the result of these visits. When I went to thank her, she talked of Father and said, "You know, he came to see me and it seemed as if he could not tear himself away." We are now wondering in what way we have been remembered. She always promised some hideous bits of tapestry which were to go to Knebworth, and promised Mother her rings. How awful it seems to be talking like this, and how dreadful it would be to have a fortune and know that all your friends and relations were counting on having it after your death!

A letter from Gerald Balfour at this time reported that the man to whom Father had confided large sums of money for investment had completely failed and that Mother would, therefore, be much poorer than she had anticipated—that her income in fact would now probably only amount to £1,900 a year, to include the money given by the Estate for the boys' schooling. I write to his Rev:

"I do not understand why we are not rich upon it, but apparently we are not. We have a comfortable home, clothes

and food, and what more do we want? Thank goodness we
have left London, so there will be fewer expenses."

On July 14th I return again to the family fortunes and say:

"Con and I are finding so much amusement out of the
smash that it is quite dreadful considering how miserable
poor Mother is. We have been laughing this morning until
we nearly died. The last idea, which is intensely comic, is
that Mother should take rooms at Hampton Court. Con is
to go into flats which are provided for poor spinsters of the
gentry class. I am to become a Maid-of-Honour! (Can't you
see me at Court ceremonies attending on some wretched
princess?) Vic will probably be provided with some magnificent house in town, and Neville will go and study art and
starve in a garret in Paris."

Booton Rectory, July 14

People judge incomes according to their own mode of
living. Those who are accustomed to thousands a year
think hundreds poverty. In my way of estimating I agree
with you that there will be enough for the degree of comfort
which I call luxury. Buy nothing but what is essential to
happiness and each of you will always have money in your
pocket. I rather hope Neville's Eton education will not be
cut short. Besides the particular advantages it offers, his
removal to another school would seem to him a descent, and
there is a risk that he would lose heart and work to little
purpose. You say rightly that it is a gain to have got out of
London before Read's final collapse was known. At The
Danes there is no need for outward change, and you will go
on as you have begun. And you escape the calls of kind friends
who come to condole with you in your misfortunes, and see
how you look under them. They put a sting into troubles
that would otherwise be unfelt. Abuse is a boon compared
to Mrs. Grundy's pity.

The Danes, July 17

We keep on making different plans for living now. Yesterday we thought of letting The Danes for three months during
the summer and taking a gipsy cart in which we would go
round the country. Mother will tell fortunes, Con will play

a hurdy-gurdy for me to dance to, Vic will take photographs which Neville will colour. I think it is a splendid idea.

I had a long talk last night with Neville about Eton. He says it is a sink of iniquity and there are hardly thirty boys in the school who are not utter brutes. It is evidently a great trial to him, as it must be to every right-minded boy, and as he gets up in the school and, above all, if he succeeds in games, which he is likely to do, the trial will increase, as it will draw on him the notice of the other boys. I am sure he has not the smallest temptation to go wrong himself, for he says he utterly loathes and despises it all, but what tries him is that it is impossible to escape from it. It goes on in school, in chapel, at games, everywhere, and even in his own room he cannot be by himself. He says it is a tremendous thing having Vic there, because he has worked his way out of it all and is no longer tormented. Neville says his object at Eton is to be hated, that all the boys that are worth anything are hated. He says that for this reason he hates Eton and would be glad to leave. He said, "Bullying is nothing compared to it; that is only bodily pain, this is mental torture."

The Danes, July 20

To show you how little we are likely to economize, Mother is now longing for a change, and says it will do her all the good in the world, and she wishes to go with Vic to Guernsey in September. No doubt the expense of the journey would not be so great, but to think of it just when we are all wishing to save in every possible way seems ridiculous.

In discussing various plans last night, Mother said, "I am afraid when the boys grow older we shall find it very difficult having women servants in the house." I replied that if there were men-servants, Mother would be getting alarmed about us, so I could see no hope for her. She owned this was the case, but it really is too comic.

Talking of the possibility of a tutor for the boys, she said to Con, "I am afraid we shall find it very awkward, especially with Emmie." Con is past being suspect. I wonder if Mother really thinks her children quite as corrupt as she seems to do?

Booton Rectory, July 21

The fear of men servants, maid servants and tutors—all for the same reason—is an extravagance hardly to be paralleled out of stage farces. I cannot comprehend the state of mind which can entertain such notions, and still less understand how anyone having the opinion should calmly avow it. It is in effect to say, "This is what I expect of you," which goes a long way towards saying that it will be nothing so very outrageous if it happens.

The Danes, July 22

Yesterday Mother said to Con: "Shall I ask Lady Ampthill to tell the Queen about our affairs?" Then, turning to me, "Are you sure you would not be a Maid-of-Honour?" I replied that nothing would induce me, but when Mother said, "It is the only work you are capable of doing, and I am sure you are just the type," I could only return this insult by telling Mother I had been considered like her. I never felt so offended in my life. I must indeed have fallen low to be considered just the type to keep company with the Royal Family. Besides, as I told Mother, I had lately become a Republican and might feel it my duty to blow up the Queen if I got the chance.[1]

A messenger on horseback arrived this morning at 8 o'clock from Hatfield, asking us all to go there next Saturday to Monday. We none of us want to go, but feel we must.

The Danes, August 1

I must tell you about the Hatfield time, which seems already like a nightmare. We drove over from here in our wagonette, and a very funny sight we were, laden with boxes and hat boxes tied up with white tape by Con. No wonder everyone who passed us smiled. We feel sure the coachman was looking forward to driving up to Hatfield in grand style, but Mother was so ashamed of him that she

[1] Needless to say this does not represent my present sentiments. In fact, it did not represent my sentiments then, since I was always an ardent Royalist and I fear that I expressed myself so merely in order to annoy my Mother.

cruelly got out and walked up to the house and told him to be sure and go to the servants' door, and all the way along such cruel remarks were made about his horse and vehicle.

The party at Hatfield consisted of the Chamberlains,[1] Mr., Mrs. and Miss Master, Lord and Lady Granby, Mr. and Mrs. Akers-Douglas, Mrs. Austin Lee,[2] George Talbot, Sir Philip Curry, and others. Mrs. Akers-Douglas was kind and shy and knew no one, and Mrs. Lee was also shy.

The first night at dinner I sat next Mr. Neville Chamberlain, who talked botany with me. He is not a botanist, but very fond of flowers and knows a lot about orchids, and he told me some very interesting things about the way they were fertilized. In the evening there was music. Con played and Lord Salisbury sat listening intently, his head wagging from side to side. Mrs. Lee then sang, and when she had done, Lady Salisbury made the most delightful and visible signs to Lord Salisbury, to induce him to ask Mrs. Lee to sing again, but he only smiled. Once he walked towards her, but only picked up Con's pocket handkerchief and returned to his seat. I got into that horrible position of trying to listen to two conversations and joining in neither.

To feel that visit is over gives me a feeling of such happiness that I can hardly contain myself. We nearly stood up in the fly and cheered all the way home.

> *Booton Rectory, August 2*

Your letter is immensely enjoyable, only there is not enough of your talkings and doings at Hatfield. I suspect you drew a good card in Neville Chamberlain. You should have pushed matters to a point which would have led him to invite you to go and see his—that is his father's—orchid houses and get a finishing lesson from examples in orchid botany. This on your part was an omission.

> *The Danes, August 4*

The boys arrived yesterday in radiant spirits. They have both taken good places, Vic second class and Neville first class,

---

[1] Neville Chamberlain and his wife.
[2] The widow of Austin Lee, who had been my father's secretary in Paris.

so Mother is immensely pleased and proud of them. Neville's pride in his hat band and flannel jacket, which are the objects he has gained, is immense. He almost chokes with pride and pleasure. Poor Vic feels rather sad not having done as well, but he is very good. It is harder to be outdone by a younger brother than anything, and Neville is much better at games.

It was most characteristic last night. Mother asked us at dinner, "Would you like breakfast at 8.30 or a quarter to nine?" We every one of us said, "8.30." "Then," said Mother, "as I know you will none of you ever be down, I will have it at a quarter to nine."

She was very anxious to read aloud to the boys in the evening the *Life of Darwin*, but happily they struck at that.

The Danes, August 5

There was a comic scene last night. Mother was anxious for a game of whist and told the boys to come and play. Neville was enveloped in *The Times* and both the boys were most reluctant to play. It seems such a very comic thing when the parent has to force the child to play games. I should have thought Mother would have been so glad to let them amuse themselves.

Yesterday they were perfectly happy playing about all day, but Mother insisted that they must be dull and kept suggesting amusements for them. The boys asked me to read to them before lunch, and Mother inquired afterwards what we had read. I said the *Indian Mutiny*, which both the boys had asked for, and Mother said she was sure her *Life of Darwin* would have amused them more.

Chapter Twelve

I NOW come to what was to prove a very important turning-point in my life. Up to the time of my Father's death I had been a rather solitary girl, having no friends of my own age, his Rev my sole confidant and friend. My father's death naturally made a great change in the life of the whole family. My mother was deeply unhappy, not only because my father was dead but because with his death her whole social position had changed. I was young, unsympathetic, longing for the natural amusements and gaieties of life, and yet my religious faith was strong enough to give some seriousness and solemnity to life. With my mother's departure to the Cape I had experienced a new sense of freedom, and begun, as it were, to spread my wings. During 1893 I began to make friends with young people of my own age and enjoyed a certain amount of frivolity. I became very much attached to Judith Blunt, and unfortunately that attachment was extended to her father. Because of my friendship with his Rev I felt much less shy with older men than with young ones. No doubt my rather flirtatious and chaffing manner encouraged Blunt to believe that I felt more friendly towards him than was actually the case at first. But he understood my feelings for him long before I understood them myself. He drew me out, flattered me, encouraged me in playful chaff, leading me on until I unconsciously found myself deeply in love with him. I was shocked and horrified when I discovered that his intentions were strictly dishonourable, and yet it took me three years before I was able to break the spell he put on me.

In this dilemma his Rev was my sole confidant, and although he fully realized my danger and my weakness, his love and tenderness and understanding, and also his patience, were unfailing and saved me from what might have been disaster. The situation was complicated by two factors: one, that I could not confide in my mother, who would most certainly have put all the blame on me; the second, that my growing friendship with Judith kept me constantly in the same orbit as her father.

At this time Blunt was aged fifty-three and was still a strikingly handsome man. When he put on an Arab cloak and headdress—in themselves very picturesque—he looked like some splendid chieftain, and romantic enough to capture any woman's heart. He had dark eyes, with which he seemed able to speak his thoughts. But perhaps it is his hands that I remember best, as they were very beautiful. Judith also has long, beautiful, sensitive hands, inherited from her father.

After a visit to Booton I went with Con to stay with the Blunts at Crabbet, and I write from there on August 22nd:

Crabbet Park, August 22

On arriving at Three Bridges we found the Blunts' carriages and were told that they themselves were coming by the next train. They arrived five minutes after we did. Con and Lady Anne drove up in the brougham, Judith in her cart, and Mr. Blunt drove me in his carriage. He seemed very pleased to see me. Judith is in every way more fascinating than ever. After tea I had a talk with her sitting in the garden and I felt to love her more than ever.

Our evening was characteristic, i.e. Lady Anne fell asleep on a sofa; Con read a newspaper, I suppose to get hints for her style; Mr. Blunt talked to me, though he was also half asleep. I feel that I shall enjoy my visit here; I love Judith more, and I feel much more at my ease with Blunt. It is nice to be where I am spoiled. Mother gave Con many injunctions about my behaviour here!

Booton Rectory, August 23

I was impatient for your letter and its contents are everything I could wish. You and Judith have made a good beginning, and each day will be an improvement on its predecessor. You have got thoroughly knit together, and there is nothing to limit your confidence and love. Therefore improve the time to the uttermost.

I smile at the injunctions to Con to regulate your behaviour. Happily the need is nothing since the effect will be nothing either.

Crabbet Park, August 23

Yesterday morning as I was going upstairs I met Mr. Blunt. He never comes to breakfast, as he gets up at 6 o'clock and has his breakfast then. He told me when I had finished my letters to come to his library and he would take me for a walk, which he accordingly did. He took me through the park to a wood which was very pretty and we sat down on a bank. He then began asking me about my novel [Judith and I were writing a novel]—what the characters were, and what the plot. I told him I had as yet no plot, and that he was to be the villain. He asked if I came into it and whether I married. I said I had not yet decided that. He then took my hand and said, "Won't you let the villain love you, the villain does love you and will you love the villain?" I told him I would see as the plot worked out. We talked on in this way, he holding my hand and kissing it, and telling me he loved me, and thought of me always, and hoped I loved him. Then he said, "Tell me about yourself, do you care for anyone?" "Lots of people," I answered. "No, but anyone in particular?" I told him "No," and he said, "Then don't." After some time I said I thought it was time to continue our walk, which we did for some way. Finally we came to a bench by a pond in the wood and there we sat down again. He at once took my hand and kissed it and stroked it, said he adored me, which I told him I was very glad of, as one did not get adored every day. He said he had loved me for two years. "What a long time!" I remarked. "Yes, isn't it?" he said. He then asked me if I had no name but Emily, as he wished to write a sonnet to me and my name was just two letters too short. He became more and more demonstrative, and then said to me, "Are you angry with me for loving you?" I told him that I was not in the least angry with him, and should not be unless he did something to make me angry. After a time I suggested moving and he said I should go if I liked. I feel more glad than ever for our talks about this subject, because but for them I should have felt shy and miserable, and knowing most people would put a bad interpretation on it, I should have felt it must be wrong. But having talked with you I was happy. I am happy to be loved by him, until I find he means something else.

Con had received injunctions from Mother that I was not to go anywhere alone with him, but it was an absurd thing to say, for how could Con prevent it?

We were back very late for our ride, which was arranged for 12 o'clock, and Con says Lady Anne was rather vexed. We had a most delightful ride. My horse went perfectly, the woods were lovely, and I enjoyed myself very much. Mr. Blunt has written an historical play in three acts which we are going to perform. There are at least ten characters, not to speak of hosts of Arabs, and there are five actors, and two people for audience. Mother would not come here because she said it was silly, but silly though it may be, we are all very happy over it. Judith is dearer than ever and I am immensely happy in the feeling that I am being loved.

Crabbet Park, August 24

Yesterday morning we had another delightful ride. The rest of the day was spent in preparing the play, which we acted in the evening. It was no doubt an absurd performance, but we enjoyed it very much. When you are with friends and happy everything you do is a pleasure. Mr. Blunt has given Con and me the most lovely stuffs for dresses which he brought from Constantinople and some Arabian stuffs also. They are very beautiful. He tried to arrange a walk with me yesterday but without success, until the evening, when he asked me to come for a row on the pond, which I did. He rowed me about for some time, and then we got off on a small island and sat down on a bench hidden amongst trees. There was a repetition of the day before, only he was yet more affectionate, until I insisted on going. I had a talk over it with Con last night and she said to me, which I feel to be true, that though there may be no harm in our present

intimacy, yet it is at a stage to lead to anything further, and
that for his good and mine I should make him understand
that our intimacy is to be one of friendship and that it is
foolish for him to spend his time only showing me his love,
but that being established we should get to something
further. That I quite agree to and if I get the chance today
I will tell him so. It is not good for him or me to go on
simply as we are doing now.

Booton Rectory, August 24

The word love being used in such opposite senses it is
sometimes difficult to say what the inner meaning of the
speaker may be. The same words may serve for the divinest
thoughts or the basest. I begin to be a little suspicious, but
if the bad were the true interpretation the enormity would be
so great that I can hardly bring myself even to speak of
suspicion.

Your letter is a delicious specimen of the minute truthfulness with which you spread out your entire life for my
inspection. I am accustomed to it, but delight none the less
in each fresh instance of your habit.

Crabbet Park, August 25

I am very happy here, and the time passes only too quickly.
Mother was anxious we should leave tomorrow, but they
are so pressing that we should stay till Monday, and I am so
longing to stay as long as I possibly can, that we shall stay.
I have had no more real talks with Judith, but we have been
very happy together. Yesterday morning she was carried off
by Lady Anne to study Arabic, and I did not see her again
till lunch time. After lunch Mr. Blunt proposed that we
should all go for a botanizing expedition in the forest, so we
started after about an hour's preparation of rugs and cushions.
Lady Anne rode, Judith drove Con in her cart, and Mr. Blunt
drove me in a Norwegian carriole, which is a carriage without
springs. We had a delightful afternoon. The forest is
enchantingly lovely and there is not a sign of human habita-
tion for miles. We got out by the side of a little stream and
walked along picking flowers. I got several new ones. I knew

that Blunt was anxious all the time to get away, and finally he said it was time to turn round, and that Lady Anne had better ride on and we would follow. This she tactfully did, and we then crossed the stream and wandered through the wood to the top of a little hill. Here we sat down and began talking. He said I had got a frown which was exactly like the pictures of Blake (the Admiral, not the poet), which was complimentary! He then grew affectionate, and I was much too shy to say what I wanted properly, so only told him not to be silly, but to talk sensibly to me. He replied, "I told you, you were like Blake." Soon after we wandered back to the others. The forest was delicious and I got all sorts of flowers and moss and ferns which I had never seen before. When we were all assembled we got into our carriages once more and drove to another part of the forest where lilies of the valley grow. Mr. Blunt and I got ahead of the others, but were followed by Lady Anne. We got down again to walk to the place where the lilies grow, and Lady Anne was coming with us, but he told her to remain and look after the horse. There is a little enclosure where the lilies grow, and they must be lovely in the spring time. While we were looking at them, Blunt took hold of my hand and said, "Have you no sentiment, Emily?" I told him I kept my sentiment in my heart instead of on my tongue, and that it was far more lasting sentiment then. On our way home he talked to me of his poetry.

In the evening Judith asked me to dance, which I did. Everyone praised me very much, and Mr. Blunt said, "To have seen that for five minutes is worth six weeks of Paradise"—but I think he was only joking.

Crabbet Park, August 26

Yesterday Judith practised my dances in the hall and we had great fun, and then went out driving together, as Lady Anne was in London and Mr. Blunt occupied with a man who had come to buy some horses. The afternoon we also spent together sitting in the garden and had a good talk over various subjects. I saw Mr. Blunt wanted me to go with him, but as he never asked me outright to do anything I could not. When I came down to dinner before the others were down and he was sitting in the drawing-room alone, he said to me, "Well, my child, how are you? I have not seen you all day. You would not come out with me this afternoon and there was a lot I wished to read to you." I then arranged to go out with him this morning at 10 o'clock, and he said he would sit in the garden and read to me. I told him I liked being read to, and I liked going with him when he reads and talks sensibly to me.

Crabbet Park, August 27

I told you yesterday that I had not seen Blunt alone at all until I came down before dinner, when he was in the drawing-room. He asked me why I had not seen him all day, as he wished to have read to me. He then said, "I should like to give you one kiss before the others come in." He then gave me a very hot embrace and said to me, "Emily, might I come and see you in your room?" I replied indignantly, "Certainly not!" and pushed him away. He sat down and said no more. His remark could only have one meaning, I am afraid. My feelings now are these. I know that he found me fascinating, and when he was alone with me, being, as he is, a man who never has put the smallest restraint on his feelings, he showed them to me in the way I have told you. As I allowed him to do it all, he most naturally took it as an encouragement and put no restraint on himself. So in a way I feel that I showed myself to him in a false light and to a certain degree my behaviour is an excuse for his. I ought to have shown him clearly much sooner exactly what my feelings were. This I determined to do yesterday morning when I went out with him. He took me to a bench in the garden and we sat down. He began trying to kiss me as usual. I pushed him away and, when he asked the reason, said I was cross with him. "Why?" he asked. "You promised not to be cross." I replied that he had said something which had made me very angry, and that if he did not know what, I could not explain. I was very silly not to have explained further, but felt as if I could not. For a long time then he read to me some of his poems, and held my hand, and I felt that was so delightful if only he could be content to care for me in a right way. When we had done reading we talked of various things, and I told him my views of friendship, and that I loved him as a friend and in no other way. We talked like this for a long time, and before we got up to go I let him kiss me once, which was foolish. When I am with him I never feel able to say what I want. Afterwards I realized that I ought to have put it far more clearly and am determined to seek another opportunity of doing so. I went down to dinner early and found him again alone. As usual he wished to kiss me, but I refused and then said to him, "You said last night something which offended me very much. You told me that you loved me; I thought that meant that I could trust you, but from what you have said I feel now that I cannot, and so I do not wish you to kiss me any more." He pretended not to know what I meant, but I saw that he did. At that point we were interrupted. Yesterday, Sunday, he told me before lunch that he had finished the poem he had been writing to me. I asked him to read it to me, and he said he would at 3 o'clock. So at 3 I went to his room and we went for a walk together. On the way he asked me my age, and when I said eighteen he expressed his surprise that I was still so young, quite a child. He took me the walk we had been the first day and we sat down on the same bench. Then he read me the poem, taking my hand and saying, "Now, don't make yourself stiff, you foolish thing." When he next tried to kiss me I said to him, though in a silly, shy, fumbling way, something like this: "I have been brought up differently from most girls, in a much freer way, and I have let you do things to me which other girls might not have allowed, or if they had you would have misunderstood them, and you have probably misunderstood me, but I want you to understand that I care for you only as my friend, and I ask you as a favour to me not to kiss me. Do you understand?" "I understand," he said, "that you are only eighteen." He went on to say he had no intention of kissing me and would not do such a thing for the world, but it was said in a tone which was meant to pique me. I replied, however, "That is all right, then." We sat on there for some time. He read me some more

of his own poems and we talked about Father and his
intimacy with him. Then I said to him, "I want you to write
to me as you said you would, but as Mother will expect to
see my letters, you must write nothing I cannot show her."
"Well," he replied, "let me know if ever you go from home
and I will write to you, and you can write anything to me,
because I don't have my letters overlooked." I answered
that I had nothing to write to him which might not be seen,
and he could have nothing to say to me. "I might want to
say that I loved you very much and was very miserable
without you." I let him hold my hand. You see I tell you all
I did, although you may blame me for it, but I want you to
know. He looked at the rings I had on, and then said he had
a ring he would like to give me and if I came down a little
before dinner-time he would give it to me. Judith and I had
agreed to dress up in the costumes we wore for the play,
that is in Arab dress, and I came down dressed like an
Egyptian woman. He was in a lovely Arab dress also. He
said to me, "I love you in that dress, Emily. I will call you
my Mahomedan wife. I don't see why I should not marry
you. Here is the little ring I promised you. I will marry you
with it." Then putting it on my finger he said, "With this
ring I thee wed, with my body I thee worship." This was
all said half-playfully, but I answered that I wanted to be his
friend and nothing else. It was a lovely little ring with many
coloured stones, though he said it was only a trumpery thing
he had bought to give Judith on her birthday. I said I would
wear it and say he gave it to me. "Yes," he said, "I want
you to wear it, and you can say it was part of the play." I
went upstairs after that for Judith to arrange my dress. I
have not seen him alone since. . . .

This morning he came to the station, where he said goodbye to me and asked me to write, and promised he would
write and tell me about his visits to Scotland.

Now that I have come away I can look over the whole time
calmly and arrange my thoughts. Perhaps I ought to have
broken off my intimacy with him altogether, but I could not,
and for two reasons. First I am really fond of him. Perhaps
I ought not to be, but I cannot help it, I am. It is quite

unnecessary to tell you that I am not in the very smallest degree tempted towards anything wrong, but I am very fond of him and it is a great pleasure to me to be with him. My second reason for wishing to keep up my intimacy with him is this. If he has a real genuine affection for me, all else apart, which I cannot help thinking he has, it is possible that our intercourse may become not only a pleasure but a good to him. I think I have shown him clearly what my feelings for him are, and I shall try and impress it on him in every way that I can. There is this excuse to be made for him, that if anyone else had behaved to him as I have done it would have seemed direct encouragement, and how was he to know that I was different from the rest? Anyhow he can do no harm to me and I might be able to turn his love into the right channels. No doubt I have done many foolish things, but they are done and now the time is over, and when next we meet, I shall be able to tell him what I feel. Sometimes he talks to me in a half-friendly, half-fatherly way which is delightful. I have told you all this at great length because I wished you to know everything. Con said that supposing he got angry with me he might let out all that had passed between us, but I think that is unlikely for all reasons, and after all there is nothing I might mind his telling.

I finished this up last night after I got home.

The Danes, August 30

When I said goodbye to Blunt at the station he said, "I shall expect to hear from you whether you get home all right," so yesterday I wrote to him. In my letter I said, "You do not like the word friend because you think it is cold and means nothing, but to my mind it is the dearest and most precious of all titles. I love it because it means the love which you say is sealed in my eyes, 'the sweetest, holiest, best.' That is the way in which I care for you." In the poem he wrote to me there are two lines which is what I have quoted from:

"Ideal love is sealed in her blue eyes,
    Love without words, the sweetest, holiest, best."
I showed my letter to Con before sending it and she said it

would do perfectly. I tell you about it because I like you to know everything as it takes place. I want to impress upon him that I do care for him, but only in a right way, and I thought it was a good thing to quote his own words.

The above refers to an acrostic on my name which Blunt had read to me:

August 27. 1893.

Enshrined within my heart of hearts she lies,
My ~~...~~ secret by the world unguessed.
Ideal love is sealed in her blue eyes,
Love without words, the ~~...~~.
Yes. She is ~~...~~ thus. But there comes a day
Looked for yet feared, when ~~...~~.
Young summer calls us to the woods away.
There will I venture my soul's passionate tale,
There kneeling crave a first unquestioning kiss.
O Sun, shine bright today on hill or dale.
Nurse O soft wind, Tonight my happiness.

—

I have not got the letter from his Rev to which the following is an answer, but he must have expressed his anxiety:

The Danes, August 31

You could not have said what you have written in a more tender and loving way. In every word I am conscious of your love, and every feeling of my heart blesses and thanks you for it. Every single word you say I acknowledge to be as true as it can possibly be. It is what I expected you to say. I long also to be able to talk to you, but I must do my best to write. First and above all I wish you to realize how sensible I am of your love, and there is not a single word in your letter which did not come to me steeped in tenderness. I will not deny that though I expected you to say all you have, and though I feel to the full the truth of every word, it has made me unhappy. I was an utter fool to think that after Blunt's behaviour to me I could bring him round to care for me as a friend, but still I did hope to do so. You have made me now realize that there is nothing for it but to break off all intimacy with him at once. I own that I still like him enough for it to distress me, but I agree that my liking for him makes an extra reason for doing so. I hate and despise myself for liking him still, but I cannot help it. I do not know a single quality in him which is lovable, and yet he fascinates me. You see I tell you my feelings without concealing anything. I feel sure that although he fascinates me it would be impossible for him to induce me to do anything wrong, but it is better to flee from any chance of temptation. I realize now that my letter to him yesterday was a fearful mistake, and I feel quite overwhelmed with the sense of having got deeper and deeper into a situation which would have been easy to escape at first and now is difficult. Of course, my worst mistake is that I have practically shown him that I understand his feelings towards me and disapprove of them, and yet I have continued to be intimate with him. However, as you say, the past is past beyond recall, and the only thing to be thought about is the future. I showed Con your letter as I have told her everything, and she advises me to do this. If I could but write an explanation I feel it would be easy; the impossibility is to say it, as I get shy and confused and never make my meaning clear; only I dislike writing down on paper things which are so private. Con says in spite of this drawback she strongly advises me to write. He will probably answer my letter in the course of a few days, and in return Con advises me to say that I have thought over the whole matter since my return home, and realize the situation, and understanding now his feelings towards me, I can never again feel safe or happy with him alone, and therefore all that sort of intimacy must end. I have put this very roughly and badly, but when I have written the letter I shall send it to you for your approval, and will do nothing without consulting you. Considering the tone of my last letter, it will seem so odd to him that I should so completely change, but Con says the explanation must come some time and the sooner the better. For the future I shall avoid him as much as I can without attracting notice. I only hope it may not interfere

with my friendship with Judith. Do you think this will put
matters right? I am sure the only way to explain properly
is for me to write to him. Of course, I see how utterly foolish
I have been, but there is no help for it now. What should I
do without you, my guardian angel? There were two things
which prevented me putting a stop to it at once, one, my
liking for him, and the other my hope of turning his feelings
into a genuine affection. He has behaved like a villain, I
agree, but there is one excuse, which is that I have appeared
to encourage him in every possible way. If any other girl
had allowed him to do what I have, I should have said she
was as bad as he was. Not that this makes his conduct any the
less horrible, but it is some excuse. It was a great thing for
me having Con at Crabbet, because I could tell her everything, which of course I could not have told Mother or even
Betty.

It is all a great worry, and I blame myself very much. I
have behaved like a fool if not something worse, but I will
try to set it right now.

I must have destroyed many of his Rev's letters during
this and the following month and can only guess at their
trend by my replies. There is no doubt that he was
thoroughly alarmed.

The Danes, September 1

I have been in great distress since your letter yesterday.
I would give my right hand to unsay and undo all that I have
hitherto done and said, but it is impossible. It is useless to
regret what is past when there is the future to be thought
of. All the same, when I think of the way in which I have
behaved and the things I have allowed and favoured, I am
overcome with shame. I have told you all because unless you
knew all you could not help me, but I feel that what I have
told you should make you not only hate but despise me. I
know, though, that your love for me is as great as ever, in
fact I feel it more than ever I did, and unless I was certain
that it would not change I could not have told you all I did.
The reason for my calmness over Blunt's behaviour to me is

this. Firstly it is difficult at first to realize the amount of infamy which is meant by words which also mean the highest and best things. Then, as I have told you, he fascinated me, and it is this liking which makes me hot with shame, and which I can hardly bring myself to confess even to you.

One thing I can see which adds to your distress is the thought that with all the knowledge I had I could allow things to get to that point, and even then was fool enough to suppose that I could change lust into holy love, and that for the future you will not feel that I am safe, not because you do not trust in my virtue, but because I have shown myself such a blind fool. But I see the full extent of my folly now, and for the future there will be experience as well as knowledge to guide me. I will never again be foolish enough to think I can turn vice into virtue.

The Danes, September 2

You have guessed rightly the reason Blunt fascinates me. He is the handsomest man I have ever met, and I think the most physically attractive. As I feel it almost impossible to realize that the way in which he cares for me is a way of which I should be ashamed instead of pleased, I still feel that his affection for me draws me to him. I think it must be all a bad dream, and that I shall wake one morning and know that things are the same as they used to be. But on the other hand I feel it is far better that they have come to a point, that knowing his intentions, I may not be led on to care for him more than I do now. As I got older I should probably have attracted him more than I do now, and getting more intimate with time, might have found it more difficult to break off all intercourse with him. I feel that he still has enough fascination for me to draw me into being friendly with him if we were much together, and therefore the only safe plan is to avoid ever being alone with him.

Booton Rectory, September 3

I opened last night a volume of the Works of Dr. Barrow, a famous divine in the reign of Charles II, and my eye lighted on this sentence, "Love is the sweetest and most

delectable of all passions, and when by the conduct of wisdom
it is directed in a rational way toward a worthy object, it
cannot otherwise than fill the heart with ravishing delight."
His expression "ravishing delight" shows that he understood
the pleasure to the full. I note the passage that we may live
up to it, not forgetting the condition of the ravishing delight,
that we must be directed by *wisdom* toward a *worthy* object.
Yet no one less needs the warning than you do now.

Our late experience has brought prominently before me
the folly of the conventional protection which is relied on
for shielding women from corruption. A particular passion
is the cause, directly or indirectly, of perhaps half the vice
and misery of the world. This passion is implanted for bene-
ficent purposes in the constitution of man, and with this
indwelling informer, besides the thousand hints, or more
than hints, that are continually cropping up, it is assumed
that innocence will be preserved by an impossible ignorance.
On this account the mere mention of the sin is held to be
almost equivalent to committing it. What sort of safety can
there be in a fictitious barrier that has rarely any existence?
And it is a little short of madness when people keep up the
hollow pretence, and trust to it. And as for the taint that is
supposed to attach to speaking plainly on the subject, this
depends entirely on the purpose of the speakers. You and I
have been writing plainly these last few days, and there could
not have been less taint in our words and thoughts if we had
been writing of the stars. We have had a high, momentous
end which has been attained by telling freely everything we
each had in us, and this momentous end would have been
sacrificed if a misguided scrupulosity had condemned us to
silence. I have never written more reverentially to you.

The Danes, September 9

You have made something plain to me in your letter
which I did not before rightly understand. I realize that the
fascination Blunt has for me is a reason beyond all others
why I should avoid him. At the same time I have felt the
impossibility of his ever persuading me to do wrong, not
because I trust to my own power of resisting temptation but

because I have never felt the very smallest temptation to do wrong. My intimacy with him has made me understand how many women fall, not from their own inclination but from the wish to give all that they possess and make even the very greatest sacrifice possible for the man they love. I am not saying that I felt this for Blunt, because I did not in the least, only I can understand the feeling. But I never for one single instant felt the temptation to go wrong from physical feelings and therefore I thought it impossible that I should be carried away even by a sudden impulse. Today you have explained this to me by saying that, though it seems strange, we are not always conscious that the physical feeling exists until it has got possession of us, and then it is too late. Now I feel more deeply thankful than ever to have escaped from an intimacy which I see might have led me into such misery however little I thought it possible.

I feel already so much happier than I did last week. My regrets are turning into deep thankfulness, and I am gradually beginning to feel calmer about the whole matter. No doubt the regrets will keep returning at times as strong as ever, but for the present I must be thankful that they are less. I look forward to Sunday, as in the beautiful service there is always peace to be found, and the contemplation of heavenly things lifts one above the trials of earth.

The Danes, September 8

You have never once since I have known you said a single harsh word to me, and during all this trying time your letters have been as full of tenderness and love as they have been full of wisdom and truth. You have told me the truth without in any way seeking to modify it, but that was kindness instead of harshness. If another person had done it, in all probability it would have been harsh, because their object would have been to make me ashamed and sorry for my folly, and, however much I might insist on my repentance, they would say: "So long as you still feel as you do towards him, you cannot be sorry for what you have done, and you are only seeking an opportunity to do it again." And there is hardly another person in the world who would not have blamed me more than him. It is an injustice which it seems almost impossible to explain that the blame and the shame should always be given to the woman, while in nine cases out of ten the fault lies entirely with the man. Why is it that a man can go on sinning again and again in that particular way, and people hardly think the worse of him, while if a woman falls but once, she is made an outcast for ever? And as a general rule the man sins from lust and nothing else, while the woman sins through love. All the pity, the sympathy, the forgiveness ought to be for the woman, and yet it never is.

The reason your letters are so helpful to me is that you understand my weakness and pity it, although you see it to be a weakness. I hope I shall soon get back into a more peaceful state of things, and I know my peace will be the greater for this trial. Already I feel wiser for it, and it seems as if years of experience had been added to my life. I feel as if I were a different being now from what I was and, I trust, a better and a wiser one. I think the first years of one's life are spent in laying in knowledge, and at the right time one begins to live and use the knowledge one has been gathering in. I have now begun to live for the first time, and my first step has been a huge mistake. This does not seem promising, but happily for me I have had you by my side to counsel and advise me, and I feel I have learned more from my mistake than if I had gone on straight. One good of this fall has been to teach me not to trust so much to myself as I have hitherto been inclined to do. So though my first step was a dangerous one, by God's mercy and your help I think I am in reality the better for it. But it is all your goodness. Left to myself I feel I might have gone wrong, but you have saved me. It is a large sum added to the debt I owe you but can never hope to repay.

Booton Rectory, September 10

Your letter is in the highest degree delightful and satisfactory. Our wits jump. I am myself feeling that this disturbing event is rich in good. At your very starting in life

16

it has come as a beacon to show you the rocks you are to avoid. The rest of your days will be the better and happier for it. Far from continuing to vex we might almost shout for joy.

Nothing is better known to me than your absolute safety on one side, except in the hidden undefined way I explained to you. But I delight to have your own declaration also giving me back my knowledge, and most of all I delight in your recognizing how subtle influences may operate in us, though not perceptible to ourselves till they have brought us to the brink of the precipice. You are delicious to deal with for a score of reasons and pre-eminently for your genuine, inextinguishable desire in everything to depart from evil.

Your own words bid me picture you today raised from earth to heaven through the influences of the day and the services. When our minds are turned to these grand contemplations the petty vexations of the passing hour are driven away. They are seen to be contemptible by the contrast. Soon they will be extinct with my darling, and she will be peacefully proceeding along her own chosen path, undisturbed by the intrusion of extraneous incongruities with which she has nothing in common.

The Danes, September 10

I feel so abjectly, wretchedly miserable tonight. I can do nothing but write to you. I have another cause to make me wretched tonight, although it is all the result of the first. Since I came back from Crabbet my mind has been filled night and day with that one thought, until it seems to have driven everything else out of my mind. I have been living in a sort of dream. I must have seemed very absent or unusually cross to other people. I am quite unconscious of how I pass my days: they go by somehow and what I have said or done I do not know.

The last few days Godfrey Locker has been staying here. Victor treats him like the dust of the earth, says everything he can to hurt his feelings, and in fact is so abominably rude to him that it makes my blood boil. It is done intentionally because, as Neville says, Godfrey thinks Vic's sulkiness a sign of his immense power and genius, and he would not admire him half so much if he were amiable. But not only does Victor try his bad temper on Godfrey but on all of us as well. I know it is folly in me to notice this, but as I have said, I seem to have lost all control over my feelings, and I give way to them without the smallest effort or restraint. This evening Victor was extra cross because Neville was absorbed in an exciting book, and accused Neville of being unbearably cross. I foolishly retorted by saying that Victor was not the person to talk of crossness when he was in a temper all the day. We had a regular squabble and Vic ended by going up to bed. I came up later and went to say goodnight to Mother. She then said I had spoiled the whole evening, that it was shameful of me to lecture Vic before his friend, that I wished to rule everybody and made the house miserable for everyone by my temper. Of course, she was angry when she said it and did not mean it all, but I feel a sort of black cloud of wretchedness over my soul which I can only work off by writing to you. I feel there is darkness all round me, with only one bright spot in my world which is the brighter for the darkness elsewhere, and that is your love for me. I cling to it as if it was my one hope, as it is my chief joy.

The Danes, September 11

We have all been in most characteristic moods lately, and last night especially. Mother has been going over old papers and letters, which have upset her a good deal, and so she was more than ever inclined to oppose whatever anyone suggested. Our dinner was one continual wrangle. Whatever the boys ate, they were scolded for taking. Finally there was a grand scene when Gobble [1] ate up Cush's [2] dinner. I flew at him, whipped him, and abused him hotly. This greatly irritated Mother, who said I was not to be so rude to Gobble, who was an angel; that if Cush annoyed Gobble, she must go. I retaliated by saying that if Gobble came near Cush I should kill him. The scene was ludicrous, and at length, worn out

---

[1] My father's dog.　　　　　　[2] My dog.

with temper, we all collapsed. Mother left the room, when there was an immediate and most extraordinary revival of the whole party. We all fell to eating and fighting again with renewed vigour.

After dinner I read to the boys. Neville was soon sound asleep, likewise Mother. Suddenly Vic perceived that there was a bat in the room. Imagine our horror! He broke it gently to Con, who enveloped herself in a shawl and fell flat on the floor. We all followed her example except Vic, who endeavoured to chase the bat from the room. Suddenly there was a piercing scream from Mother, who had been woken up by all our noise. "Oh, I have been stung by a wasp, and it hurts so. I don't like it. I don't like it." Thinking from her first scream that the bat must have returned, we again prostrated ourselves on the floor. On discovering that it was only a wasp, and Mother being the only person stung, we all expressed great relief, which did not comfort poor Mother much. We were so worn out by all out exertions that we felt bed was the only possible thing.

The Danes, September 12

I have had a letter from Blunt this morning. I expected him either not to write but to seek when I next went to Crabbet to begin the same thing all over again or else to write in a joking way as if he had not taken my letter seriously. The letter he has written is far better than I hoped it could be. I have read it to Con, who while agreeing that it is better than could have been expected, says that of course he has written what he thought would be most acceptable to me, that she thinks he probably guessed someone has been advising me, and that he is anxious to harrow my feelings by calling me unkind. Con can read the letter from an unprejudiced point of view and so will you, and you will probably not be the least convinced by it. Needless to say I am, I cannot help it. I am sure that he understands my feelings and will not try to overcome me again and that we can still be friendly towards each other. I feel that matters are now so established between us that my path lies clear and plain before me. I have told him my resolution, he has agreed to it, and the rest is easy. You, like Con, will probably see in his letter fresh proof of his hypocrisy and baseness; I, who cannot judge, never felt so fond of him as I do today. I say it with shame, but I must say it because it is true. I believe I am writing arrant nonsense, but forgive me, for I really do not know what I am saying. His letter has changed all my ideas, and I no longer see him as a villain. Not that this alters my resolution, as I have said before, only it fills my heart with a tenderness when I think of him which no doubt is all undeserved. However, I cannot help it. He certainly knows how to influence me, and he could not have written a letter to give me a better opinion of him.

He says that he has taken some days to think over my last letter, and at first could not understand that I had written it; "It was so strangely unlike you and unkind. I think, however, I must answer it, if only to say that I shall never write again." He then goes on to say that he does not blame me for what I have resolved. "Love," he says, "sentiment, friendship, whatever we may call it, is a dangerous thing to play with and ought not to have been talked about between us. For that I blame myself. I am sure, however, that when you are older, you will be sorry for the hard things you have written in this letter. When I first talked to you about other things than the nonsense we have always talked, I saw that you were fond of me in some way, perhaps childishly, perhaps like a woman, but differently from others. That was what attracted me so much to you, and but for it (and I saw it in a hundred little ways) we might have talked and laughed together all our lives and I should have told you nothing more. I had no design to make you love me in one way or another, only I was enchanted when you told me it was so." He ends by saying, "For the future it shall be exactly as you wish. I will see as little of you as circumstances allow. The thing I loved in you was that you loved me. And since it is not so I shall not seek you out. This need not hinder our remaining friends. My thought of you will always be kind and tender, and I hope yours will be kind for me. As for our few days together last month, you will not be unhappy about them and I shall, I hope, forget."

At this point I went to Booton, as I evidently felt that I had more to say to his Rev than could be expressed in letters. On my return home I write:

The Danes, September 28

Letters are a poor substitute for talks. The more I think over our time the more perfect I feel it to have been. I had a most peaceful and happy day yesterday, living over again all the delicious bits with you, and trying to keep to my new resolution of being patient and cheerful.

The boys go back to school today. They are very depressed and in consequence very cross, and Mother is the same, so there are a good many rows between them. It seems strange that sadness at parting instead of drawing them together should only make the rows worse. Mother objects to everything the boys propose, and when they insist upon having their own way, she comes to us almost in tears to say that the boys bully her so fearfully she does not know what to do. The last days of the holidays are always very trying for this reason. It would seem the natural thing to say to the boys: "These are your last days at home. Make the most of them and be as happy as you can." Instead of which Mother acts upon this: "These being your last days I must make the most of them and order you about while I can." No doubt in a large family there would always be at times quarrels and irritations, but half the trials of our home come solely from one person wishing to rule everyone else.

The Danes, October 2

Another day and a letter to match it. Yesterday was as peaceful and happy as I had anticipated it would be. We had our Harvest Thanksgiving, which seems very late in the year. I brought to it a heart bursting with thankfulness for innumerable blessings. When I think over my late trouble, the marvellous escape I had, the blessing which it has produced in place of curses, I do not know how to show my gratitude. God has indeed been good to me, and I see this more every day. While I was at Crabbet I never realized any actual danger, but I see I was all the while standing on the brink of a fearful precipice. I should not have realized this to the full even now but for our talks at Booton. When occasionally our feelings alter about certain things, as mine have altered about this affair, and we can see clearly what curses we almost prayed for, it helps us to trust more to the infinite wisdom of God in cases when we do not see the harm of what we pray for. All round I have learnt an invaluable lesson.

Booton Rectory, October 2

I keep up my rejoicing at the thought of you restored to your old pursuits. Now you have passed through a few days of turbulent excitements, uneasy in themselves, and which only attracted you to disappoint you, you can better realize the charm of blissful occupations. Your late experiences have their compensation in teaching you what is genuinely valuable, whereby you value it the more. Shameless profligates are only plausible so long as they deceive. They varnish over their foul purposes by clothing them in the language of the purest affection, and you do not at first perceive that what pretends to be love is what Walter Scott, in his *Lay of the Last Minstrel*, calls "fantasy's hot fire, whose wishes, *soon as granted, fly.*" No wonder that, judging the language of others by the meaning it bore to yourself, you should have been distracted by mingled belief and misgivings. But even so the misgiving poisons the belief and spoils the pleasure before the full baseness is unmasked. There is nothing to be got out of that world of fleshly desires. Whatever delusive form it may put on for a while it can never be your world.

Chapter Thirteen

My sister Con, in order to help the family fortunes, had now taken to reviewing books for various newspapers and also writing articles for a women's paper. I was apparently horrified by this activity, which shocked my social prejudices, and in various letters to his Rev I comment unfavourably on my sister's activities.

The Danes, October 3

I see that Con will soon develop into a regular newspaper correspondent, which is painful to think of. She has been asked by her editor to write on the etiquette of Ambassadors and Governors. To think she has come to this! It is really most melancholy. At any rate, when I am obliged to make money, I will not have anything to do with newspapers. I think I should prefer the workhouse. It is generally considered as the least degrading occupation a lady can take up, but I think it is very low.

I don't think that even were I starving, and certainly not before, that I could descend so low as to write articles for a miserable paper.

I cannot myself understand how she can bring herself down to such a level. If there was any real necessity and we were starving, I can understand sacrificing one's pride for the sake of one's family, but when there is not the smallest necessity, as there certainly is not in Con's case, I could not bring myself to associate with such a vulgar paper. Of course, Con must manage her own affairs, but I wish that in a case of this kind, she would remember that our name is the same, and that we are in a measure dragged after her. Anyone knowing she subscribed to such a paper would suppose her family approved, which they do not by any means.

Mother is beginning to make objections to Con writing for it, so I feel bound to stand up for it, but I really do not understand how Con can do it. I think it quite unnecessary that Con should write at all in our present circumstances, but as she will she might at least keep to a respectable paper like the *Saturday Review*, which pays her so highly.

The fuss that is made over spending pennies does seem to me so absurd, and in a way distressing. I do not intend for one moment to blame economy, because that is only right whatever our income might be. But considering the money we have got and the way we live I do think it is excessively mean to be always borrowing from those poorer than we are and grudging every penny that is spent upon other people. Mother talks in the village here as if only with the greatest difficulty could she manage to scrape together a few shillings to give to a charity, and then treats it as some generous gift. I cannot understand myself how she has not sufficient pride to prevent this. She occasionally says how distressed she is at accepting so many presents, but she accepts them all the same, and we never give anything to anybody. Betty with her small income is infinitely more generous than we are. Of course, I don't know the exact state of affairs, but I do think we are unnecessarily mean.

Booton Rectory, October 4

Betty explains to me that Con is paid £2 2s. a column, and as her articles commonly fill two columns, this amounts to £4 4s. a week. It shows what a title is worth to such a paper. Of course, the ordinary rate of payment is barely a fourth of what Con receives. The rest is paid to her title. With readers of the upper and middle classes a title prefixed to such an article would not enhance its value. Rather the reverse. It is otherwise when you drop lower. Fanny tells me that our servants take in three Society Papers, and they like to have their news and sentiments fresh from the Queen herself, or her associates. This explains the pay, which is to me a novel fact in modern literature. As titled contributors multiply the pay will diminish. The wisdom is to earn a fortune while golden harvests can be had.

I should require some thousands at least to compensate me for my loss of self-respect. I am obliged to be glad that my Lady is beginning to take alarm. I am alarmed myself, wondering where this making common cause with vulgar journals will end.

The Danes, October 6

Con has written an article on the feeling of honour in men and women, instead of the wrongs of women versus men, which, however, I believe is to follow. Apparently the wrongs she is going to write about are on the labour question. She got very excited the other night, giving me a long account of what women had to complain of, and certainly they have a right to complain if all Con says is true. No doubt her article will give the solution to the whole question.

Mother and I go on Saturday to the Derbys. I am rather looking forward to the visit, as they are a very jolly family. From there we go to Lathom, which I do not care for so much. Wherever I go there are comedies to be seen and enjoyed, and when I can write and tell you about them, it adds to my enjoyment.

The Derbys and Lathoms, living very close to each other as they now do, will be full of abuse of each other. I enjoy a change, even though it may not be a change for the better.

Booton Rectory, October 12

I am curious to know Con's opinion of honour in women, and beg you to send me a copy of her article. Years and years ago, while Lord Bath was still a bachelor, I had a discussion with him on the characteristics of women, he depreciating them, and I upholding them, till at last he said, "At least you must allow that they have no honour in a man's sense of the word." My experience obliged me to concede this point. A woman and a man have a bitter quarrel. The woman blazes abroad all the evil she learnt of the man through her intimacy with him; the man holds his tongue on the kindred weaknesses he learnt of the woman. You tell a man something in the strictest confidence and he does not reveal it. Tell it to a woman, and you find you might as well have

printed it in a newspaper. A state secret oozed out in the
reign of Louis XIV through Marshal Turenne, who excused
himself to the king by saying, "I only told it to my wife."
The king replied, "I did not tell it to *my wife*." The difference
between men and women in this particular is only true in a
general way. Many women are as secret as the grave where
secrecy is required, and many men are as leaky as a sieve.
But as far as I have seen, men have on the whole the
advantage.

My mother and I were going on a round of visits, ending
up with Crabbet, and I write from The Danes on the 13th:
"We are all very busy and very cross this morning preparing for our departure tomorrow. As Mother and I share
a box I foresee many fights. The ink bottle is sure to break
and ruin some precious article of Mother's, which she will
put down to my bad packing."

Our first visit was to Knowsley, the home of the Derbys,
from where I next write.

October 14

We started from home early yesterday and got into an
express at Hatfield which was being stopped for the Salisburys. We had prepared for the cold of the North by
putting on every species of wrap and were in consequence
nearly suffocated. Most of the country round here is dreary
in the extreme, flat, bare and when we came through it
wrapped in a fog. There was only one pretty bit and that
was lovely, which was round Sheffield. There are the most
beautiful wooded hills. This house is enormous and very
rambling. There are something over 80 bedrooms, all very
small. None of the house is pretty, though some very old,
but it has been so patched and pulled about by different
owners, especially the last Lord Derby, that it is really
hideous. It is built of a dull red brick. The rooms are all
small, with the exception of one dining-room which is
enormous and a very fine room, only terribly modernized
and spoilt. Inside it is very comfortable and nice. There is a
fascinating library, a suite of little rooms lined with books

and ending in a large odd-shaped room, something like the long room with books at Longleat.[1] The present owners abuse right and left all that was done by the last Lord Derby, in a way which I think is very unkind and disagreeable, especially considering that he was a brother. They have jumped into his shoes and can only abuse him. The only people in the house besides the family, which consists of the Derbys, Isobel,[2] one son and a secretary, are Lady Emma Talbot, Lord Derby's sister, and her husband, neither of them at all lively. Cousin C.[3] has the family failing of abusing everybody in a very nasty way. Lord Derby is rather like a boy, very jovial and full of bad jokes, but I should say without much else. Isobel has not changed a bit. She has pretty hair and a very pretty skin. She is rather clumsy in her movements, and is still what she used to be, a tomboy. This spoils her. Judith, even when she was most fond of riding and driving and sports of all kinds, never for a moment lost her feminine nature and was always the gentle, refined, graceful girl she is now. Isobel, on the contrary, is too much inclined to be like a boy and has in consequence lost much of her feminine charm. This, I think, is partly owing to the fact that she has seven brothers and has been accustomed all her life to romp with them like a boy. This to my mind spoils her, but apart from that she is very cheery and good-natured, talks well and seems very intelligent. She seemed pleased to see me and has been very nice. I will make the best of her good qualities, but feel we have nothing in common with each other. They all seem very fond of each other and are immensely cheery, which is pleasant. The mother and father seem more like a brother and sister to their children, and they evidently get on perfectly. All the same they make me fearfully shy and I do not feel in a particularly lively mood. My cold makes me feel more than usually stupid, and it is very difficult to join in their jokes. I try my best but at present do not feel very comfortable. I seem to have no interests in common with them. They know

[1] The home of the Marquis of Bath.
[2] The only daughter.
[3] Lady Derby.

none of my friends, and I know none of theirs, except our
mutual relations, whom they only talk of to abuse, so that
it is rather difficult to get on. One thing is nice, which is
that Mother seems really happy here. She enjoys her talk
with Lady Derby and enjoys the luxuries of servants and
carriages and large dinners. I am very glad of anything
which gives her pleasure.

We drove to church this morning, it being some little way
off. After church we were taken round the house and its
ugliness was roundly abused. This afternoon we went to the
stables, which are magnificent. An old coachman who has
been here for years and is a great rogue, although a great
character, showed us round with the most tremendous pride.
They have over forty magnificent horses. The stables are
kept spotlessly clean, which they ought to be considering
that they have twenty men to look after them. The gardens
are large and ugly, and these require twenty-four gardeners.
Thank goodness I am not obliged to live here. The luxury
of a small home and a few servants can only be properly
appreciated by coming to a house like this. The whole house
and stables are lit with electric light, which is nice. On
Tuesday we are going into Preston to hear Lord Salisbury
speak, which will be something to tell you about. . . .

I meant to send this letter today, but it will reach you as
soon by tomorrow's post, so I keep it to tell you my latest
news. I have just had a talk with Isobel and begin to like her
better; she is perfectly natural, which is always attractive.
She is very much surprised to see how much I have changed
and evidently thinks I have degenerated very much since old
days. I told her I adored children and was never so happy as
when I had a little baby in my arms. I don't know whether
contempt or surprise was the strongest feeling in her mind
that anyone could be so foolish. There is a lovely little
grandchild here, only she never comes down. It is far more
surprising to me how people can be so indifferent to children.
I think Cousin C. is as surprised as Isobel at the change in
my character and much disappointed with me. She said she
thought it a great pity that I had ceased to be a tom-boy. I
think I shall like Isobel very much.

The electric light has just gone out and there being no candle in the room except the little scrap which is usually given to one to light sealing-wax, I am almost in the dark . . . Happily as I write it has come back.

I will certainly send you Con's article. Her argument is that women have no code of honour, while men have; that so long as a thing comes within the limits of that code a man will behave honourably, but that apart from that his natural sense of honour is not so great as a woman's. She quite agrees to the fact you mention, that after a quarrel with a man a woman will reveal facts which a man would not, but this, she says, must be ascribed to a woman's passion for talking and telling secrets, which unquestionably is greater than a man's. As to cruelty she gives a very good instance. A man who is naturally tender-hearted and humane will yet do a brutal and cruel thing without the smallest compunction if only it comes under the head of sport, which he might scruple to do if it did not. A woman, she says, is not influenced by such a thing, but to her cruelty is always cruelty. I shall like to see her article on the subject. Certainly men do behave at times in the most base and dishonourable ways without it being thought anything of, while a woman could not do such things.

I am finishing this letter before going to bed, as it will leave early in the morning. I count with pleasure another evening gone. I do this at nearly every place. At this sort of house I long to bring in someone like Margot, who will shock and horrify everybody, and not having Margot I long to do it myself and dare not. There are some people I cannot help longing to shock.

Booton Rectory, October 16

Life in visits is dull unless you establish friendly relations with somebody. When you go to a new house I speculate upon how you are getting on. The family in the present case is familiar to you, but the mode of living will be on a bigger scale, and the guests perhaps numerous, and the surroundings generally will be different. I hope your shyness when strangers talk to you will not prevent your being gracious.

Advances towards sociability are a sign of goodwill, and you should respond to them in kind, and not answer drily and curtly, and look in another direction. I am eager for your first report, which I may possibly get tomorrow.

I read this in an agricultural newspaper. A retired farmer who had saved money and was anxious to settle his daughters said he would give £1,000 to the youngest, aged twenty-five, when she married, £2,000 to her elder sister, and £3,000 to the next, who was turned thirty. A young man standing by in the market listened thoughtfully and after a pause enquired anxiously of the farmer whether he had a daughter of fifty. The world grows mercenary.

Knowsley, Prescot, October 16

Another day has passed successfully. I walked with Isobel this morning and drove this afternoon. It is a very fine park, although, I think, dreary. It is full of red deer, which are such splendid animals. I like Isobel really very much and think she is a thoroughly nice girl, but I am certain I could not make a friend of her. At present she is full of fun, and I should imagine does not have a serious thought. She is thoroughly contented with her life, has no wish to marry and no wish for a friend in our sense of the word. She would think friendship very silly and absurd.

I cannot say I am happy here, though certainly not unhappy. It pleases me to see Mother happy and I make the best of what is enjoyable. I am sure Lady Derby has taken a dislike to me. I am not a bit offended, for it only amuses me, but I know she thinks me very dull and spiritless and a great muff in all ways. She is not very gracious to anybody and snaps a good deal at me. Although I only want to laugh, it does not make one feel happier.

The Salisburys come on Wednesday, and I am thinking how nice it will be to have Lady Gwenny here. Isobel asked me today what Gwendolen Cecil was like, and it seemed so strange for anyone to ask after her in that way. I have got to thinking she is a being of a higher order than most human beings and can only be spoken of with the deepest respect.

Cousin C. is very anxious for me to stay next week when Mother goes to Lathom, but I think a fortnight would drive me mad. Happily, Mother wants me.

I am bored with having a cold as, though it is much better, it makes me feel heavy and stupid, and also I look more than extra pale, which distresses Mother and adds to Cousin C.'s irritation. There are some people who seem to look pale on purpose to annoy one, and I know I am one of those people. I annoy myself so frightfully.

Booton Rectory, October 17

Your letter is a good description of house, establishment and inmates. I knew that Knowsley was large and not stately. I have now a visual picture of it. Big establishments would alone have sickened me of wealth if they were its necessary accompaniments. I never in the least got reconciled to the spectacle of waste, and the want of domestic snugness in the whole cumbrous machinery. Some proportion must be kept between the needs and comfort of man and his dwelling and its appurtenances or the comfort vanishes. I often used to say of particular houses when I was in them that I would not take them at a gift on the condition of living in them.

A male cat is called a Tom Cat; a masculine girl a Tom boy. What can it have been in the Thomases of the world that the name should have been specially selected to designate masculine characteristics? I must have quoted to you Milton's view of the distinctive qualities of man and woman:

"For valour he and contemplation formed
For softness she, and sweet attractive grace."

The gentleness, the tenderness, the refinement, the delicacy of a woman are her charm, and the traits to which she owes the chivalrous homage of the man. He is bound to treat with courteous deference the soft graces which demand his protection as well as his admiration. But when the woman apes the action of the man her claim upon his chivalry is gone. She has come down from her eminence, and has converted herself into an inferior and very trumpery sort of man. Nothing out of nature pleases. A masculine woman is a deformity. Being

a girl you may legitimately wish you had been a boy, but try
and turn yourself into a boy and you will be a failure. We
shall not join in Lady Derby's lamentations that when you
had passed the age in which boys and girls are much alike
your sex asserted itself, and you grew into a delicious
woman.

The Stanleys for many generations have usually been a
sporting tribe, cock-fighters when cock-fighting was fashionable and then racers. The last man was an exception. The
present set with their increased means may be expected to
draw to the turf, which may account for the number of
horses in the Knowsley stables.

Rogers, the poet, described the English country gentleman
as saying, "It is a beautiful day, let us go and kill something."
An inexplicable propensity to me, to whom killing would be
torture. I protect life wherever I see it. Animals commonly
reckoned noxious are safe here. But Con is right as to men in
general. Call slaughter sport and they rush into it with glee.

Knowsley, October 18

All the gentlemen went last night to a dinner given by
Mr. Birley, the Chairman, who is to preside over the meeting
in Liverpool. I should think few of them felt inclined for a
big dinner at 5 o'clock. We had a most excellent meal in
an hotel, where the Lathom party also dined, only in a
separate room, as Lady Derby was most anxious to be
independent and have her own way. It is very comic the
pride she takes in her new position and her delight in
lording it over Lady Lathom, who is fearfully jealous. It
is also comic the way Mother brings forward her glory
in India and Paris, and each tries to outdo the other. Only
with Mother it is also very pathetic, as it is a terrible trial
to her to see Cousin C. in such a splendid position and to
feel that hers from a worldly point of view has gone. She
is wonderfully good over it, but I know she feels it very
much. I was glad that yesterday she was also put well in the
front and shown great respect. The meeting in the evening
was a wonderful sight. The huge hall was packed; they said
there were 8,000 people in it, and thousands more tried to

17

force their way in. Forty policemen were fighting with the crowd and kept them out with great difficulty. Though noisy at first they kept as still as possible during Lord Salisbury's speech, and were most appreciative, seeing every point. They gave him a most enthusiastic reception. Mr. Birley, who gave a little opening address, read out a letter from Sir Henry James, which was most comic, as he could not read the handwriting at all, and made long pauses over it and many mistakes, while of course the people shouted with laughter. The heat of the hall was suffocating, and it must have been terrible to speak in it. I thought Lord Salisbury's speech exceedingly fine. He has a beautiful voice, and his manner is perfectly quiet and dignified and yet very impressive. He makes hardly any gesture. All that he said was put into the best and purest English, and not one word that did not tell. The contrast between his speech and those of the other wretched speakers was wonderful. It was a great chance to hear him. He speaks very slowly and deliberately, but never seemed at a loss for a word. His speech took exactly an hour. I have only read a very few of his speeches, but all I have read were splendid, and so infinitely above Gladstone's which are all words and are meant to put himself forward. In every word you feel what a great man Lord Salisbury is. His speech was received with great enthusiasm. After his speech was done the meeting became dreadfully tedious. Mr. Hanbury's speech was popular but, I thought, vulgar and commonplace. Lord Derby was received with immense enthusiasm, and one man shouted, "Good boy, Fred." He is very popular in Preston.

I have given you a dull account of it but can do no better. I got no chance to see what the town of Preston was like. The crowds were wonderfully well behaved, but like most great crowds they were a ghastly sight, from the number of miserable and wicked faces. The women in Liverpool, and I suppose in all Lancashire towns, go about with shawls pinned over their heads and no hats, which I like very much, and in Liverpool as we drove through, half the people seemed to go about barefoot.

I am much more at my ease now, and I like them all much

more. One thing which is very pleasant is the friendliness which exists between parents and children. They all seem devoted to each other and the children are as easy with their parents as possible, and all work together in the most perfect harmony.

Booton Rectory, October 18

A very dear letter indeed. You give a faithful picture of the dullness which pervades parties in big houses. They are for the most part a blank. The manners are rather formal, the conversation flat, and the performers walk tamely through their parts. Some people like the dead-alive proceedings, others endure them, and many detest them. I have heard haters say that they would rather spend the time at the treadmill. I do not expect you to enjoy yourself. You can only resign yourself and take your chance of now and then a brighter bit than ordinary. The one hope beforehand is that you may find a congenial spirit with whom to pair, but that hope is apparently over for the present.

I spoke yesterday of the probability that the present Stanleys would return to the family love of the turf, which was not among the propensities of the last Lord Derby. The gambling element is at the bottom of the passion, as appears in Lady Isobel's announcement that she will bet directly she comes into her money, and it is the hope of winning that gives gambling its charm. She will probably add one more to the numbers who ruin themselves in the desire suddenly to fill their own pockets by emptying the pockets of others. Gamblers in high life have told me that the greed for gain is always the chief factor in the business, and if it is so with well-to-do gentlemen there is no need to enquire into the motives of the rest.

Knowsley, October 20

I am much more at home here now. Yesterday Isobel took me boating on the big water and we were very friendly together. Lady Alice Stanley, the eldest son's wife, is here now, and though I do not care much for her, she is so nice to me I quite like her for that. Then the last two evenings there have been big dinners, and I can get on much better talking to one person instead of joining in general conversation. Last night I sat by Gwenny, which was a treat. I have not seen much of her, but merely to know she is there is nice. We were going yesterday to see the watch-making at Prescot, which is a trade that has been revived there, only they feared there might be some disturbances from the miners, who are out of work, or anyhow there are so many people starving they thought it would not be right to go in smart carriages to see the town, and so it was given up. The misery must be fearful. About 100 miners were out yesterday with the shooters as beaters, and they say they seemed extremely cheerful and were capital men. They thought the strike would not be over for some time yet. Col. Talbot, Lady Emma's husband, says he once commanded a regiment of men composed chiefly of miners, and that if treated with tact, they would do anything for you and were splendid soldiers; proud of themselves, their regiment, their commander. But if they were treated tactlessly they became unmanageable.

The present Stanleys are all mad on racing, and Isobel tells me her father's great ambition was to be rich so that he might race, and the eldest son, Eddie, told Mother last night that he could take no interest now in his parliamentary work as he was so keen on racing. He has just bought a beautiful horse for a large sum, and the horse fell suddenly sick of some internal inflammation. It has been watched over day and night, and to keep up its strength it was given a bottle of port, a bottle of brandy, and three dozen eggs every day, and in spite of this the poor thing died last night. It must be fearfully expensive to keep racehorses if you feed them in that way when they are ill.

There was a large dinner-party last night with the Lord Mayor and his wife, and the Bishop and his daughter, and just before dinner out went the electric light. Happily there was gas in the passages, but it was a great nuisance. Everyone, though, enjoyed the joke, and the light came on again during dinner. These luxuries have their drawbacks.

Knowsley, October 22

Cousin C. yesterday gave me a splendid present of £20. Is it not generous and good of her? I do not know how to thank her sufficiently, I feel it is so kind. She said it was as a little remembrance of my first visit to Knowsley—I feel a millionaire. My chief pleasure is that now I can have both botany and dancing lessons during the winter. I feel able to supply my family with presents and anyone who is in need of money, at which rate I shall soon be in debt. They have all been very kind to us and I now feel quite at home, and sorry to leave. I am not looking forward to Lathom [which was to be our next visit]. The Stanleys are all thoroughbred and all get on together without a disagreement. Also, now that I have got rid of my shyness, I am quite happy here and dread beginning again in a new house. The drawback of relations is the way they abuse each other, and as they do it before everyone else, I think it is very bad taste.

It will be very comic when we go to Lathom and hear all this family abused when all this week it has been the Wil-brahams who have been torn to pieces.

Lady Derby is bursting with pride and says how foolish her sisters are to be jealous of her, when she herself is fearfully annoyed if anyone seems to be above her. I think she treats Mother very rudely. That is, she snubs her and is always airing her great position as compared to Mother's. This makes me very angry with her in spite of her great kindness to me, but, happily, Mother seems unconscious of it. The whole thing is very ludicrous. I do think ambition is the most absurd passion. Whether gratified or not, it makes the person ridiculous.

Lathom House, October 24

Here I am in very different surroundings from Knowsley. We arrived yesterday in time for lunch. Lady Lathom gave us a most warm welcome. Of all the three sisters [1] she is the only one really nice to Mother. She is so sympathetic, so interested in all her interests, and above all in Father's poems, and I think she makes Mother very happy. She is

[1] Lady Lathom, Lady Derby, and Lady Ampthill, daughters of Lord Clarendon.

also charming to me. The only visitors in the house are Lady Headford and her two daughters and a Mr. Fitzclarence. They ask much after Knowsley and are very disappointed that we don't abuse it.

We have tea every evening in the bowling alley, and play afterwards till nearly dinner-time. The post is generally in when we return to the house. Tonight I rushed to the table where the letters are generally put, and found none for me. I had been counting so on your letter, all through the day. The thought of it made the day go by quite happily, and when there was none, I crept upstairs almost in tears. At that minute I felt that I simply could not live through the evening, that everything was hateful to me and everyone odious. At that moment my eyes fell on your letter, which had been put in an odd corner of my bedroom. I nearly screamed for joy, and immediately I loved everyone and have spent a pleasant evening. The happiness of my whole day depends upon your letter, and when it comes it always surpasses my highest hopes and expectations.

Lathom House, October 25

Yesterday evening arrived Lord Dunmore. He gives a lecture tomorrow in Liverpool at the Geographical Society on his late travels in the Pamirs. He has told us many of his adventures, and showed us this morning some deeply interesting and most beautiful sketches of the country. They give one a great idea of their beauty and grandeur. He also took many photographs of great value, some hundreds, and these, with all his collection of butterflies and other interesting things, were lost in a great snowstorm. It must have been a fearful loss. Before this journey he was a very wild man, fond of drink and gambling. He has completely ruined himself, and his wife and five daughters live in Cashmere in some desert.

Lathom House, October 25

We got home last night something after eleven, and I only kept awake long enough to tumble into bed. The lecture was not very successful. Lord Dunmore seemed very nervous, which surprised me, and coughed very much and spoke fast and huskily. What he told us was interesting, but he had told it better before.

He told Mother that when the Russians heard in the month of October that Gladstone had come in, they exclaimed joyfully; "Now we can have what we like and go where we like and no one will interfere with us." Lord Dunmore had his right eye shot out some years ago and was very plucky over it. Lady Lathom remembers him laughing and saying he should have a crystal eye put in with his coronet and monogram upon it.

I am made to take long walks here, and we play bowls each evening for two hours, so I get plenty of exercise. I have also danced twice in the evening, which they all seem to like.

I think the visits have been a success. If I have gained nothing else I have at least gained £20. I shall certainly hoard it carefully, but I mean to have a good set of dancing and botany lessons. I can have a course of dancing lessons for £2, and the botany lessons are ten shillings a time, so you see I am well provided with the means. I shall learn skirt dancing, which I have been most anxious to do. It will be splendid exercise for the winter. I cannot walk much, it tires me so and does me no good. Mother tells me I get paler and paler, and I don't know what to do. I know exercise is the best thing, but walk I cannot. It is not laziness, but it makes my back ache and does me no good. Nothing helps me so much as dancing, so I shall be grateful for a new set of lessons.

You will get this letter on Sunday morning, and on that day above all others we are near each other, and you know how my love will be going out to you.

Lathom House, October 28

I am too sleepy tonight to write much, having played bowls vigorously before dinner and danced with equal vigour most of the evening.

When I realize that in a couple of days I shall be at Crabbet, and think of all that has passed since our last meeting, I cannot but feel a mixture of hope and fear. There has been considerable talk here about the Blunts, and when I described some of their eccentricities, and the way he came down to dinner in Arab dress, everyone exclaimed that they must be raving mad. I said that when I stayed there I also dressed as an Arabian woman in a veil, which I did twice last time, and I have now been put down as equally crazy.

My next visit was to be to Crabbet, and I write to his Rev:

"When I go to Crabbet please write to me all you have written before, and more; drive it into me that I may see only his villainy and see it in the blackest light. I like that you should know all my weaknesses, even those I am most ashamed of, and so I tell you this which comes only from a wretched vanity. When I am here and feel out of everything and know I am neither much liked nor admired, I naturally think of those who do like me, and I think of his admiration for me with pleasure. I think to myself: 'If Blunt came into this room full of people he would single me out and I should know he admired me most and liked me best.' There you have my feelings without any concealment. I have told you them in their broadest light, and even writing I blush for them. If I did not tell you all you could not help me, and yet I am bitterly ashamed of my vanity, for it is nothing else."

To this letter his Rev replies:

"Presumption only doubles the risk from danger. Over-confidence takes no precautions. Our security is in seeing the danger and guarding against it. In this you are grand. You indulge in no deceptions towards yourself or towards me, and I honour you for it. The majority have a way in certain cases of scouting the possibility of transgressing. It may be a point in which human nature is specially fallible, and they will assume in their language that any tolerable nature is beyond temptation, and that it would be an extravagance and an insult to think the contrary. When we are dealing with individuals it is criminal to adopt these fictions. We are to take human nature as it is, or we betray those we ought to shield from evil instead of protecting them. No one can know your virtues better than I, or can have a steadier faith in them. Religion, principles, temperament, conduct all speak loudly for you. And it is part of your very virtue that you scrutinize yourself rigidly, and honestly recognize that with your eager yearnings for a spotless life you have a fallible element in you. It is against this that you are longing with the whole force of your being to be secured, and I love you with a bigger love for your delightful candour in recognizing the danger, no less than for your zeal in combating it. In revolving the subject afresh I had come to the conclusion before I got your letter this morning that the chief risk was from the subtle workings of vanity, that is from the impulse to regain or to keep his admiration for you. You are aware now that it is a polluted admiration, but flatters you still, because not appealing to pollution in you, you receive it divested of its base and loathsome ingredients, and only realize them by an effort."

Crabbet Park, October 31

It seems strange after all our talks and letters to think I am really here at last. We arrived about tea-time. In the hall we were received by Lady Anne and Judith. After about five minutes Blunt appeared, gorgeously dressed in his Arab dress. The hall was rather dark and I was the last he greeted. I can say to you honestly that not once this evening have I given him a look which could have displeased you. I realize now how much we spoke by looks, and having given him none this evening I seem hardly to have seen him. He is evidently desirous of attracting my notice; that is, he has spoken to me by looks. I hardly know whether they were looks of admiration or reproach, but they were not looks of indifference.

Judith looks more beautiful than ever and more fascinating. She is as affectionate to me as I could want and we both revel in each other's company.

Crabbet Park, November 1

I must write to you my daily chronicle as briefly as I can. This morning Blunt, Lady Anne, Judith, and I went for a ride. We started with a gallop, in which Blunt and I found ourselves some way behind the other two. He said to me,"I want to say a few words to you today, by which I don't mean a quarrel." I made no answer, as the others rode up. Towards the end of the ride we again found ourselves in the rear, and he began, "I want to know why you wrote me that horrible letter." I replied, "I explained my meaning fully to you in that letter and you ought to understand." "Well, it was a horrible letter. Did you write it of your own accord?" "Yes," I said, "entirely." This is the substance of what he then said. "Well, I thought it a horrible letter and not at all nice of you." I answered, "I did not intend it to be nice. I simply wrote you my opinion. You yourself in answer approved of it, and therefore it is useless to quarrel with it now." "Yes," he said, "*au fond* no doubt it was all right, but still it was not nice." After a pause, "Did you tell your Mother about it?" "No." "Or anyone else?" I made a motion with my head, in doubt as to what I should say. This he took to mean no, and said, "That is all right, then. But tell me now, then, why did you write that letter?" I then saw he would try and coax me. My feeling was this: If I let him think I have no adviser, he will conclude the letter was written in a moment of virtuous resolution, which he will now try and overcome by persuasion and reproaches. If on the other hand I tell him I have an adviser, that means a strength he cannot touch, and the knowledge that his conduct is known to another will make him more careful. So I said to him, "Although I told Mother nothing, I did tell someone else." "Oh," he said, "did you tell them before or after you had written that letter?" "Never mind," I replied, "I told you I wrote that letter entirely by myself and no one dictated it to me." I added again that he had approved of it. "Yes, it may have been wise, but it was not nice." "I prefer to be wise. From that letter you know my opinion and no more need pass between us."

I wonder so if you will approve of what I did. I think I can have done no harm, and I spoke decidedly and without any signs of wavering. Besides, you will be glad to hear that while we talked I felt none of his charm, but only realized his meanness. He did not then attempt a single excuse or explanation, but simply took refuge in reproaches.

Crabbet Park, November 2

Blunt spent the day in London yesterday, so after breakfast I did not see him again until tea-time, and from then we were rehearsing and acting our charade. At breakfast yesterday, speaking of his dog, he said, "These little creatures are not inconstant like human beings, continually changing their affections," and as he said it he gave a meaning glance at me. He may well reproach others with inconstancy when I suppose he has never cared for anyone for long. Mother said to me later in the day, "It pleases me that you no longer chaff Blunt as much as you did. I am very pleased about it." I was glad that I had made a visible change in my manner, for it is difficult to see oneself.

Crabbet Park, November 3

Another day has passed in safety. I have had no chance of a private interview, nothing to avoid. I wish, I wish I could say that being in his presence I hate him, but I cannot help feeling the old fascination still. I know that it is a sin in me, but I cannot help it. Do not let this alarm you, it makes me more alive to my danger.

It is strange the things people will say unknowingly. Mother begged him to read aloud tonight. He replied the only thing he had to read was a poem he had written to Pamela Wyndham, a beautiful young lady who is apparently a new love. But he refused for some time to read even this, and finally Judith said, "Do you want me to leave the room, because I am quite ready to do so?" "No," he said, "I should like Emily to leave the room." "Delighted," I replied, when Judith said to me, "I expect he is afraid you will be jealous." It would have mattered nothing to anyone else and really mattered nothing anyhow, but knowing what has passed, it seemed strange.

The Danes, November 4

I could not write you proper letters from Crabbet for two strong reasons. First, while I was there I was suffering from a kind of nervous excitement which made me almost unable to sleep, and quite unable to eat, and still more unfit to write. It was a horrible feeling, a kind of perpetual internal tremble. I hardly knew what I was doing. Another reason which prevented me writing fully to you was the fearful struggle that was going on within me. Had I told you the exact state of my mind, I was afraid it would make you uneasy about me, and so I waited until I was in safety to tell you all my thoughts and my folly. During the conversation I repeated to you, I felt no difficulty in telling him all I did, and was only conscious at the moment of his utter inability to excuse or defend his conduct. But being with him again I was as conscious as ever of his charm. Knowing all I did about him, knowing that everything in him should make me hate and despise him, I was again fascinated. I have no intention of excusing myself; I know the feeling was wrong, wicked, that it was made up of vanity or something worse, but there it was and I could not help it. I cannot analyse all my sensations; they are not all vanity, so I suppose they are physical, but again I say I am not conscious of any defined physical feeling or of the smallest temptation to evil. But supposing he had again made efforts to win me, and I had been forced into private talks with him, should I have kept to my resolution of scorning his attentions? and when I put the question I feel very doubtful of the answer. I cannot say that I never looked at him, for I did. He treated me with indifference, his vanity was wounded, and he wished to pique me, but from his looks I know he is not indifferent to me, and I know that I could win him back if I tried. If not in looks at any rate in thought I have been wrong and am wrong still. You will not blame me, I blame myself. I know every argument you could use; I use them myself again and again, but these feelings are not to be overcome by reason but only by patience.

You would think that a man, inordinately vain, inconsiderate, and profligate, must be universally hated, and yet I suppose Blunt has numberless devoted slaves. Lady Anne is one, Judith another, and many, many others who suffer from his tyranny and yet kiss his feet. Human nature is very

strange. Judith says he has not the smallest consideration
for her or anyone else, and yet I am sure the kindest father
that ever lived never had a more devoted daughter.

Mother said to me today as we were coming away, "Did
you thank Blunt when you said goodbye to him?" "No," I
replied, "what was I to thank him for?" "Oh!" she said,
"for his kindness in letting you hunt, and for all the trouble
he has taken to make you happy, and besides he was so
gushing to you all the time." Gushing he certainly was not.
I thought, if Mother did but know how little I have to thank
him for. She now takes the line that I have been rather
neglectful of him, and should have been more cordial, which
is a proof that my conduct in public was markedly changed.

The Danes, November 7

Your letter of today is another proof of your endless and
wonderful goodness to me. I cannot thank you for your
patience and tenderness with me; the grateful, devoted love
of my whole heart is the only return I can make you. It is
wonderful that you can be so patient with me in spite of
everything. If you could but know the burning shame with
which I tell you of my weakness, or rather of my sin, for sin
it is. Directly I am away from him and can think everything
over once more in peace, I cannot in any way account for the
fascination, and wonder how I can be so foolish, so blind, so
wicked, as to care for him at all. If I kept back from you the
extent of my infatuation and pretended an indifference which
I did not feel, you could not help me, but at the same time
when I have written you an account of my feelings, I say to
myself, "What must he think of me? Knowing all that I am,
is it possible that he can love me still? If I could but keep   .
back the extent of my wickedness." And then I get your
answer which assures me beyond all doubt that bad as I am
you can still love me. The only thing left is to fight against
my feelings with all my might. Religion, virtue, reason,
nothing seems to have power over them.

This one subject so entirely fills my mind that I am
forgetful of every other duty. I am cross and selfish to Mother,
and never seem to do a single thing I ought. I feel altogether

to have sunk so low that I wonder whether I shall ever rise again. Your love is my one hope and strength and joy, and while I have that I will fight against my sins without wavering.

Booton Rectory, November 9

Your letter yesterday brought many tears to my eyes from the way you speak both of yourself and me, and it is the same today. I should have been right glad to have spoken all that I have in me of love and praise, for I have heaps of both for you, but a succession of interruptions only allows me to jot down this hasty line or two. But knowing that the love and praise are in me, and are silently bestowed upon you, you can wait for the rest, my dearest darling.

The Danes, November 9

Every fresh thought increases my shame for what I have done. Had I been told last year that I should have been placed in this position I should not have believed it. What distresses me is to think that on the very first occasion he kissed my hand I was horrified, shocked, indignant, and at that moment I genuinely detested him. I had been fond of him as a kind of playmate, and when he revealed himself to me under a new aspect I was revolted. It is sad to think how soon this right feeling wore off, and when he came to kiss, not only my hand but my face, I no longer felt myself outraged. It is a very painful thought. Had I gone all lengths with him I could not be more ashamed of myself or feel more guilty than I do.

The Danes, November 11

Your yesterday's note was so full of love that I think that I can feed on it for another day. I want to tell you all I feel in return for your goodness, your tenderness, your patience with me, and not one word will come. You must be content to know that all I am capable of feeling of love and gratitude I feel for you. No outward act of homage could express my feelings. To kneel and kiss your feet which I do in spirit, is but a feeble way of telling you my thoughts.

I had a long letter yesterday from Con on the subject, and amongst other things she says this, "I will hide nothing that strikes me from you. I think it very unfortunate that Judith, your greatest friend, should be his daughter and that she goes abroad with him. However, even I could not recommend your abandoning this really precious friendship, and I know that you would not even hear of it. But it will make your work harder. I can't help thinking that *some* of the charm (if only a little) she has for you is due, not to her being *Judith* but because she is the daughter of Blunt, lives near him, looks at his face every day, speaks to him of you and to you of him. Even if this conjecture has no truth in it, as regards your love for her, the fact that she is the only link between you and Blunt when he is away, and that she is very much of a link, will make it more difficult to put him out of your life and thoughts. Letters at least we can control. I think I should not ever allude to him even indirectly in your letters to her, unless something she has written makes it quite impossible not to do so."

I think all this is very true. With regard to my feelings towards Judith being influenced by the fact that she is his daughter, I think at first it did have something to do with it, but all the great love I feel for her is given her for herself quite apart from anything else.

The Danes, December 8

Mother and I are getting on pretty well, though I think Mother feels I am a poor substitute for Con,[1] and she tells me frequently what a help Con is to her and how much she misses her. I try my best to help her too, but I do not pretend to help her as Con does, for Con thinks of things to please her almost before Mother has had time to wish them for herself. What I find most difficult is to be genial. Mother takes no interest whatever in my interests and only crushes them if I bring them up, and try as I will I cannot find anything that interests her, so we are almost reduced to silence. I do really try, but I find it is very hard. However, I know that often I snub her when she is wishing to talk, so

---

[1] Con had gone on a visit.

it is really as much my fault as hers, or more, because I can help it and she cannot. It is difficult to get on comfortably in a house if you cannot share any of your interests with the people in the house. If I tell Mother anything about botany she is fearfully bored and changes the subject, if I tell her I wish to make bread she says I am not to do so, if I talk to her about Judith she says Judith is a bad friend for me. I am scolded for the heavy way I walk and want of energy I show. I hate walking and can never walk energetically. When I am by myself I run, and if I pass a gate I try to vault as Judith has shown me how. This is all better exercise than a walk and amuses me into the bargain, but I cannot do it when I am with Mother, as she says I am unkind to leave her if I run, and if I suggest vaulting she says I am much too big to behave like a child. But you know the difficulties as well as I do, and we have talked them over scores of times, and it is useless for me to repeat myself. I do not mean to complain, because we long ago settled that the trials were trials, and as Mother cannot change, my duty is to be patient. All that I have been saying sounds impatient, but it is only a passing feeling and I try to control it.

Mother was dreadfully upset by Professor Tyndall's death, and now this morning there are the details in the papers that his wife gave him by mistake an overdose of chloral. Mother has also had a broken-hearted letter from Mrs. Tyndall with these words, "Darling friend, is this not more than human heart *can* bear! to have *done* it myself! His Louisa." I think it is the most terribly tragic thing one can imagine. Fancy the poor woman's feelings when she realized what she had done. It is awful to think of. Poor woman! I suppose it was a most painless death, and though it seems as if it might have been different but for the mistake, I always think we die at the appointed time, and things are not really accidents. However, no thoughts can make it less dreadful for the poor wife. We heard that the day before yesterday there were placards all over London with "Professor Tyndall poisoned by his wife." It seems too dreadful, but no one reading the papers could feel anything but the deepest pity and compassion for her.

Booton Rectory, December 9

I knew Tyndall pretty well some forty-five years ago. He was an amiable man, very anxious for fame, and working hard for it. His powers were not great, but he did well what he undertook, which was to give popular lectures on the first elements of Natural Philosophy. The manner of his death is a fearful calamity for his poor wife. With little blame and perhaps none to herself she will be torn with self-reproaches for many a long day. Some fifty years ago I was at the house of a clergyman in Somersetshire, who a little before had been taken ill in the night. His wife fetched some medicine from her closet which turned out to be a poisonous mixture for cleaning plate. He is still living, but nearly died from the poisonous dose. A clergyman who was present with me as he related the circumstances said, "I suppose she gave it you by mistake," and he drily answered, "I hope so."

The Danes, December 15

I hoped last night that being alone together (Mother is in London) Con would be sociable, and that we should have a pleasant evening. But no, of course she must read the novels she is to review, and though not in words, yet by her looks she requested me not to talk to her, and the evening was passed in gloomy silence. She relaxed so far as to talk to me during dinner, but I was sure she was wishing to read. She has grown perfectly unbearable, there is no other word for it, since she took to reviewing. She is at present reading two novels, three volumes each, to be reviewed for the *National Review*, and last night arrived *sixteen* volumes she is to read and write upon for the *Saturday*, and having done these sixteen more will be sent. She reads on an average one volume a day and sometimes more. Is life worth living on these terms? I should say certainly not. I cannot imagine a worse Purgatory. It makes my head ache to see Con reading reading all day. Betty seems to think it is a far more intellectual employment than darning stockings, and says that for that reason Con should be encouraged in it. If she lived with Con she would not say so. While you are darning stockings, your mind is at least free, and your thoughts may be on the

18

grandest subjects. Also you can talk and be agreeable while darning. But surely there can be nothing intellectual in passing your whole day and most of the night in the study of trashy words, which prevent all thought upon higher subjects. I can imagine nothing more intellectually lowering, not to mention that as a companion she becomes intolerable. If she sits in the same room you may not speak to her, and generally she sits alone. I sometimes feel positively wild with rage it maddens me so.

Booton Rectory, December 16

The effect of an occupation upon a person's pleasantness and usefulness in the family in which she lives is a very important element. The effect of it upon herself is obviously of the first importance also. You justly test the novel reading and reviewing by both these circumstances, and by both the function is condemned. Nobody, however able, could give himself up to the pursuit of reading drivel day by day with scarce any intermission and not lower his intellect to the same level. As you justly remark, darning is exempt from the objection of interfering either with thought or sociality. I value very much these light mechanical pursuits. They have an interest of their own and help the mind instead of degrading it.

I remarked to Lord Salisbury when we were standing before a large collection of scientific works in the library at Longleat that I believed there was not a single one that anybody would read now, and he said, "No, for they are the history of *error*!" However, happily facts remain, but science, or what is called such, is largely made up of hypotheses, theories, or by whatever other name you may like to call the conjectures ambitious men desire to pass off for discoveries, and it is these which are superseded by fresh comers who refute the old guesses and substitute equally baseless guesses of their own. You, with your sections and your microscope, are on safe ground.

The Danes, December 16

Con was telling me yesterday of a discussion which took place while she was in London, on the subject of the independence of girls. Mrs. Horner and Miss Grant Duff were the chief talkers. Miss Grant Duff thinks no limit should be put on the independence of girls, and that it is ridiculous prudery not to allow girls to come home from parties at night alone in a brougham with a man. At the same time she says that she could not sit in the same room with a man who had been guilty of kissing a girl. Did you ever hear such rubbish? They then quoted an instance of what had happened somewhere. A young lady was at a party in a house a few doors off her own. The evening was so wet she could not walk home, and a young man possessing a brougham offered to take her in his carriage and drop her at her house. She accepted his offer, and the man, as I think, most tactfully and delicately, himself got on the box. Mrs. Horner and Miss Grant Duff both thought that his behaviour was positively *disgusting*, as implying that the girl would suspect him of bad motives if he got in the carriage with her. I should like to shake that man's hand. Con says, "Call the convention which obliged him to do it disgusting if you like, but his conduct was most honourable." I do not even call the convention disgusting, but approve of it. Since you have opened my eyes to so many things, and shown me more of the baseness and audacity of men, and shown me moreover how many profligates are in the world, my ideas on the independence of girls have much changed. If they knew all I do, they are as safe as any woman ever could be, and I should imagine their feelings would be what mine now are, and desire to avoid the possibility of harm. As men will take advantage of *any* opportunity, the only safeguard is to give them *no* opportunity. I am quite coming round to the parent's side. Only I say that in this as in everything else concealment is what does harm. To keep a girl very strictly and give her no reasons for so doing is cruel. Explain *everything* to her, and the girl will herself take the necessary precautions, and this seems to me the only right and possible way. Give a girl liberty but teach her to make a right use of it. Don't you think this is the proper way to treat girls? Knowing all I now do, I perfectly understand a mother's feelings. I also understand how many girls who wish for independence are all the other way as soon as they are married. They then realize the awful dangers.

Booton Rectory, December 18

The way to judge society rules is to generalize them; for what society allows to some it must allow to all within its own circle. Suppose it then the rule that a young man, or if you please a middle-aged man, should take a young woman in his brougham at night, no third person being present, can it be taken for granted that the man will always behave with perfect propriety? The women who are simple enough to think it are not fit to be trusted alone at night with men in broughams. I should suspect that those who argued for the arrangement were, for the most part, the reverse of simple, and as eager for the opportunity as the laxer class of men. I think with you that the gentleman who took his place on the box showed his refinement of feeling, showed it to such an extent that the girl, when he opened the door to let her out, would have been almost, if not quite, warranted in kissing him to show her sense of his delicacy. I am thankful that the course of events enabled me to show you how little men in the lump are to be trusted, and the amazing extent to which they abuse the smallest openings for licence. It is nothing that many men would far rather die than be guilty of the least outrage to a woman when you are making rules for mankind at large, since you cannot part off the honourable from the dishonourable, or tell in a multitude of cases which is which. And further this also is clear, that when there is so much at stake the social rules should lean to the side of safety.

Chapter Fourteen

As usual there are none of my letters during the first few months of this year (1894). But my state of mind may be gathered from the following entry in my diary, which shows how much my attitude to life had changed. I no longer found consolation and inspiration in reading the Bible, and my interest in cryptogams and phanerogams gradually declined.

"I think we begin life very near to God, with a real sense of His presence. The world does not yet mean much to us, and God means everything. In our childhood we have very little real communion with our fellow creatures and we draw entirely upon the spiritual side of our nature and live in a world of idealism and imagination. We judge ourselves severely because we have a high standard to go by, which is good, but it leads inevitably to harsh judgments of other people, and to a great narrow-mindedness. We live in an atmosphere which although pure is entirely self-made and we have neither pity nor sympathy with those who live for the world only. But suddenly there comes an age when the spiritual and ideal world no longer fills our minds entirely. There grows up in us the craving for human love and sympathy, and from a stern indifference we suddenly change to a yearning love for all human beings, the longing for a love which is substantial and real. And with this love our minds open and we begin to find excuses for the faults of others, Love sees only virtue, and love only wishes to serve. Perhaps this is the finest time of life, while we are still stern with ourselves and tender with others. But of necessity the reality of life and love draws our thoughts from the ideal and spiritual world. It seems at first like a falling away from God, until we remember that we are meant to serve Him, through our fellow creatures, and the years of communion with Him were intended to fit us for the service of mankind. But as no human things are perfect, so we find that life is not what we had hoped. We do not wonder much that the 'whole creation groaneth and travaileth in pain' until the pain begins to touch ourselves. There is the pain of death, but oh, how far greater is the pain of living. For death there is a cause which we can understand, a remedy which we may believe in and hope for. But for the infinite pain of life, what reason? what cause? what cure? That sin should bring its own curse and punishment we can understand. But the mystery of life and its burden is the sorrow and the pain which fall upon the innocent, the crushing of our noblest hopes and ambitions, the ruin of love, the mockery of hope. Love at least, one would think, should be free of pain. When two lives are so merged in each other that each only lives for the blessing and the good of the other, when every thought of self is forgotten, it would seem that the perfection of good is reached, that the human, through Love, almost attains to the divine—and then comes the misery no human wisdom can explain. It seems as if a law went forth and said, 'Because you love so that each completes the other's being, because through your love you are lifted up to all goodness, because you have become necessary to each other, you shall be divided and separated, your love must be overcome, the good in you must be trampled down. What is dearer than life and self shall be torn from you, and a cloud of black, bitter, hopeless despair drawn over your sun. Live your life alone, because another has become necessary to you.' What comfort is there for this misery, what hope, what reason? It is said that in another world you will be united. Love wants to share sorrow and pain and live, and in the world beyond we are to hope there will be no pain.

There are moments when the whole world seems to ring with mocking laughter at one's pain, and there is no hope, none—in time or Eternity. We need to have a strong, great faith to live.''

The three letters of his Rev's which follow give a good picture of him and his life at Booton:

Booton Rectory, January 11

Today I have had an old family Bible given to me with the entry of my grandfather's children on the blank page. They were twenty-six in number, and now after Fountain there is not a male representative of the family in the direct male line.[1] One of our late visitors, a widow, had eighteen children, all by the same husband. My grandfather was twice married and only seventeen of the children were by the second wife, enough, though, to satisfy even you.

Booton Rectory, March 8

I went this morning to buy some wallpaper at Reepham for papering a cottage. It is sold in what are called pieces, each piece being 12 yards long and 2 feet wide. I selected what I took to be the prettiest and costliest pattern, and asked the price. Twopence-halfpenny a piece. The cheapness of some things astounds me. Here are 12 yards of a handsome flowered fabric, cost of material, cost of workmanship, profit of manufacturer, profit of wholesale dealer, profit of retail dealer, carriage, etc., and all for 2½d. I bought one piece as a sample to ascertain whether the cottager approved of it, and the shopman wrapped it up in a large sheet of paper that was alone worth the money to my eyes.

Forster used to tell how Macready, the actor, went into the shop of one Moon, a stationer and print-seller, to buy a quire of note-paper, and before he came out had been persuaded to buy print after print to the amount of £1,200. Something like this happens to me in cottages. A newly-married woman, with a charming baby in her arms, complains of the draught from a door. I examine it and say I will send a carpenter to set it to rights. Having got her desire with respect to one door, she begins on a second, which she says is as bad, and then proceeds to a third. I promise that all the doors shall be made air-tight, upon which she calls my attention to the walls of the sitting-room, and tells me that she is ashamed to let her friends come and see her until they are repapered. I agree to the papering, and immediately she invites me to walk upstairs, and let my own eyes convince me that the bedrooms need papering even more than the

---

[1] Fountain had no children.

sitting-room. I assent to this also, and finding that she gets her way at every stage she boldly proceeds to the fabric and suggests that the gable end being damp had better be rebuilt. I promise the evil shall be rectified, and fly before she can introduce her next demand. This was yesterday's work, and today I have begun to redeem my pledges, which was how I learnt that 12 yards of very attractive-looking paper could be bought for 2½d.

Booton Rectory, March 28

I have for some years wished to buy a mangle for parish use. To iron everything, big sheets and tablecloths, as well as small miscellanies, is weary work for the poor mothers. But suppose a mangle, and who was to have charge of it, and what order could be kept when twenty women were clamouring for it at the same moment? It seemed that a mangle in common would be a source of endless dissention, worse than the toil of ironing. However, I have ventured at last to try the experiment. I have bought what is reputed to be the best mangle going, and myself and William the carpenter have set it up in the village this very day. Nobody knew it was coming, and the villagers look at it with equal surprise and admiration, and declare that they would not think of such a thing as quarrelling over it, but will arrange among themselves the order of using it, and will be thankful and amicable. I have my misgivings, still I am glad I have taken courage and given them the chance of getting some good out of it. We tested its capabilities by mangling a tablecloth (the work of a minute) and comparing it with a well-ironed duplicate, and the mangled specimen had a hollow victory, to the exceeding delight of the assembled community.

During the winter months when the Blunts went to Egypt my mind grew calmer and I was able to settle down to my ordinary pursuits. But with the spring they returned and so did my difficulties. They were increased by my growing friendship with Judith. We corresponded daily and saw each other constantly, and although her father was not often present at our meetings, nevertheless he was always there in the background and I was liable to run into him at any moment. In this way his attraction for me was kept alive. It would, of course, have been better if I could have confided everything to my mother, but I was sure that she would have blamed me far more than Blunt and she might also have tried to stop my friendship with Judith. In the end I did tell her that Blunt was inclined to flirt with me and that I wished to avoid him as much as possible.

My first letter this year was on May 17th, telling of a visit of Blunt's to The Danes. I was staying with the Derbys and write from there.

Fairhill, Tunbridge, May 17

I think the Blunt visit went off satisfactorily. Con assured me my outward behaviour was just what it should be, and Mother said to her how I had changed my manner to Blunt. I talked with him in an easy and friendly way. I was several times left alone with him. He sat by me in the garden in the morning and we were repeatedly left alone in the drawing-room. During these times I felt his eyes fixed upon me steadily, but I kept mine on my work and never once let my eyes meet his gaze. I also kept the conversation to general subjects. Had I returned his looks or appeared conscious of them, he would immediately have ventured on the old style of talk. On saying goodbye to him yesterday I gave him my hand, which he kept and pressed, but I abruptly withdrew it and turned away from him. He talks to me with his eyes more than in any other way, and if I answer with mine, they tell him what my lips deny. Therefore I studiously avoided meeting his eyes, and I found this easy. Last year the effort of appearing indifferent when I felt his eyes upon me was greater than I could bear. This year I easily avoided him. Also last year when he pressed my hand I insensibly returned the pressure. This time I found it easy to pull my hand away. When I think of this I hope I have nothing with which to reproach myself, and yet I do for this reason: I am still terribly sensible of his charm and feel too much pleasure in his presence. I hate and despise myself and try to hate and despise him and I do try very, very hard to eradicate the old affection from my heart, but the feeling is still there and I do

not see how I can help it, though I can fight against it. What
I cannot do is to be stiff and cold. I felt the immense benefit
of my conversation with Mother, for he was anxious to go up
to London by the same train as mine, and on Tuesday there
was a question of my remaining at home instead of lunching
at Hatfield, when I should have had to entertain him for two
hours alone. In both these cases I appealed to Mother and
she arranged matters for me. I have promised you to avoid
him whenever I can and my promise I will faithfully keep.

The other day I wrote to Betty and told her of my talk
with Mother and at the same time begged her not to ask me
questions as to my feelings for Blunt and the result of our
meetings, as it only did harm to keep on discussing the
subject. She answered like an angel that it should be as I
wished, only begged me not to keep my feelings secret
from you, for it would only make me deceive myself. Of
course, I have not a single feeling in my nature that I ever
desired to keep secret from you, or that I could, for to tell
you my thoughts seems the same as thinking them. I lay bare
every feeling before you, although I do it with intense shame.

You know, without my saying, that I never desired him
for a moment in an evil relation; my love was pure and is
pure, and that I still care for him is not a proof that my
affection was evil but that it was good. My weakness brings
its own punishment. With my reason and my conscience I
am obliged to own him a villain, deserving of all contempt,
and my heart cries out: "May I not have one kind thought
of him, may I not see one virtue to love?" and the heart gets
the worst of it, for reason and conscience answer none. My
own Rev, let me still have your love and trust and I will go
on fighting hard against my own weakness.

Booton Rectory, May 19

From your earliest childhood onwards you were noted in
your family for your absolute truthfulness, and the virtue has
lost none of its virtue in you since. You have never favoured
yourself in anything you tell me. What I read in your letters
is exactly what I should find if I could read the thoughts as
they rise in your heart. And knowing this the account which

comes to me this morning from Fairhill rejoices me. You
have behaved bravely under circumstances to try you
severely. I could hardly have expected you to get through
situations so often repeated, and of such duration, without a
single step backwards. Your resolution is the more note-
worthy that you still have a sense of charm which, though
the evil never sleeps, may still be separate from the evil
intertwined with it. Feeling the charm it is harder for you to
defy and repel the evil, and you have done your duty splendidly in spite of difficulties. You take for granted I should
not desert you if you failed. Certainly I should do the reverse.
Love does not withdraw itself when most needed. But when
it is good or evil that is in question, I must be exultingly
grateful to and for you when the good prevails.

The reason I interpret your actions differently from what
some would do is because I know you better. I know you
better in a double sense. I have your account of yourself,
your acts and feelings, and have a certainty that your repre-
sentations to me are truth itself. Independent of this I have
a complete acquaintance with your disposition, and have an
assurance that with a craving for true love you have a
detestation of evil passion. My faith in you follows the facts
and is entire.

The petition which appeals most forcibly to my own needs
is "Lead us not into temptation, but deliver us from evil."
And if the temptation comes notwithstanding, there is no
more powerful preservative than to have this petition in our
hearts, and silently on our lips, supposing we are where it
cannot be openly spoken. Then the power of the Almighty
encompasses us, for our will seconds it, and without our will
there can be no virtue. We have to look to ourselves as well
as to the protecting might of the Redeemer. You know I do
not say this mistrusting you, but only to help you.

The letters from me to which the following are answers
must have been destroyed:

Booton Rectory, June 12

Bless you for your honest, truthful letter. It is the greatest
proof you could give me how much you are a friend to me,

and how fully you are convinced that I am, heart and mind, a friend to you.

I believe the situation may be summed up in a sentence. You would not willingly afford him an opportunity but if an opportunity occurs you are lost. This is a momentous change from the former state of things. In circumstances such as might easily occur you would be in his power, and he knows it. The change in your feelings will have shown itself in ways unconscious to yourself, and will be super-abundantly manifest to a practised profligate like him. His very language to you, his open proposals, since you keep on friendly terms with him notwithstanding, tell him that he has only to persevere and you will be an easy victim. That you do not wish for the catastrophe is but a small protection, since it would cease to be any protection at all when the catastrophe was possible. It is plain that your sole safety is in breaking with him. You ought not to stay at Crabbet at all, for there must be risks in a visit at his own house, nor be alone with him for an instant anywhere, nor keep up the least pretence of friendship or cordiality with him. His whole design towards you is that of a demon. Consider what you are in yourself, a lady in the most cultivated sphere of society, in the first bloom of youth and charm; consider his relation to your family, and his obligations to them; consider the awful and undying misery he would entail upon them— upon mother, sisters, brothers; consider that he would degrade you to a condition that would bring the hiss of the world upon you, that he would consign you to infamy, and that your entire life would be blasted and filled with self-reproach and untold woes; consider that all this, and more, is as well known to him as to you, and that the knowledge does not divert him for an instant from his purpose, but that year by year he steadily continues bent upon effecting your ruin, and that the whole of his pretended affection has no other object but to accomplish it; consider these things and you will feel that you might as well ally yourself with Satan in person as to keep up intercourse with him. His mere attentions, meaning what they do, are an intolerable insult to you, and when you realize the truth of my feeble summary you can brace yourself up, by God's grace, if not by your own human will, to the conclusion that you ought to be in haste to shake off this foul fiend when by tampering with him and tolerating him you are sealing your own doom. The events of last year have not alienated you from him. You have been drawn closer to him. Let the intercourse continue and you are undone. He sees this and is simply watching for the moment that will enable him to take possession of his conquest.

No; I do not think hardly of you. In some respects you showed your self-control and your higher instincts in a praiseworthy manner. But your efforts are incomplete because you have a divided mind. This is the reason why I say that your only security is in avoiding his society. Away from him you can muster up resolution to refuse an invitation to Crabbet, and to dinners and teas. In his presence your resolution is imperfect. You are pulled contrary ways, and it is he that will decide for you which way is to predominate by taking the matter into his own hands. There is only one safe course, as it seems to me, that gives you even a chance of escape.

It is a disadvantage of society life that it breaks in upon the intercourse with Heaven. It is very difficult with the jaded feelings that heartless, empty parties engender to sit down to read the Bible, or to kneel down to pray and in thought to realize the presence of Father, Son and Holy Ghost. Intermitted these aids are lost to us. At The Danes you will have them without abatement, and it is under divine teachings and promptings that you should set yourself to form your final determination in regard to all your relations with your tempter, who is one of the basest of men. A viler seduction was never planned.

My most darling Emmie, you are endlessly good to me. The confidence you give me is of itself sufficient to touch every tender feeling within me. For you I have nothing but affection upon affection, and you will see in what I write only one desire—that of guarding you from the most terrible tragedy which could befall you.

Booton Rectory, June 14

I entirely approve of your projected letter to My Lady. Put as strongly as you feel you can the need you have to be protected from his love-making. It is fearful to think how in a minute or two a woman may be plunged into unutterable wretchedness for life, and this in general proceeds from the fact that people persuade themselves that they need not take any extreme precautions. Thus they tread the brink of the precipice till the moment when they suddenly sink from top to bottom. The ruin is instantaneous and it is complete. It is worth anything that you should be kept from this awful risk, and I am grateful to you for the honesty which calls forth the protection. No second motive could add to my zeal on your behalf. I have it from my zeal for yourself, and it is incapable of being rendered greater. But if the first motive failed of being complete I have a second in being under a bond to My Lady, for I have twice, and perhaps oftener, in reply to letters of hers pledged myself to your safety from the knowledge I had of you, which enabled me to say that absolute trust could be reposed in you. And my trust in your own nature is the same as ever. It is not altered in the smallest degree, though for the reasons which have intervened I no longer think it safe that you should owe your protection to yourself alone. And as this is your own opinion there is no need for another word.

I do not know to what letter from Betty the following refers:

Booton Rectory, June 15

I had Betty's letter this morning. I learn from it that both she and you are quite convinced that Blunt is not trying to seduce you. I wish that I could share the conviction. I have the entire belief to the contrary. We shall now drop him from our correspondence. Either I could not comment on anything you told me, or what I said would appear to you unfounded and extravagant; for there is the difference in our views between innocence, however imprudent, and enormous guilt. I could render you no service whatever, while the information while rousing my apprehensions would be pain to me. But happily you have Betty to go to. Her tenderness and zeal are unbounded, and she has ten times the means of serving and shielding you that I could ever possess. I expect she will not be long before she takes some precaution on your behalf. In every circumstance through the many months that I have advised you to the best of my light and experience you have been a model of the sweetest patience and forbearance, and I have the memory of it as a lasting tribute to your desire, your deep-seated desire, to keep yourself unspotted. No one, under what I consider to have been fierce temptation, could have manifested this virtue more completely than you. It was your unvarying aim. I had absolute trust in you from the first, and the whole course of events confirmed the justice of my faith in you. In taking final leave of the subject it is with beaming satisfaction that I set this down as the summary of my impressions from beginning to end.

The Danes, June 16

Your letter has made me abjectly miserable. I have made myself out to you a horrid ungrateful wretch, answering all your tender love and goodness to me by saying, "I can get on best without your advice." This is what I must seem to you from your letter. Oh, my own adored Rev, if you could but see my heart at this minute, and know how I love you more, a great deal more, than I have ever done, how my whole soul is yearning to show it to you. If I really had to cease telling you about Blunt, or pouring out my feelings to you, I should be lost. For one thing I could not do it. To have my heart and mind full of a subject and not communicate my thoughts to you would be an impossibility. I do not know what Betty said in her letter to you, but if she implied that Blunt had no intention of seducing me, she went much beyond my opinion. But I think that his proposals to me to go off with him were never intended seriously as an offer to elope with him, and it is necessary to know Blunt to understand the manner in which he said them. I believe I misled you on this point in my last letter. Also I do not believe that that is his one object with regard to me. I think he has a genuine fondness for me which is innocent, but in my presence, as he never attempts to control his feelings, passion gets the upper hand of him and then his desire to seduce me overcomes his better feelings. If he had no evil desires there would be no danger, and do you think I could make the sacrifice of his company, of going to Crabbet, which is one of my chief pleasures, unless I felt that I should be in fearful peril if I did? It is such pain to me that only fear of the worst would induce me to make the effort. All that I wished to do, and felt that Betty could do better than I could, is to say that Blunt is not altogether the villain you think him. He has behaved meanly, dishonourably to me, but he is not entirely eaten up with animal passion, and there is a higher side to his nature which is very charming. He has the possibility of grand things in him, but he has allowed the lower side of his nature to conquer the higher, which makes him a man not to be trusted, but he has not been able to kill entirely the better side of his nature. I wanted you to realize this, not in any way to change your opinion of Blunt's untrustworthiness, but merely to show that there were things in him which justified my loving him still. If he was altogether the low and degraded creature you think him, my love for him, to exist at all, must be equally low and degraded, and it was this thought that made me so miserable. The reason why I wanted Betty to tell you these things was that, coming from me, you would naturally say, "She is blinded by her love," but coming from Betty, who is certainly not prejudiced in his favour, I thought you would believe it more.

If it was to spare you pain I would gladly agree never to mention Blunt again, but if for other reasons, seeing I agree with you as to the main facts, you will let me tell you my feelings still, and you will continue to show me what is my duty, won't you, my Rev? But for you I should never have strength to do my duty, and it is when I think you know all and I can feel behind me your approval, your love, that I have strength to do right. You have helped me to fight every battle of my life, do not desert me in this one, the hardest perhaps of all.

I wrote to Mother last night saying that I had just a word to say about Blunt—that as I had told her, he was inclined to be foolish over me, which might become a bore, but also I felt that he was an attractive man, and his liking for me naturally increased mine for him, and I felt that if I saw a great deal of him I might become too much attracted by him. That she was not to think that I was in love with him, only it was better not to play with one's feelings, and therefore I wished to be careful. That for all these reasons I wished to avoid him as much as possible and would she help me.

Booton Rectory, June 17

I have but an instant, which will suffice, for I am able to say without an atom of reservation, "Be at rest." I have no objection to make of your view of the case. As I misunderstood the matter from Betty's letter I could have been of no further service to you, for all my arguments to you would have been based upon suppositions which you yourself repudiated. I could no longer have urged them, and if I did they would have been futile. You will have seen, I am sure, from my whole letter that the supposed divergence of opinion did not diminish in the slightest degree my estimation of yourself, and whatever change there might have been, there could be none in that respect. Upon reflection I find that I have not another word to say on the momentous subject which has been troubling us. Your whole conduct shows you to be the same Emmie I have always known you to be— high-minded and resolute—and I have no other language for you than praise for the self-denying measures you have taken to secure yourself for the future. You have acted nobly.

The protection and blessing of Heaven is sure. Trust in that and you can go on peacefully day by day, leaving the morrow to the disposer of all things. My loving solicitude for you is greater than ever and in this is my rest.

The Danes, June 26

I am beginning to feel that unless I come to Booton soon, or have a visit in prospect, I shall commit suicide.

I was very depressed yesterday, I am very cheerful today. It seems strange why at one moment everything should look

19

dark and gloomy and the next all bright, and apparently no reason for either. Happily depression never lasts with me more than a day or two at most.

The country seems steeped in the peace of Heaven and its influence soothes and calms one's feelings agitated by the vanity and vexations of the world. It is not easy all at once to go back to worthy pursuits, to reading the Bible, to quiet thoughts and occupations, but it comes gradually, and when one has got back to them, the so-called pleasures of the world do indeed seem empty and worthless compared to them.

I never trouble myself as to whether I get on in society or not. Mother was complaining that I did not, and I was justifying myself to her and saying that all things considered I got on extremely well. I enjoy myself more or less wherever I go, and it does not trouble me much whether people like me or not. I have quite a sufficient number of friends not to trouble about the rest. I have no great intimacies, but society is not the place for becoming intimate, and it is not therefore my fault that I do not.

When I tell you that I want to marry, and that there is a blank in my life which will not be filled until I do, I know you understand me. Other people would conclude either that I wanted to satisfy my passions, or coveted a worldly position, or that I had other reasons people have for wishing to marry. I have only one, which you understand, the longing for a complete and soul-satisfying love. No other love can satisfy this instinctive longing, or I should be satisfied, for no one in the world has love in such abundance as I have, or such friends as you and Judith. But the mere fact alone that your lives are separate to mine shows that they cannot complete my life. I crave for a love which will be all and only mine, and which will be my life. I am content to wait if the love comes at last. For all reasons I am thankful it has not come before, and I know it would be better to wait some time longer. But at times I grow to think it will never come, and it is that depresses me. I think of myself as a good deal older than I really am, and it is only when I see someone else of my own age that I am conscious of how young I still am. I think to myself, when I am low, that year after year goes by and I am no nearer to it than I was before, but of course it is not a thing which comes gradually, but suddenly one day it happens.

The Danes, August 3

There seems but little time even here to read my Bible, and I cannot do it as I wish. It is impossible to read in scraps amidst interruptions, but my delight is this. A short time ago had I read for hours in perfect peace it would have been no pleasure to me and done me no good. When one's mind is filled with the worries and vexations of the world it is impossible to fix them on heaven. I read without taking in a word. Now I am so happy because if I only read for a few minutes, but a page, I am filled with the joy of what I read, I seem lifted into a higher world, and even when I stop reading and go about my other occupations, I can lift my mind into that higher world, and the peace of heaven seems to have entered once more into my life. And this is the state of mind which makes me happy, when I can lift my thoughts to heaven without a fierce struggle first to drive out the thoughts of earth.

The boys came home yesterday very flourishing and much grown. Vic is really now as tall as I am. We do not yet know what place they have taken in trials, but what is far more important is that Neville has got his colours for cricket and has great hopes that in two years' time he may be in the eleven.

Betty reported to me an intensely comic remark of Mother's, who said to her: "There are so many complications about going to Crabbet. Emily declares she will not go if Blunt is there, and I will not go if he is not." She is in reality bitterly disappointed that it has all come to nothing, and is dying to bring us together again. She told me she had talked to you a little about me, and asked you if you could not suggest a way to get me married! She then added: "I am sure you will have to change and soften down a lot before you fascinate men. They hate a great, strong, chaffing woman, and like a quiet, gentle, sentimental woman, who will make a submissive wife." I assured Mother I could be very sentimental if I tried. The conversation made me roar with laughter. She added: "To succeed you must try and like everyone. Betty always did." This is nice, considering how she used to complain of Betty's fastidiousness.

We were staying at Cromer and I write from there:

Marlborough House, Cromer, August 22

I was saying to Con this morning that I am beginning to feel so painfully conscious of my ignorance upon all subjects. Con crushingly replied: "Only now." But I have not realized it before and I do now, and it is very painful. I am generally feeling very depressed at myself because I do feel that I waste my life so. Day after day passes and I never improve myself in any one respect or do any good to anyone else. And my life being more or less empty I grow inactive and depressed, which makes me feel ill, and feeling ill makes me more than ever disinclined to do anything, and so it is a kind of vicious circle. I am sure the reason of this is that I have no settled employment or absorbing occupation. I had my botany and I have dropped it. I might take up a hundred other things and I do not. One day I have a wild craving to learn something and do some kind of work no matter what, I begin to do something, and at the end of a week I drop it. This is partly owing to the fact that I am naturally indolent, but chiefly the impossibility of doing things alone. Life becomes empty and desolate when there is no one to share it. No one in my family takes the smallest interest in what I do and my days are spent entirely alone, except when we go for constitutional walks and at meal times. I know you are interested in what I do, as in my botany, and this is a great help to me, but it is not the same as someone living with me. I do not care to do anything because no one else cares.

If I had the right sort of stuff in me I suppose I should have some employment and stick to it in spite of everything, but as it is I do nothing and I know nothing, and I think I am fast becoming an absolute idiot.

Back at The Danes I write:

September 5

Much as I love Neville he occasionally drives me absolutely wild by his utter selfishness. It is impossible to knock into his head that it is a duty ever to think of other people. I am sure it is the ruin of boys to have sisters, for a sister is always a slave. I sometimes sigh for a family of boys and girls that I may bring them up properly, the boys waiting upon the girls instead of the girls upon the boys.

Booton Rectory, September 6

Though a bright day I had strong evidence immediately before dinner of the change in temperature. Ann came to me and said in a solemn voice that alarmed me, "May I say something to you?" I thought she was going to ask me to elope with her, or to make some similar request embarrassing me to refuse and impossible to grant. I felt I was in a tremor, but assented, and here is the result: "May I go upstairs and get you a thicker coat? That Alpaca is not fit for you now, it is thin. I am certain you will catch cold and be ill. Do let me get you a proper coat." I was as warm as toast, and am very unwilling to part with the Alpaca, which is light as gossamer and loose and suits my tastes every way, but I see that opinion will be against me, that I shall have to sacrifice my comfort and shall be told that it is for my own good. Advice to take care is thrown away. No one acts on it.

The bondage of sisters to brothers seems speculatively to be against nature, but in practice it falls in with nature, for it is universal. I reckon it myself to be a law of perverted nature only. To be grateful for loving service, to return it as lovingly, and to exact nothing appears to be the proper instinct.

Great talkers are great bores. They ought to be conscious of it from a hundred visible evidences. Yet they persist in the inane belief that they commend themselves by their tiresome chatter, and think you put out their light if you stop it. Poor deluded creatures. I take warning and pull up.

The Danes, September 7

I am delighted to hear that Ann has induced you to take to a warm coat. Being light as gossamer is scarcely an advantage in this weather. I have taken to all my winter clothes and feel much happier in consequence. We have also taken to fires in the day-time, which makes life more bearable. If you took as much care of youself as I did I should be perfectly satisfied.

Neville is painting a portrait of me while I write, which is an exceedingly painful operation for me, for he has put me into such a position that I can only see my paper by squinting, and he swears horribly at me if I move so much as an eyelid. He has also tried to rearrange my hair, which is anything but pleasant. Even his remarks about my looks are anything but flattering; he has just said that my nose would do for a lighthouse on a cliff, and that he shall send my portrait to the British Museum when finished, as a representation of the missing link. I think my only revenge will be to draw him afterwards.

The Danes, September 12

Family conversations on whatever subjects generally consist of arguments, for as no two members of the family ever entertain the same opinion it is impossible to agree. But when the arguments are carried on amicably they are enjoyable. They are hardly instructive, for we all talk at once and only benefit by the sound of our own voices. Mother always refuses to discuss any subject, for directly she is getting the worst of it, which is generally, she leaves the room, saying, "I never argue—you will know better some day."

Booton Rectory, October 25

I said the other day to a man of my own years, "You don't look your age," and he answered, "No, perhaps not, but I feel it." And that is the case with all old fellows, even if those who, in their ambition to appear young, pretend not to feel it. In busy times you are doubly conscious of it, and I sometimes wish that measles were less catching and patients fewer, that proper church roofs were less massive and the

erection of them less tedious, that bits of business did not
spring up in endless succession like weeds, and that England
was less populous and callers fewer. Fanny and I often praise
the wisdom of a Mr. Harman who was our neighbour when
we lived in Somersetshire. His habit was to go to bed as
winter came on and not get up again till spring was well
established. For it aggravates some of the occupations which
I have mentioned as unwelcome to decrepit age that they
involve wading through muddy roads under driving rain,
which youth reckons nothing, or congenial to superabundant
energy. You may guess how I have been using the morning
hours. All the same I have been free from care and abun-
dantly happy, and am hoping to hear this afternoon that in
spite of minor drawbacks you are richly happy too.

As usual there are no letters from me during the first few
months of the next year (1895). I have come to the conclusion that in the winter months when there was a fire handy
his Rev burnt my letters. In the summer months, having no
fire, he probably pushed them into a drawer, where they
remained to be returned to me after his death.

In May my mother, Con and I paid a visit to Florence.
Although I greatly enjoyed this, my first visit to Italy, the
letters in which I record my impressions are of very little
interest. I describe the scenery and the pictures as they
presented themselves to my very uneducated eye. I also
describe a very violent earthquake which left a far more
vivid impression upon my mind than the finest works of
the great masters. I was very indignant with his Rev, as he
did not take this frightening experience seriously enough.

In July of this year my brother-in-law, Gerald Balfour,
was appointed to the post of Chief Secretary of Ireland, and
my sister and her family moved to Dublin. His Rev writes
of this appointment:

Booton Rectory, July 10

All Ireland is opening to you. The news excited me tremendously. It gives Gerald just the start he needed. He will
fill the office splendidly and because of the difficulties success

will gain him great distinction. If the elections go in favour of the Government he will be in the Cabinet before the Ministry comes to an end. Betty will be a wonderful hostess. Poor Lady Cadogan will be nowhere. I shall enjoy seeing Betty presiding over her admiring guests, and if I were not on the wrong side of ninety I would make a voyage to Dublin for the sake of an evening with her. She will be worshipped. In bad hours say to yourself, "There is Dublin at hand and be merry."

During the winter I went over to Ireland to stay with the Balfours. Dolly Parry came with me. Only one incident of the visit stands out in my memory. Dolly was a very good actress, and with my sister's approval and connivance she and I dressed up as two elderly women come to beg for some charity. In this guise we were introduced into Gerald's room and managed to play up to our roles for some time while Gerald looked sterner and sterner. At some point he must have discovered who I was, but without for a moment changing his severe expression he suddenly clapped me on both cheeks and gave me a kiss which somehow seemed more of a rebuke than any words could convey.

I had evidently described a visit to Guinness's Brewery, for his Rev makes the following comment:

"The part of your Dublin experiences that I envy most is your visit to Guinness's Brewery. I used to think his porter the finest drink ever brewed and I should have asked to be served with a big tankard of it in its best state. It was not altogether to your credit that you were able to walk home, though unsteadily. I should have had to be carried."

As the years went by I think his Rev must have got very weary of the subject of Blunt, as he could not understand why, when once I had realized that Blunt was a villain, he could still have any attraction for me. At the same time he very much encouraged my friendship with Judith, not realizing perhaps that this also kept up my contact with her father. So gradually I ceased to write to him about a subject which still, however, occupied my mind.

In the summer of 1895 Judith and I were staying at the
Lockers' at Cromer, and I must have suggested to Blunt
that he should join us there for a short visit. I remember we
played the letter game in the evening and I sat beside him
and held his hand under the table. This, I suppose, convinced
him that I would now yield to him in every way. Happily I
locked my bedroom door, as I heard someone trying to open
it some time during the night. However, I got up to see him
off the next morning without revealing to him what I had
heard.

In the beginning of our relationship Judith seems to have
been quite unaware of what was going on between us, or
indeed of her father's infidelities. In the winter of this year,
however, she was to discover his real nature under circumstances which were very painful to them both. When I
realized, as I did in the following year, that she had found
him out, I told her of all that had passed between us, even
telling her of his attempted entry into my room at Cromer.
She took me off to see a priest, who gave me some good
advice, but before taking any step I wished also to consult his
Rev. Hence the following letter from me in May, from
London, followed by a visit to Booton.

                                          67, *Addison Road*
You must have forgotten my handwriting by this time,
it is so long since I have written to you. But though I have
not written I have thought of you all the same, and I simply
ache to hear something of you, which I hope to do from Betty
tomorrow. I am writing now to ask a favour. I greatly want
your help and advice. It is impossible to put into a letter,
and I should be so deeply grateful if you would let me come
to Booton, if only for one night. I am half afraid to ask it lest
you should feel unable to refuse me, and perhaps it would be a
worry and annoyance to Mrs. Elwin to have me there, and
to you. She may not feel up to having any guest yet,[1] and I
beg that you will tell me honestly and truly if this is the case.
Nothing is important enough to justify me worrying her or
you in any way. But supposing you had no objection it would
be an immense relief and satisfaction to me to talk out my

---

[1] She had been ill.

mind to you. Do not hope I am going to be married and want your help to make up my mind. It is the old matter.

I cannot tell you how I pine for the sight of your face once more. There has been a long silence, and, as it were, gap between us, which can only be bridged over by a meeting. My love for you is the same as it always was, but we have all the same slipped apart, and I want to get close to you again. My life has been a blank to you for the last year, and I want to fill up the blank. Perhaps you do not feel so interested in filling up the blank as I do. If I do not see you I shall write again soon and tell you something of my doings lately.

Later that month Judith, out of pure love and friendship for me, confronted her father, and when he tried to excuse himself at my expense, stating that all he had done was to try and make me happy, Judith then asked him why he had tried to get into my room at Cromer last summer, and found the door locked. He was staggered by this revelation, as he had no idea that I had heard him. He said that he would write a letter to Judith which she could show to me. In this statement he tried to excuse himself and lay all the blame on me. I replied that having seen it I never wanted to see him or speak to him again, and at last I meant it and kept to my resolution.

I write to his Rev on June 11th, 1896:

The Danes, June 11

I hope that the whole business is over at last, and in the best way it could possibly end. But there have been some very painful scenes for poor Judith to go through. She returned him his letter and my answer, and he came up on Monday and made an awful scene. He said that my conduct was monstrous in writing as I had done, and he could not believe it possible that I had so changed. Judith asked what use it was to discuss the matter further, and he said he must have it out or it would end in a quarrel between them. He refused to take any hints and put on an air of perfect innocence. Judith told him in plain terms what she thought of his chivalry, his morality, and his honour, but he pretended amazement and incredulity, said he would never have done anything against my wishes. He admitted candidly that had I encouraged him he would have done wrong with me, but it was to have been for my happiness. After this Judith said she was obliged to point out in plain unvarnished terms that I had always refused to have him in my bedroom. He said this was the case, which showed that there was nothing wrong in our friendship, as he would never have gone against my wishes. After this there was only one more card to play, and Judith asked him point-blank why he had tried to get into my room in the middle of the night at Cromer, and why he had found the door locked. Judith said she had never seen anyone so completely overcome with confusion. He stammered and stuttered but found nothing to say for himself. He never had any idea that I heard him, and mercifully I never told him, so that the blow was totally unexpected and left him speechless. All that he could say was that he was convinced that my seduction would have made me *permanently* happy. He assured Judith that there had never been any harm in my affection for him, and she replied that she knew that perfectly well, and the question was not my love for him but his for me. He insisted that she should read my letters to him, and was again somewhat overcome when she said by all means, that I had specially told her to do so. So on Tuesday morning she went to him, and was given all my letters to read. I am thankful to say she thought them much less incriminating than I had led her to expect, and told him they were just in the style I wrote to her, and much less affectionate than the letters I wrote to you, which seems to have annoyed him! He ended by begging Judith not to say anything which could make matters worse between us, and gave her his solemn promise never to try and see me again. He also wrote a letter for her to show me, in which he says that he never intended to reproach me for anything, as I had been an angel of goodness to him, and he knew that my love had been the pure love of a girl. More in this style and finally a promise to avoid me. Before Judith left she burst into tears, being overcome by the interview, and this happily had a

good effect on him, for he kissed her tenderly, and I hope the
quarrel between them is over. Judith will tell him that I
have seen his last letter, and I have told her to say that no
one is more anxious than I am to bury the past and forget it,
and I have no wish for any quarrel or bitterness to remain
between us, and there need be none if he keeps to his promise.
I have promised to make it easy for him, if he will help me.
If he wants to come to The Danes and see Mother, I have
asked him to tell Judith a few days beforehand that I may go
away. If he will behave well and tell her his plans and really
try not to see me, it will all be quite easy. And I think it
could not have ended in a better or a happier way. Goodness
knows I only want peace. I have loved him far too much
for it to make me happy to be unkind. And so I think the
matter is really over, and I will try and forget it. It has been
the centre of my life for three years, and I hardly know
whether it has given me most happiness or misery. At least
there is one good which has resulted from it, and a good
without any bad, and that is my increased friendship for
Judith.

Chapter Fifteen

My life now seemed to have come to a full stop. The love affair which had occupied so much of my thoughts and emotions was at an end. The gaieties of social life had lost their charm. I could not settle down happily to any of my old pursuits. I was unhappy in the present and had lost hope in the future. I therefore decided to take up some social work —that last resource of the desperate—and had been advised to go down to the women's branch of the Oxford House at Bethnal Green. I write to his Rev at the end of June, 1896:

"I have broken to Mother my plans for work in London and she took it like an angel and made no objection at all, said to me that no one was happy without some serious pursuit. The only thing she asked was that I would not do anything till the season was over and I had more time. In this I quite agree, as I feel much too tired to be up to any work. Betty has talked to Gwenny on the subject and she is strongly of your opinion that it is most important to begin with a good organization, and in London she thinks I probably should be wanted to undertake a girls' club one evening a week and amuse them. But I will try and arrange something when I am up with Betty in July.

"I was amused in talking over the matter with Con when she said to me: 'The harm to other people would be so small compared to the good such an interest would be to you.' I asked her to explain what harm she expected me to do, and she implied that all that kind of work was rather a sham and she personally thought it a mistake to go out of one's way to do good. Some people may make a sham of it; but that depends on the person, and as for going out of the way, who would do anything unless they went out of their way? Anyhow I know it is the only work which would really

interest me. I feel so far more sympathy with the poor than
with my own class. In society the more people pretend the
more they are liked, and it maddens me the way everyone is
tested by their intellect instead of by their character. Betty
may scold me till she is black in the face, but I shall never
love people for their intellect, when they have no other
qualities to recommend them."

24 Addison Road, Kensington, July 4

I had an interview the other morning with Miss Harrington, the head of St. Margaret's House [1] at Bethnal Green.
She is quite charming and most kind. Apparently one can
work with perfect freedom at what one likes best. There are
girls' clubs most evenings to superintend, district visiting to
do, and many other things. I am going to begin work on
Tuesday by going there for the night to see one of the clubs.
She says this particular club consists of factory girls and they
are extremely rough and require a good deal of management.
Their chief pleasure is dancing and talking. At most of the
factories they are not allowed to talk, and Miss H. says they
often tell her that their first thought on Tuesday morning is,
"Tonight we shall be able to talk." Miss Harrington goes
away soon and I do not feel I should like to stay there
without her, as I am too ignorant of what to do. I told her
that September would be the best time for me, and she says
I should be most useful then, as most people are away. I was
altogether delighted with the interview and liked her
enormously. The house is quite nice. I feel now that I have
really made a start in life and I need not trouble about my
future as I have an interest in the present. Mother has been
quite angelic and says I may go and stay there when I like
and she will pay all expenses. She has been too dear about it.

24 Addison Road, July 14

I must now tell you my experiences of Bethnal Green,
which I have not had time to do before. I am very thankful
that I did not stay longer than one night for the first time.

[1] Headquarters of the Oxford Mission.

It is a dreadful and depressing part of London, and I felt that
if I had remained an hour longer I should have gone mad.
Do not suppose from this that I have changed my mind in
any way about working there. I am more anxious than ever,
and I feel the organization is splendid and Miss Harrington
a most charming person. But when one is suddenly brought
into contact with a squalor and misery which one has never
fully realized before, the first impression is depressing. I was
sent around to investigate cases for the children's holiday. It
made me very shy, as I felt so impertinent asking these
inquisitive questions. Every woman was surrounded by about
seven dirty children and generally expecting another. They
were all most amiable to me and every one of them had most
perfect manners. They answered all my inquiries with the
greatest civility. In the evening there was a girls' club,
attended by about fifteen of the roughest factory girls. It was
very interesting, as they were all as free and easy as possible
and said whatever came into their heads. Many were beauties
in their way and all of them as sharp and bright in conversation as possible. There was none of the stiffness and forced
conversation of a London party. Their chief delight is in
dancing and nothing else pleased them. I was amazed to see
the beautiful way they danced. They were all graceful in their
movements and some of the steps they did were wonderful
to watch. How they learn I cannot think.

I am not going to stay there again till September, when
I shall go for a week or so. In the meanwhile I have promised
to look out cottages for the children to go to in the country,
and look after them while they are there. In this way I can
do something and make the children happy. I hear ten
children can be put up in our village.

But happily for me I never returned to Bethnal Green,
either to do good or to do harm. Instead I went on a visit
to the Webbs at Milford in Surrey and there met my fate.
That visit changed my life.

Mr. Webb—Bob to his friends—was the Squire of
Milford. He was a very stolid, ponderous, typical English
squire, very kind and good, possessing a dry sense of

humour. His wife, Barbara, was a sister of Sir Alfred Lyall (Indian administrator and minor poet). She was a woman who, without being beautiful, had immense charm, and her marriage in middle life to the somewhat pedestrian Bob Webb had come as a great surprise to her many friends. The Lyalls had been friends of my family in Indian days, and Barbara and my sister Betty remained on close terms of intimacy.

Among the near neighbours of the Webbs at Milford lived the Lutyens family at Thursley. Ned Lutyens, then beginning to make his name as a promising young architect, was a protégé of Mrs. Webb and at some time during the summer she had introduced him to me at a musical party in London. He always declared that he had fallen in love with me on that occasion because I looked so cross and unhappy and he resolved there and then to make me happy!

We met many times at dances during that summer. I found him an amusing but somewhat eccentric young man and a good dancer. He talked a great deal about his mother, said that he was assured of a place in Heaven because she, being so good, could have no other destination, and it would not be Heaven to her without him. I therefore assumed that his mother was a widow and he her only son. It was somewhat of a shock therefore when I later discovered that his father and seven brothers and three sisters were alive!

Ned had confided to Mrs. Webb his feelings for me and had obtained her promise to invite him to Milford should I ever come there on a visit. And on a visit I came in September. But at that moment I was more interested in Gerald Duckworth (founder of the publishing house of that name) and rather hoped he was interested in me. I had arranged to spend the Sunday following my arrival at Milford with Gerald and his family at Hindhead. Of this day's outing I write on September 20th to my mother, who was in waiting at Balmoral[1]:

Milford House

I have not seen Barbara yet, as she was bad yesterday after a long drive [2] and is not yet up. Bob is very kind and

[1] My mother had been appointed lady-in-waiting to Queen Victoria.
[2] She was seriously ill with cancer, from which she died the following summer.

nice and I find conversation quite easy. A Madame Vitelleschi is also staying here. She has told me all her family troubles and all her ailments, and exactly how much she perspires at night. I am very full of sympathy and get more details. She plays rather well and it is a change from conversation. I got up to breakfast with Mr. Webb at 8 this morning and it is now 9.30. The day is divine and will be perfect for my ride. I start at 11 and Mr. Gerald is going to meet me somewhere quite near here, so I shall not get lost. Mr. Lutyens arrives here this morning.

I continue my narrative next day:

"I had a perfectly heavenly day yesterday. Started from here at 11 (luckily twenty minutes earlier than I had intended). Mr. Gerald had given me a map and Mr. Webb directed me most clearly. There seemed to be only one possible road, and would you believe it, I lost my way! Went about two miles along a lovely common, no one in sight to ask my way. At last I came upon a solitary female, whom I nearly frightened out of her life by addressing. She was of course a stranger in these parts, as people always are when you want to know the way. I nearly cried with despair, when a cyclist came along behind me. I stopped him, asked the way, and found I was quite wrong, and then said to him, almost tearfully, "Would you allow me to show you this map?" I did, and explained where I had gone wrong, and then the dear kind man said, "Would you allow me to turn back and show you the way?" I nearly hugged him, and we turned and tore back to Milford. He being a regular scorcher I was afraid of not keeping up with him and we went like blue murder, as Neville would say! He then put me on to the right road and three minutes after I met Mr. Duckworth. It is only about five miles to Hindhead, but uphill all the way, and Mr. Gerald made me walk and rest several times, so we only got to the house at 1.30 in time for lunch. The whole family were there.[1] Stella looked lovely, and the two

---

[1] Mrs. Leslie Stephen had three children by a previous marriage, George, Stella, and Gerald Duckworth. There were also two Stephen daughters, Vanessa (married Clive Bell) and Virginia (married to Leonard Woolf).

20

half-sisters promise to be very pretty later on. Is Mr. Leslie
Stephen an idiot? He is quite deaf, which made me horribly
shy, and he never said a word at lunch, but groaned and
grunted and heavily sighed. . . . The rest is in my next
number, as I am going out bicycling with Mr. Lutyens."

I write again on September 22nd:
"I will now continue my history of Sunday [at Hindhead].
In the afternoon we all went out for a short walk to the tip
top of the hill, where the air was so fine it nearly blew one
to bits. There is a little path round the garden and they were
all racing round on bicycles with their feet up. The result
was a spill of course. Vanessa, the eldest of the Leslie
Stephens, came a tremendous cropper with the bicycle on
top of her. She was happily only bruised. Mr. Gerald rode
back with me and was very nice."

When I returned to Milford that evening I found that
Ned Lutyens had arrived in my absence. He did not allow
any grass to grow under his feet. After dinner he proposed
that he and I should bicycle to see a house he was rebuilding
for Mr. Webb in the neighbourhood, called Warren Lodge.
There was a full moon and by the light of that moon we set
forth on the first of our expeditions together. I little thought
that night that in the following year I should be honey-
mooning at Warren Lodge with the same young man! We
broke into the house through a window and wandered all
over it.

About this adventure and others which followed I write to
my mother on September 22nd:

Milford House, September 22

The whole household is overcome with our behaviour on
Sunday night. Vitelleschi said to Barbara: "I don't like these
goings on at all. It is quite different from the way you and I
were brought up!" Barbara assured her she thought it
scandalous and disreputable! Lord Tennyson,[1] who came

---
[1] Son of the poet.

over to lunch yesterday, was immensely amused at our adventure. But we were still madder yesterday evening. In the morning Mr. Lutyens took me to call on Miss Jekyll,[1] who lives about four miles from here. She is the most enchanting person and lives in the most fascinating cottage you ever saw. Mr. Lutyens calls her Bumps, and it is a very good name. She is very fat and stumpy, dresses rather like a man, little tiny eyes, very nearly blind, and big spectacles. She is simply fascinating. She lives in a little cottage [built by Mr. Lutyens] with a small kitchen and a parlour, and a big room which is her workshop. The big room is full of drawers and cupboards and everything is huddled together in the tidiest manner and yet all untidy. There is a huge old-fashioned fireplace, with chimney-corner seats and big blazing logs.

Well, when the rain came down yesterday we suddenly thought we would go and have a surprise dinner with Bumps. We spent the afternoon buying mutton chops, eggs, sponge cake, macaroons, almonds, and bulls'-eyes, and turned up about 6. Getting out of the carriage I of course dropped all the eggs and smashed them! We reeled into the house shrieking with laughter. Bumps has about six cats, three quite kittens, and they romped about the room.

Bumps bore the shock splendidly and was delighted to see us. We set to work to cook the chops and peel the almonds and make tipsy cake, and then we sat down to the best dinner I ever ate. After dinner we sat in the big ingle-nook and drank a variety of intoxicating liquors, brewed at home by Bumps, ending up with hot tumblers of elderberry wine, the most delicious stuff you ever drank. It was altogether the most heavenly evening you can imagine.

Mr. Lutyens has gone this morning but returns on Thursday.

So after those first hectic days Ned Lutyens returned to London and to work, while I remained at Milford to miss his gay company and to wish for his return.

In the meantime Barbara gave me some good advice about not encouraging Ned too much—"for," said she, "he is

[1] The celebrated expert on gardens.

inclined to be bumptious!" So on his next visit I showed much attention to a cousin of Barbara's who was also there, called Julian Spicer. We played the guitar together and sang songs and Ned was a little bit left out in the cold. Nevertheless we had some fun together, and I write again to my mother on September 26th:

"Mr. Lutyens came back yesterday morning and we went off on our wheels to see an old church at Compton and a new chapel being built by Mrs. Watts,[1] rather interesting but very odd. In the afternoon we made an expedition to Guildford, which is a delightful old town, and saw all the sights. We went another cycling excursion this morning and got wet through, which was unpleasant. Mr Lutyens has gone off to some work but returns for tea. It is delightful having him here and we have great fun together. Will you ask him to The Danes one day? I am sure he would come and he is so nice and very clever."

I was beginning to realize that he cared for me, and this belief was confirmed when after his next departure I received the following letter:

In the train from Frome to Paddington, October 17
My dear Lady Emily,

It is with your little pencil that I write. I felt wretched in the train leaving you this morning, and now how I regret—Bumps or no Bumps—that I did not have the courage to play truant to my work and stay by you, but then I should have broken away and you might have hated me.

I would have told you how I loved you. Would you have laughed? Except my love I have nothing to offer you. I am poor, unknown and little altogether.

My life's work would be yours, and I shall now work the more earnestly so that I may, in time, become more worthy of your dear self. All that I have is at your feet.

I love you ever so. I dare not ask anything of you. The little hope I have in me is so large a stake to lose that the very thought of it makes me feel ill and sick.

One word from you would turn my world to one great

---

[1] Wife of G. F. Watts, the painter.

sphere of happiness and I would become a man. Give me some chance to prove it.

Before I realized your name I loved you, and being with you at Milford House has only made it grow the more, so that my whole horizon is filled with and by you.

I am in a coupé at the end of the train. The receding landscape through the windows draws with quick perspective my very hope, even as I write. Everyone must love you, so that I can be only one of many others. I could write miles to you, but I dare not persuade you, and after all I cannot say more than that I love you, I love you.

Yours Ned Lutyens

To this I replied from Milford on October 19th:

Dear Mr. Lutyens

Your letter has touched me very much. Why did you think I should laugh? At present I can only say thank you for what you say to me. My mind is too uncertain for me to say more one way or another, and I can only ask you to wait and give me time to think it over. But whatever I settle I hope that you will believe that my interest in you and your work is very real and deep. Bumps is quite right in what she says. I do not want to be a frivolous influence in your life, but the reverse, and your work is what will always interest me most. No one will be more pleased than I am to hear that you are getting on and making a name for yourself, as I am quite sure you will in time.

Does my letter sound horrid? I hope not, but it would not be fair if I said more when I know so little at present what I feel.

Yours very sincerely,
Emily Lytton

6 *Gray's Inn Square, October* 20

Dear Lady Emily,

I felt so unworthy in all respects that laughter would have brought me no surprise. It is no frivolous influence that you have on me. Your influence is great and I know full well how good. If I frivol when with you, it is with the happiness of being with and near you.

That you should be kind is all that I could expect from what I know to be you, only I have so little to offer you— a small white house and my poor life. I always see you in that wee white house, with a red cabinet. It is not size that helps in life—so long as all one would have is there. How I would give that I might have your love. Your "one way or another" gives me one little gleam of hope. May I hold to this? It is enough for me to work for—for I have no heart to press you to do ought but what you would, and I will wait, only don't let it be long. If you marry, let it be some good man who would worship you as I do and would. I dare not say all I feel, it all seems so selfish, even the good you bring to the surface and make in me.

Bumps is lovable, only don't let her abuse me. She knows nothing of how much you are to me, and if she did even Bumps would see that you could make me man and give my work the serious touch it wants. Help me. Without you all seems dreariness, a hearth without a fire.

I can only pray God to bless you and give you of the best. Here I shudder, knowing how small a manner of thing I am.

I cannot write, I feel flat and the world about me flatter still.

I stand as on some drear little hill alone and desert round me. The lovely valley seems to rise and give me warmth and you. Then I wax strong and great and worthy of you, nothing there is between us and all seems beautiful. Then I realize, to wake and turn cold and bleak, and though the valley is still beautiful it is too far distant and I alone.

It is so hard to be righteously unselfish when I want so much, although I cannot say how well I wish you. What can I do?

Yours sincerely,

Ned Lutyens

The Danes, October 23

Dear Mr. Lutyens,

I have been thinking a great deal over your letter and have told my mother about it, and I feel that I ought to tell you at once that it is hopeless for you to think of me any more. You probably do not know that I have no money of my own, and you tell me that you have nothing but your love to offer. Under these circumstances you will feel yourself that it is hopeless to consider the matter any further. If I saw any hope I would give it you, but there is none. Mother says that she would rather we did not meet, or write or see each other again. It may seem hard but it is better so. You will feel this too. We have had some happy times together which we shall both like to remember.

I want to say something to you for the future if only I knew how. It is this. You have said that I could make you a man, and give your work the serious touch it wants. I may not help you in the way you want, but I should like to tell you how much I believe and trust in your power to become a distinguished man some day. I feel so sure you will if you only try your best, and put your whole life into your work. You have it in you to do great things, I am sure of it, if you will only believe in yourself as I believe in you. And when I hear that you are getting on and making your name known, I shall feel so proud to think you cared for me, and that I have been something in your life. I will pray God to bless you and give you strength to prove before all the world that I was right to put my faith in you.

All that I write seems so cold and horrid, but you will know I do not mean it so. I suffer in the thought that I have brought you only pain, but you will know how much against my will it was, and will forgive me. I shall hear of you sometimes from Mrs. Webb, great things I hope and believe.

I should like to hear from you just once again to know that you understand what I have said so badly, and that you will take comfort and courage, and go forth like a knight of old (as you said) and conquer a name and fortune for yourself. I ask it of you, though perhaps I have no right.

Goodbye and may God always bless you. It is the prayer of

Yours? (I cannot write "sincerely")

Emily Lytton

Munstead House, October 25

Dear Lady Emily,

I received your kind letter here last night. It already seems years ago.

I understand too well, and thank you for all you are to me. It never for one moment occurred to me whether you had money or not. I should have remembered only that I had none, but what I can make and save, but I forgot everything but that you existed.

I will try, if only for your sake, to obey Lady Lytton loyally. It is hard. I can't write . . .

If only, like that knight of old, I could have seen some hope, some "Grail." How I would fight!

I want no name, no fortune for myself, but I will, as you have asked it of me, and my prayer will be that I may win some deserved happiness.

May you never have the sorrow that is mine and may God keep and bless you. You must not suffer for me: that you should suffer makes it worse. I cannot bear that thought. There are things in this world which are inevitable and by these things man may prove himself man.

I will trust in the God you pray to.

Oh! to know you could have loved me so as to have remained

Yours ever,

Ned Lutyens

The Danes, October 28

Dear Mr. Lutyens,

Would it comfort and help you and give you the gleam of hope you need, to know I could have loved you, oh, so well? which means, I suppose, that I love you now. If it is wrong of me to have told you, God must forgive me. I could not bear that you should suffer all alone, and I thought it might make you happy to know that I too cared, and that I felt your pain, not merely out of kindness. I had not the strength to resist the happiness of making you happy.

I trust you not to ask more of me, but on the contrary to help me to be good and obedient to Mother's wishes, though it is very, very hard. The present must remain as it is, the future is in better hands than ours, and God is kind.

I dare not tie myself or you. We may both wish to change. If you could love someone instead of me, someone who could bring you more than I can, you would know that I should be the first to rejoice at what could bring you joy. You would feel the same for me, I know.

But should all be as it is now, come to me when you feel that you are man sufficient, and that like that knight of old you have proved your knighthood. For the present I trust you to be patient, and to keep as a secret in your heart the secret of mine.

I dare not speak of the future I can only trust. But if you will take comfort in the present, I shall feel that all has been right, and that I was not wrong to write this letter.

I will not say goodbye. Have hope and courage for my sake.

Yours,

Emily Lytton

Ned's reply came quickly:

16 *Onslow Square, October* 28, 12 *p.m.*

My darling, your letter brings me hope and great joy.

I fear no vow—I love you so—but you must not bind yourself. I will work and come to you without doubt.

Should you ever be in trouble you must turn to me—without fear or doubt.

God bless you. I feel so unworthy—there is much before me—pray for me.

I cannot—dare not write all that I would say to you. I must honour your own mother for your sweet sake, and God forbid that I should ever ask of you anything but what is right.

Only I want so to be near you. God bless my darling and keep all harm from her.

I have prayed so hard for your love and now I pray for more with courage—will you join me? My prayer would not have been answered if there was wrong in what you did.

I have seen the *Holiest* Grail and I can now go forth with great comfort. Pray that I may hold it.

How I shall work for *you*. How I look to the day I may come forward—and in the space of silence—do not forget me—I trust you as I trust God. Is this wicked? I don't mean it so.

Do you remember that we thought the world a flat place? I find it is round, quite round, and full of hope and blessing, with more yet to come. I must now go back to my shadow, but I know now what you have said and I am wondrous happy, knowing that light will come undimmed. I have hope, I have courage, and God will yet bless us.

I love to say "us" and I may say

Yours Ned

At the same time my mother wrote a letter to Mr. Lutyens which is very characteristic of Victorian tradition. It was impossible to know anyone who had not been formerly introduced!

The Danes, *October 29*

Dear Mr. Lutyens,

Emily has kindly and frankly told me of your meetings at Milford and of your writing to her after your last visit there. It has all taken me much by surprise, as of course you are quite unknown to me, and I cannot even remember having been introduced to you.

I feel it only right to tell you that Emily has nothing but a very small allowance which I give her, and even at my death will have only a small sum of settled capital which her father left her, and therefore I must beg you not further to seek Emily in any way, and try to overcome your kindly feelings for her. I had thought of asking you to come and see me in London, but as I have only these few words to say, I thought it would be less painful to both of us just to say it on paper.

Believe me, dear Mr. Lutyens,

Yours very truly,

Edith Lytton

Happily, "dear Mr. Lutyens" would not take "no" for an answer, and wrote back:

Munstead House, October 30

Dear Lady Lytton,

I must thank you for your kind and considerate letter.

I cannot alter my love for Lady Emily, but I understand full well how you wish well for her and I can say nothing against it.

I will be loyal in this. I should have remembered that I have practically nothing to offer, beyond the income I make of some £1,000 and the possibility of a life insurance, at present.

I do not see how else you could have written and I thank you sincerely for having written it so kindly.

If only I could have had some gleam of hope.

Yours very truly,

Edwin L. Lutyens

I naturally turned to his Rev for advice, and though none of my letters remain, his answers show the difficulties which had to be overcome and how they were finally surmounted.

Booton Rectory, October 22

The immense majority of weddings take place under circumstances less promising. Men ordinarily count upon reasonable *prospects*, which is all that the course of nature, that is the appointment of Providence, usually permits. If men waited till they had *made* their fortunes, few would marry under fifty or sixty, when they had better remain single. Mr. Lutyens has both income and prospects. He has already established himself. You have no cause to fall back upon the hackneyed line, "But love can hope where reason would despair." Reason may rationally hope upon the sober basis of ordinary experience. Look into things all round and you will find that *certainties* are not the rule of man's life.

I know you wish for my opinion, and I give it accordingly

without qualification upon the supposition that the facts are what you apprehend them to be. But it is not with me you have to deal, and you are already face to face with the usual difficulties, which must be natural or they would not be usual. I predict they will yield before long to patience and forbearance. They might equally yield to violence and defiance, but the gentle are the only right methods, and these require resolute self-control. The fervour of love will generate impatience, and unless you shut up feelings of exasperation within yourself by ever-watchful efforts you will discredit your better nature without advancing your cause.

Love in all its departments—heavenly, matrimonial, paternal, filial, the love of friend to friend, and neighbour to neighbour—is the crowning blessing of existence, and if you have attained to that form of it which is the consummation of domestic joy I shall congratulate you with my whole heart, even though marriage shall entail upon you the hardship of having to share with your husband and future encumbrances a beggarly twelve hundred a year, which is four times more than I ever cared for. I have nothing further to say today.

Here leaps into my mind a passage in a letter from Thackeray to a friend about to marry upon a fraction of the income you name: "Though my marriage was a wreck [because his wife became insane] I would do it over again, for behold, Love is the crown and completion of all earthly good. A man who is afraid of his fortune never deserved one." The very best and pleasantest house I ever knew in my life [his own] had but three hundred a year to keep it. And it was a house in London too, with the rent to pay.

I think marriage good both for man and woman, and the result of this opinion, if I had the ordering of matrimonial affairs, would probably be that the number of imprudent marriages would be enormously increased. My chief demand would be that the love should be deep, and promised to be lasting. I am a bad adviser. I have faith in your destiny, and on the next occasion you will not be asking me for imprudent advice, but for radiant congratulations.

I must have written back very despondently to explain the letter from his Rev, which follows:

Booton Rectory, October 31

You know the old saying, "To love and to be wise is not given to man," for all other qualities are extinguished by it. Never mind if the usual law has come true of you. You share the common fate. I will say no more about it, nor speak, of it to anyone, nor think about it myself. Bury the dead and begin afresh. This is the last word on the subject.

But happily this was not the last word. I suddenly decided to appeal to my uncle, Lord Loch, and to place all the circumstances before him. He was most kind and sympathetic and suggested to my mother that a life insurance policy might make up for Mr. Lutyens' lack of capital. I wrote to tell his Rev of this latest suggestion, to which he replied:

Booton Rectory, November 5

I think it a reasonable provision for marriage if, as you have £5,000, he insures his life for another £5,000. An over-heavy insurance is not desirable. The premium eats up too much of the income. It is better to take the chance of life and save.

The decision of the question does not belong to me. I can only say what would appear to me the rational course if I were arbiter, and it would be this. I should advise you to wait a year with a view to see whether further acquaintance confirmed the love, and whether Mr. L.'s business at the end of that period confirmed his present expectation. If both these questions were answered in the affirmative, then I should be for a marriage without further delay. It would be an engagement in the interval as regards the intercourse between you, but a provisional engagement from which either might recede. Objections may be made to this course or any other. In a practical way I think it is the mode of proceeding which will best reconcile all the momentous interests concerned.

Philip Hardwick, the architect, deferred marriage till he

had realized, as Murray used to say, £200,000, but I take
this to be an exaggeration. He used often to talk to me of his
wife and young children, and lament the impossibility of his
living to bring the children up to manhood and womanhood.
"I think I have done very well as regards my wife," he has
said to me, "but I married too late, too late." Let your
architect beware of repeating the error.

My sister Betty also greatly helped my cause by the
following kind and wise letter which she wrote to my mother
from Ireland:

Chief Secretary's Lodge, November 12

And now, darling, as it may be long before we meet I
think it best to keep silent no longer on this new crisis in
Emmy's life. Whatever may be the outcome of it all, I think
it is no use ignoring it. Let us face the fact. Lutyens has
proposed to her, is—from his letters—clearly in love with
her, and she believes herself to be wholeheartedly in love
with him.

He is a gentleman, he is four years older than she is, and
he has made a remarkable start in a profession which a
gentleman of ability may be proud to follow. That he has an
exceptional gift is evidenced by the fact that at twenty-six
with no social advantages at the outset he is already making
£1,000 a year at his profession. As to his means—he has no
capital. No more have half the professional men of the world,
no more has Neville, yet I hope he will not die a bachelor.
This means, however, that any provision for children must
be put by out of income, and this is of course a risk. But
between risk and imprudence I think there is a distinction to
be drawn. I have talked it all over with Gerald and he said if
you ever wished to have his opinion he would tell you that
the minimum he would advise you to ask, before marriage
was contemplated, would be an insurance out of income for
the amount of £10,000. But if this could be undertaken he
would not himself advise you to forbid the marriage on such
terms.

Now as to character. Barbara—who of course never in her
dreams contemplated such an event, but who has long hoped

he would marry a woman worthy of him, and who has talked
to me freely about him—Barbara has convinced me that he is
exceptionally pure-minded and honourable. I have seen
enough of him to believe this from my own observation and
I think him attractive and lovable. So far I think his defect in
my judgment has been a sort of frivolousness of talk which,
attractive in its way, seemed to indicate a sort of absence of
seriousness. But this may have been purely superficial and a
great genuine love would bring out all that is deep and
determined in his nature. Finally there is the great and far
the most important question—is their love of the highest and
most lasting kind? Now I think you could put this to the test.

If I were you I would send for him or write to him, let him
feel he has incurred a great responsibility in telling your
daughter of his love. Tell him straight out what are the
money conditions you would require before you would
consider marriage anything but wild imprudence, and tell
him that until those conditions are fulfilled you will trust to
his honour not to speak or write of love to Emmy or to seek
her except in so far as you suggest or as the society of which
they are both members naturally throws them together.
Personally I should be against forbidding them to meet
altogether, for this encourages the nourishing of an ideal
and if you are to test the truth of their love they had better
get to know each other better. To such conditions I believe
they would willingly submit and be grateful for the test it
would impose upon them. They are both very young and
waiting could do them no harm. Especially as I believe he
might be able in two years at longest to fulfil the conditions.
That the whole affair should be a distress and disappointment
to you I understand well. I don't pretend to think that Father
would be delighted about it. But after all, Grandfather did
not sympathize in *his* engagement, but he lived to bless it.
After all, a girl who leaves her family when she marries can
do little for it even if she married a millionaire. To marry a
gentleman in heart as well as birth, to love him passionately
and faithfully, and to give up all things to follow him through
life—that seems to me an ideal which can only bring honour
to any family that holds it.

Negotiations between my mother and Lord Loch and Ned continued throughout December, while I was in Ireland with Betty. Mother at first proposed that a year should elapse before an official engagement, and that during that time Ned and I should not meet or correspond. It is to this arrangement that his Rev refers in the following letter:

Booton Rectory, December 18

I got your letter yesterday morning and my impulse was to answer it out of hand, but had not the chance. I rejoice that matters have reached their present stage. You have now a future full of promise. It may be the fact that long engagements, or long probations without an engagement, are not desirable, but in the majority of cases they are inevitable. I myself was engaged for near three years, and the result has been fifty-eight years of unsurpassed married blessing. You are sharing the lot of the majority, and there is every reason to anticipate that the rather lengthy road will lead you to the same happy result which we of this household have attained. In my term of waiting I had the alleviation of unfettered correspondence and long periods of living in the same house as Fanny. Personally I think that long periods instead of prudential severance answer no other end in many cases than that of making two lovers uncomfortable and I wish you could have the same indulgences as to writing which I myself enjoyed, but your wisdom is to accept the situation which is made for you with cheerful submission, since you would only do harm by attempts to alter it. Very likely the course of events will favour you.

How can you best learn to be economical? Why, by never spending sixpence on anything you do not *want*. You may *wish* for a hundred things, but ask yourself at every turn, "Will life go on as prosperously without this and that—is it a necessity?" and the money which has hitherto flown about like chaff in a wind will lie snugly at the bottom of your pocket ready for an emergency.

How do I advise you to set about learning something of architecture? I answer at once, by consulting Mr. Lutyens. Probably the best method will be for him to take you to see particular buildings, also to his office where plans and designs are in progress and to lend you books with general instructions for using them. My Lady and Lord Loch must see the propriety or rather the necessity of this if you are to be a helpmate to your future husband.

I have not properly put into words my delight at the position of affairs. I believe the marriage to be as much settled, cautionary measures notwithstanding, as if you were returning from the altar, and I am radiant at the result.

Chapter Sixteen

THEN suddenly in January the clouds rolled away and my mother gave her consent to my immediate engagement. On January 30th Ned came to The Danes as my accepted lover. My mother walked to meet him through the snow. It was the first time they had met, and he won her heart at once. She was terribly concerned lest the patent leather boots he was wearing should suffer in the snow! And before they had reached the house she was already consulting him about a house she wished to build at Knebworth. The friendship between them established that first day continued to her life's end. It was also very typical of her sudden changes of mood that she wrote a letter to Barbara Webb thanking her effusively for having brought us together.

I had written to tell his Rev of the happy solution, and this was the answer:

Booton Rectory, February 6
A twelvemonth without engagement or intercourse was a preposterous arrangement and impossible to be maintained. I am glad in the highest degree. The change from harassing doubt to radiant certainty is enough of itself to fill your life with joy, and it is delightful to me to picture it. I relish too your account of my Lady's beaming view of the situation, and the charms that grow out of it. We are all familiar with these fascinating moods.

You ask why it is of the thousands who marry so few are happy? Dean Swift said it was because women were more skilled in making nets than cages, which is probably true in the majority of cases, but the remark does not help an anxious enquirer. Nor do you belong to that class. You are absolutely

sure that your marriage will be everything that heart can
desire. There is no reason why it should not be. My fifty-
eight years of married life have, on account of that marriage,
been years of unsurpassed blessing.

Blessings and blessings on you.

The following is the first letter I wrote to his Rev after
my engagement:

The Danes, February 12

I have wanted to write to you before, but there have been
streams of congratulatory letters requiring answers—and I
am only now free from them—and can write in peace to
you. I cannot put into any letter the depth and intensity
of my happiness. It is beyond all expression—only you
will understand. I long for you to see my darling Ned,
and if he is obliged to go to Cromer on business, may we
come together to Booton? I think you would love him for
himself as well as for my sake. I long too for him to see the
church.

I have found a companion more perfectly suited to me than
I ever thought possible. Everything I have ever dreamt of
or imagined, I find in him.

Our plans are still uncertain. He is anxious to save money
so as to start comfortably, as the expenses of setting up
house are very considerable. We hope to marry in September
—but it may be later. We want to live close to Gray's Inn
where he has his offices—such lovely old rooms looking out
on a garden where the rooks build, and seeming quite shut
in from the roar of London traffic. If we can only find a house
small enough—we only want just the number of rooms that
are absolutely necessary. Mother is distressed at this plan—
she thinks it so dreadful to live where no one else lives, and
thinks we shall lose social position in consequence! We
neither of us care for position except where it concerns his
profession—and it is most important for that to live in a
working atmosphere. Besides our great joy is to escape from
everyone else and in that part of the world there will be no
one to criticize the way we live. I would not for worlds live

in the clutch of my relations—or his—though they are all that is beloved. We only want each other. We want two servants—and think a Frenchman and his wife would be very delightful. I think we shall have an amusing establishment. Our house is to be all white and everything in it of the simplest kind and yet all beautiful. Ned likes nothing that is not simple. He says the most beautiful things are always the simplest.

I have a large new family. Father and mother, seven brothers, and three sisters—all total strangers to me until the other day. The father was a soldier and now devotes his life to painting. He has discovered what he calls the Venetian Secret—and is a little cracked on the subject. The effects of Nature, he declares, can be measured as accurately as the effects of sound—and he has invented an instrument for measuring tone and colour. But he can get no one to listen to him—and he is cut by his fellow painters. The sad thing is that his pictures, painted by the aid of this secret, are not very good, though he thinks them masterpieces. He is a splendid old man, very tall, with white hair and beard. He has no regard for conventions but acts in the way that seems best to him. He has the nature of a child, perfectly pure and simple. He thinks all his children paragons. The mother is Irish and was a great beauty—she is beautiful still, with a soft, gentle face and voice. She is very religious of an Evangelical turn—but though she talks of religion quite freely, not a word jars upon one, and she has not one touch of cant or hypocrisy, and her creed seems an unbounded love for all human beings. They do not go at all into society. The mother thinks it wrong, and the father is never happy away from his wife and his home.

Ned has a great deal of work on hand—and I hope very much people will give him more now they realize what an old and serious man he is about to become!

I can hardly believe yet it has all come right. It seemed so far off and improbable, and we both suffered so much. But we are the happier for it now.

I know my beloved Rev will be happy in my happiness— and I hope we may come to you together some day.

I give here a letter I wrote to Ned soon after we were
engaged, as he so perfectly fulfilled by his life and work all
that I then urged upon him to be and do:

The Danes

God bless you, and help you to do great things. Don't
work for money, but only for your work itself. I shall not
feel proud if you only make a fortune, or a name before the
world. I want you to be able at the end of your life to look
back upon your work, and know in your own mind that all of
it has been very good. Work only for the glory of your
art. Be your own judge, and satisfy your own most critical
mind, and then my wishes for you will be satisfied, and my
pride complete.

In that miserable time when I told you there was no hope,
I was wretched at losing you because I loved you so, and I
wanted your love more than anything in the world, but my
pride suffered too, because I knew that some day you could
be a great and wonderful man, whom everyone would kneel
to and admire and praise. And then I thought you would have
found someone else to love and would have forgotten me, and
another woman would have had the right I longed for, to be
proud in your greatness and success. And I thought you
would come to me and say: "You would not trust me when
I said I would become a man, and now you see I spoke truly."
And I could not have told you then how I had trusted and
believed in you all the time, and known that it was in you
to become a great and glorious man. I imagined such a
beautiful tragedy and wept so many tears over it! And now
the tragedy is swept away and turned into a beautiful and
glorious poem. And some day I shall share your success and
no other woman.

After the many unhappy letters from Ned which I have
quoted before our engagement, I give these happy words
written soon after all had come right:

"I feel that I am so much a part of you, our lives are woven
like threads in our linen, together and inseparable, making
one great sheet of glory, made in heaven (not Belfast), so

that it shall last till heaven ends, far beyond the end of this tired world."

I have said before how Ned and my mother became friends on that first day of my engagement, and in the following letter to me he expresses that love which he felt for her to her life's end:

"And your dear, sweet, pretty mother. I used so to dread her and feel such fear of her. Now it has all vanished, and I see her face only as one I have always loved.

"I do hope your mother will always love me and that I may bring warmth to her heart these coming years. I feel a robber taking you, but she must learn that she gains me and you must teach me how to teach her that. I don't want ever to say one word to hurt or trouble her. Should it happen that our loves for you, darling, should prompt us to differ, then will be the time I shall have to prove my love and respect for her, your mother, yet what I hold right by you, my one and only darling, my wife, I hold tight. I shall have to show my strength. Will she be kind and trust me? I think so, her nature is so generous and noble altogether."

In April, after a severe attack of influenza, I was ordered by the doctor to the sea, and accompanied by Con I went to Cromer and naturally proposed a visit to Booton. His Rev writes:

Booton Rectory, April 8

It is an age since we have seen you, and longer still since Con has favoured us with her presence, and it would be absurd to come here for what you call the day. You must arrive in the morning of one day and not leave till the afternoon of the next or the interchange of mind will be so hurried and incomplete that we shall have no comfort in the visit. I am longing to see dear Con, not to refresh my memories, for none of them have faded, but to add to them. If all goes well we will be joyful together and have a radiant holiday.

After my return home, I write:

The Danes, May 4

I have been wanting to write to you for days, but have had my time so filled up it was difficult. It was a great joy seeing you and I feel it is far easier now to write. I have been in London since I saw you, staying with Ned's married sister, as Betty's children are all stricken with whooping cough, poor little things. Now I am home again with Mother, who has had a very good time at Cimiez, and looks much better for it.

I find everyone thinks me looking much better but still delicate. I take great care and feel very well myself. I stay here now for a bit and Ned comes down for Sundays.

I grow daily happier and more in love. We have looked at several houses, but seen none to suit as yet. It is not easy to find the exact thing one wants.

The Danes, May 14

I went to see my doctor when I was in London the other day, and he thought me marvellously better—and asked me to let him know what tonic he had given me, as he had forgotten. He evidently means to try the same thing on his other influenza patients! Judith, who is here, says she never remembers seeing me look so well—and Ned keeps enquiring if I am flushed, my cheeks look so red! This I feel you will be glad to hear, my own dear Rev. I am feeling really well and strong now. The doctor advised me to continue my tonic— and as it seems to agree, I do so. It is some iron mixture. I will get change of air if I can—but I think the quiet life here suits me better than going about much. We live on a hill and the air is very bracing, but keeping early hours is what helps me most. I shall have a quiet summer here and hope to get quite strong by August.

Booton Rectory, June 17

I was longing to hear from you, and your delightful letter tells me exactly what I wanted to know. Far above all things I wanted news of your health. I rejoice to read your account of it, and your happiness is an assurance that everything else is favourable to your marriage in August. That will be *your* Jubilee. I am deeply thankful. This is the chief thing I have to say to you, and the rest will wait till the bustle of the next few days is over. All blessings be with you. I am always your debtor and always your loving friend.

The Danes, June 26

My wedding day has now been fixed for the 4th of August. There only wants one thing to complete my happiness on that day, and this depends on you. Can you, will you, come and marry me? I hardly dare hope for a favourable answer. I know how you hate to leave home, and that it is a long way to ask you to come, but still I ask because the joy would be so great. Mother says it would crown the day and make it perfect, and I feel this too. If you could come I know the new Rector at Knebworth would be overjoyed and put you up, and we should one and all welcome you with open arms. I know you will come to me if you feel it to be possible, so I do not press any further. I can only repeat that it wants but your presence to complete my joy and bless me on the happiest day of my life. I feel that it would be like God's best blessing to have you with me the day I begin my new life.

Booton Rectory, June 30

Tell my dear Lady I am exceedingly gratified that she should wish me to take the Service at your marriage, and that her wish would of itself be a law to me. I have, as you know well, the same to say of your own wish. There is a third commanding motive, that if I am present at the marriage I shall once more see you all together, an event not otherwise to be hoped for. But I have hesitated nevertheless. Southey truly said that of uncertain things the most uncertain is human life. At my years the uncertainty is great indeed. The "sand of my glass must anyway be nearly run out." What touches me far and away the most is that the life of the blessed Mother [1] is to outward seeming more precarious than my own. I undertake nothing, even for the morrow,

[1] His wife.

without the predominant inward qualification—if I am alive.
Therefore I doubted whether I ought to assume that in the
ordinary course of things I could be at Knebworth on August 4,
and I have waited to see the conclusion to which two or
three days' reflection would bring me. Well, unless there is
some marked change between now and then there is nothing
against the pledge, and so I answer, according to the
appearances of the hour, that I joyfully accept the privilege
my Lady and yourself have assigned me.

The Danes, July 2

I don't know how to tell you in words my joy at the good
news your letter brought me this morning. It will crown the
day with blessing to have you. I cannot tell you enough
how I thank you and how I shall love to have you, but you
know, my own Rev, without words of the depth of my
gratitude to you for all that you have ever been to me, my
best guide and counsellor. And now you will bless me on the
first day of my new life and my happiness will be complete.
Of course, I understand your reluctance to leave the dear
Mother even for a night, and if even at the last moment she
wanted you—you must not think of me. She comes before
everyone. But if she can spare you it will make me so super-
latively happy.

But alas! after all his Rev was not to officiate at my
wedding.

Booton Rectory, July 26

The vice of old age, or one of its vices, is that no
dependence can be placed on it. It may do pretty well in
favourable circumstances, but goes to pieces by changes of
weather, or habits, or things too small to be noted. This has
happened to me at the present moment, and I am hardly
more capable at this minute of making a journey to Knebworth than a voyage to the North Pole. All my belongings
here tell me that I should be mad to think of keeping my
engagement with you, though to write this is as great a
wrench mentally as any journey could be physically. I cannot
dwell upon it. Necessity has no law and I simply yield to it.

Amid much that I shall miss there is one satisfaction undiminished—that, if we are spared, we shall be able when you come here to talk out all weighty topics after your marriage to as much purposed pleasure as we could have done before. Enclosed is my very diminutive wedding offering,[1] which I send with the barren wish that it could have been better proportioned to the occasion. Every blessing be with you on your wedding-day and every day, and be sure, in the little time which remains to me, that I shall be as always your loving friend.

I was married on August 4th at Knebworth, very much regretting the absence of his Rev.

The first few days of our honeymoon were spent at Warren Lodge, the house into which we had feloniously entered during the previous autumn. From there we went to Knebworth on August 9th to celebrate my brother Victor's twenty-first birthday, leaving after the ceremony for Holland, where we spent the rest of our honeymoon.

*   *   *   *   *

Mrs. Elwin died in February of the following year (1898), after a long and painful illness. In answer to a letter from me his Rev writes:

Booton Rectory, February 26

You have said everything in your letter that heart could say. I am astonished at myself. I expected the blank to be terrible and it is as nothing in comparison with my thanksgiving that the blessed Mother has her wish, and, safe from the fleshly pains and weariness that must have troubled her had she lived, has got to her lasting home. This is the sixtieth year of our married life, and we were engaged for three years. The long line of happy memories are of necessity pathetic now, but intensely joyful too, and I live in them, as they are a presence to me. So I am not lonely, and when I join on to them the thought of where she is, and what she is, as I sit musing on her, I renounce my yearning to keep her, which absorbed me throughout her illness, and am grateful

[1] He sent me £20.

that the issue was far superior to my torturing, because almost hopeless, hopes.

I rejoice that your marriage has equalled your expectations. It could not go beyond them. Betty told me that the business prosperity rivalled the domestic, which last will be further increased when you are one more in family.

I was expecting my first child in August of this year, and had asked his Rev if I might bring the baby to be christened at Booton.

Booton Rectory, July 20

The decay of old age begins, I think, with the memory, and mine is in a dreadful state of dilapidation, but some impressions I hope are indelible, and at any rate I cannot suppose them possible of extinction while life remains. You will find my feelings as fresh as ever. The warmest welcome awaits you, your child, and your husband, and I shall think it a privilege to baptize the baby if you continue to be so minded. My heart will be in the service.

The number of people who have a settled income are as nothing compared to the millions who depend for their bread on their daily employment. And for the most part the employment itself is precarious to this extent, that you cannot see one month that it will continue in the next. Nevertheless it comes to the diligent and deserving. I long ago learned the wisdom of living for the day in respect of enjoying the blessings in hand instead of marring them by speculations on the possible troubles of the morrow. Prudence is an abiding principle with rational beings, but it is not helped by anxious forebodings. The more you cultivate peace in the present the better you can afford to dispense with wanton extravagances. You are today, to say the least of it, in a position when you may rationally bury your fears in your hopes.

Ours is a *little* village church, and we have tried to give it the aspect of a place for prayer. In this sense it has answered its end for some persons. It is the one principle which has governed us in every part of the building. But in no other way has it any pretentions, and you must not lead Lutyens to suppose that it can have any architectural interest for him.

Whatever disappointments you may have, your welcome here will not be one of them. I speak for Amy and Fountain as well as myself, and specially for myself.

My eldest child, Barbara, was born on August 8th. His Rev writes on the 10th:

Booton Rectory, August 10

The joy appointed by Providence as a recompense for the pains of child-birth, and to ensure maternal devotion in the bringing up of off-spring, comes to you in its fullest measure, pressed down and running over. You were devoted to other people's children, when they were not too old to be caressed with fervour, and your delight in your own child will know no bounds. You need no outside contribution to your happiness. I like to tell you notwithstanding that I am joyful in your joy, and am grateful that the penalties you pay are past and that you are safe and probably better than could be expected, judging by the ordinary after-results. You were always capital in facing troubles, whether mental or physical, and your radiance will hasten your recovery. You will settle your coming here for yourself. The rooms are only occupied for brief periods, and they are always safe to be secured in a day or two. I will do my best to see the Mother in the Daughter and love it accordingly. All blessings be with both Mother and child.

On returning to London in October I received this, the last letter I ever had from his Rev:

Booton Rectory, October 7

Beloved Emmie,

Your letter was delicious and put my heart in a glow. The happy memories are past counting up, but I owe most of your language to the liberality of the donor, and not, alas, to my own deserts. That you should cherish the Booton associations both for yourself and your little Darling is, however, a high delight. It was an enormous enjoyment in your visit to see day by day the realization of your fondest hopes. That you are not disappointed now that the dreams of your imagination have become a fact is good evidence that your wishes were rightly framed. Domestic peace and a healthy baby, growing in weight week by week, is the nearest approach that a right-minded mother can make to Paradise.

Blessings on you, beloved Emmie.

I am your old unchanged friend,

Whitwell Elwin

His Rev died on New Year's Day, 1900. He was planning to go into Norwich on a charitable errand for a parishioner. He seemed perfectly well when he was called, but as the usual hour for his coming downstairs passed without his appearing, his servants got uneasy, and going up to his room, found he had fallen back on his bed in the middle of dressing. Death had evidently been instantaneous.

Who's Who

AMPTHILL, LADY: born Lady Emily Villiers, daughter of the Earl of Clarendon, was my mother's first cousin. She married Lord Odo Russell, diplomatist, created Lord Ampthill in 1881.

BALFOUR, ARTHUR JAMES: Prime Minister 1902–1906. Raised to the peerage as Earl of Balfour 1922. Died 1930.

BALFOUR, GERALD: born 1853, succeeded his brother as Earl of Balfour in 1930. Member for the Central Division of Leeds 1885–1906. President of the Board of Trade 1900–1905. In 1895 he was appointed Chief Secretary for Ireland. He married my eldest sister Betty in 1887 and died in 1945. They had one son and five daughters.

BALFOUR, EUSTACE: youngest brother of Arthur and Gerald, was an architect.

BALFOUR, LADY FRANCES CAMPBELL: daughter of the 8th Duke of Argyle, was the wife of Eustace Balfour.

BLOOMFIELD: Born Georgina Liddell, was the youngest daughter of Lord Ravensworth, sister of my grandmother. Her husband, Lord Bloomfield, held many diplomatic posts.

BLUNT, WILFRID SCAWEN: diplomat, traveller, politician, and poet, first became friends with my father in Lisbon. In 1869 he married Lady Anne Milbanke, daughter of the 1st Earl of Lovelace and granddaughter of Lord Byron. Lady Anne became Baroness Wentworth in her own right in 1917 and died the same year. Blunt, born in 1840, died in 1922. He founded the Crabbet stud of Arab horses.

BLUNT, JUDITH: the only child of the above, married my brother Neville in 1899. They were divorced in 1923. She became Baroness Wentworth on the death of her mother. She has carried on the famous Arab stud with great success.

CECIL, LORD ROBERT: (Bob), third son of Lord Salisbury, later created Viscount Cecil of Chelwood, in recognition of his work for the League of Nations.

CECIL, LORD EDWARD: (Nigs) fourth son of Lord Salisbury.

CECIL, LORD HUGH: (Linky) fifth son of Lord Salisbury, created Lord Quickswood in 1941.

CECIL, LADY GWENDOLEN: younger daughter of Lord Salisbury, wrote the life of her father.

CRANBORNE, LORD: was the eldest son of the 3rd Marquess of Salisbury, whom he succeeded in 1903. He married Lady Alice Gore, daughter of the 5th Earl of Arran.

DERBY, FREDERICK ARTHUR STANLEY: succeeded his brother in 1885 as Earl of Derby. He married Lady Constance Villiers, daughter of the Earl of Clarendon, my mother's first cousin. Their only daughter, Isobel, married the Hon. J. H. Gathorne Hardy.

EARLE, MRS. C. W.: born Villiers, was my mother's eldest sister (Aunt T. to me). She made a name for herself quite late in life through her books *Potpourri from a Surrey Garden* and *More Potpourri* and also *Memoirs and Memories*.

JEKYLL, GERTRUDE: made a name as a landscape gardener. She greatly helped and encouraged my husband in the early days of his career. His nickname for her was Bumps, the mother of all bulbs.

LATHOM, EARL OF: married my mother's first cousin, Lady Alice Villiers. He was appointed one of our guardians by my father. The family name was Wilbraham.

LOCH, LORD: Sir Henry Brougham (born in 1827), married my mother's twin sister Elizabeth (Aunt Lizey).

LOCKER-LAMPSON. FREDERICK: Locker, a man of letters and civil commissioner of Greenwich Hospital, married as his second wife Hannah Lampson, daughter of Sir Curtis Lampson, and took his wife's name (1821–1895).

LOCKER-LAMPSON, GODFREY: son of the above, was a contemporary and friend of my brother Victor at Eton.

LUTYENS, EDWIN LANDSEER: my husband, born 29 March 1869, was the ninth son of Charles and Mary Lutyens. For details of his life and works see *The Lutyens Memorial Volumes* by A. S. G. Butler and Christopher Hussey.

LYTTON, ROBERT: My father, was son of the novelist Bulwer Lytton. He was a distinguished diplomatist holding many posts in the diplomatic service. He was appointed Viceroy of India by Disraeli in 1875 and returned home in 1880 when the Conservative Government went out of office. In 1887 he was appointed Ambassador in Paris, in which post he died in November, 1891. He was also a poet, writing under the name of Owen Meredith.

LYTTON, EDITH: born Villiers, my mother, was one of the twin daughters of Edward Villiers, brother of the Earl of Clarendon, and Elizabeth Liddell, daughter of Lord Ravensworth. Both my mother and her twin sister lived to the age of ninety-five. My parents were married in 1864, and had seven children. After my father's death my mother lived in retirement until in 1895 she accepted the post of Lady in Waiting to Queen Victoria and at her death was offered the same post by Queen Alexandra and remained with her until 1905, when she retired to live at Knebworth in a house built for her by her son Victor and designed by my husband, Edwin Lutyens.

LYTTON, VICTOR ALEXANDER: my eldest brother, born in India in 1876, succeeded to the title on my father's death. He was educated at Eton and Cambridge. He held many Government posts and in 1922 was appointed Governor of Bengal, which post he occupied till 1927, acting as temporary Viceroy from April to August in 1925. He married in 1902 Pamela Plowden and they had two sons and two daughters. He died in 1947.

LYTTON, NEVILLE STEPHEN: my youngest brother, born in India in 1879. He was educated at Eton and from there went to Paris and studied at the Beaux Arts as a painter. He took part in the 1914–18 war, attaining to the rank of Major on the General Staff. He was wounded, and received the O.B.E.(Mil.) and the Croix de Guerre. In 1899 he married Judith Blunt, who divorced him in 1923, and in 1924 he married Alexandra Fortel. He succeeded his brother Victor and died in Paris in 1952. He had a son and two daughters by Judith, and one daughter by his second wife.

LYTTON, ELIZABETH EDITH: my sister Betty, born on 12 June 1866. Married Gerald Balfour in 1888, died in 1945. After my father's death she wrote a volume of his Life and Letters and also an account of his Indian administration.

LYTTON, CONSTANCE GEORGINA: my second sister, took a leading and active part in the movement demanding votes for women. As a militant suffragette she was three times imprisoned, her health being seriously impaired by forcible feeding. From this experience she never fully recovered and remained an invalid until her death in 1923.

RAYLEIGH, LORD: the eminent scientist, married Evelyn Balfour, Arthur's and Gerald's sister.

SALISBURY, MARQUESS OF: succeeded his father as 3rd Marquess 1868. In 1874 became Secretary for India under Lord Beaconsfield and later Foreign Secretary. In 1885, after the death of Lord Beaconsfield, he became Prime Minister, but was defeated by Gladstone 1892. Re-elected Prime Minister 1895.

VILLIERS, EDWARD: my grandfather, was a brother of the Earl of Clarendon and married Elizabeth Liddell, daughter of Lord Ravensworth. He died young of tuberculosis, contracted from his brother.

WEBB, ROBERT: (Bob), was the Squire of Milford in Surrey. Married late in life Barbara, sister of Sir Alfred Lyall, Indian administrator and minor poet.

WEBB, BARBARA: wife of the above, had known my parents in India and always remained a close friend of my sister Betty. She did much to help and encourage my husband as a young man. She died of cancer shortly before we married. Our eldest daughter was named after her.

Appendix

SOME LETTERS FROM THE REV. WHITWELL ELWIN TO HIS WIFE

Old Hummums, Covent Garden
Thursday Night. Dec 2: 1858.

My most dearly beloved Wife,

I have to be at Albemarle St. at a ¼ to 10 tomorrow morning to meet the carriage which takes us to Wimbledon. It is not therefore probable that I shall be able to write in the course of the day and I give you a line instead before going to bed.

Thackeray was at Forster's and as there was no one else it promised a social evening but Thackeray was silent, and apparently out of spirits. He has just brought me in his carriage to the Old Hummums and told me on the way that the cause of his reserve was the apprehension of getting on the subject of Gates (the man who was expelled from the Garrick Club for libelling Thackeray) and provoking an explosion from Forster. The letters written by Gates were thought by Thackeray to be extremely offensive, and Dickens has just addressed a note to Fr. stating that he (Dickens) was the author or adviser of them. This makes Thackeray indignant with Dickens whose cause Forster would be sure to espouse, and hence T's fear of an angry scene. Thackeray says that Dickens is mad, in which opinion I think he is not far wrong. As for Forster, T. declares that he behaved so ill some time ago when dining at T's house that nothing except Forster's entreaty that he would dine in Montague Square induced him to break bread with him again. He uttered his old complaint of Forster's being perpetually acting so that you could never trust to what he said or did, or separate what was real from what was artificial.

In consequence of the constraint there is little to report. Yet the evening was not unpleasant. There is one Mahoney, an Irishman, who writes under the name of Father Prout, and who is now resident at Paris. Thackeray knows him well and likes him and gave this trait of him, that he goes about saying, "You know Thackeray has a brother that is transported but the family never allude to the subject." These are the fellows from whom Thackeray draws his Irish portraits. He laughs at their lying and finds food for mirth in it—I suppose because they have no malignant intention.

Thackeray's mother has broken her leg. His daughters are in attendance upon her and he himself has to pass backwards and forwards between France and England. This he says makes the "Virginians" hard work to him. He tells his mother that if she will live in Brighton he will hire her a house and keep her a carriage. She says, "No, she prefers Paris." Yet if you have a fingerache, he rejoins, you expect us all to come over to you, and she answers "Yes."

I asked him how the Virginians sold. He said better now than at first. "I lingered too much over the dining scenes—a good deal owing to ill health." I suppose, I said, you meant to take us into the literary society of that day now you have got the bookish brother to England. "Certainly. I shall send the other youngster off. He has hampered me terribly. You can have no idea of the trouble the book is to me. It is not like describing the scenes in which I live. I have to read for everything, and it is not worth the toil. I will never do it again."

I was about to tell him what I admired in the Virginians but he cut me short with his old phrase, "You are not a trustworthy judge."

Speaking of Douglas Jerrold he said, "He hated me like the plague, and I scorned him as I should a dustman."

He said at dinner that when he had finished the Virginians he meant "to fly a flag of his own." "That is, I suppose, you mean to start a magazine." "Yes," he said, "something of that kind. I shall write a story for it at starting, and then afterwards I shall have nothing to do except superintend and contribute a trifle now and then."

He told us that the other day at the Garrick Club one member insulted another upon which a man—whose name I forget—said "I should treat it with silent contempt just as I myself treat Jackson." "What Jackson?" said Thackeray. "Why *that* Jackson," replied the man, pointing to a person who was smoking quietly at the opposite side of the room. Really the ways of the world are very odd. I asked how Jackson received the observation. "Oh! there," said Thackeray, "the curtain drops. He bore it quietly at the time." I am afraid this is all there is to tell.

At dinner at Brougham's on Tuesday, B. Ker mentioned that the present purchasers of luxuries of the victuals and drink kind in London were the trades-people. Lord Hertford used to dine with Lincoln, of the firm of Lock & Lincoln, Hatters in St. James St., because Lincoln's cook was better than Lord Hertford's own. Ker twitted his tailor with his Epicurean habits and the tailor replied—"What other luxury can I have? If I went often to the play, my customers would say, 'Hang that impudent tailor of

mine he is always at the theatre whenever I go there.' I could
well afford to keep a carriage but you would call me an impertinent
fellow if I drove to your door in a carriage when I came to measure
you for a pair of pantaloons." Brougham said that when he went
the Northern circuit there were frequent prosecutions of persons
for a breach of the game laws in killing grouse before the 12th of
August. He used to ask the witnesses on these occasions at what
price the birds were sold. "A guinea a brace." And who were the
purchasers? "The *weavers* of the manufacturing towns." I repeated
this at Forster's and Thackeray added that enormous prices were
given for lamb very early in the season and that the purchasers
were from the labouring classes. This is a new trait to me.

Lady Cranworth, in B. Ker's hearing, said to Lord Cranworth
when he was Lord Chancellor—"Robert my dear, if it is not a
great secret would you tell me so and so." "I have been now 6
months in the cabinet," answered Lord C., "and I never heard
but one secret there. I would tell it you but I have forgotten it."
All who know Lord C. who is a simple, honest but rather weak
man, would be aware that this was no artifice to stop the inquisi-
tiveness of his wife. It was the truth and it is a just representation
of the usual state of affairs. There are and can be no secrets in
politics now-a-days except underhand intrigues of which the
contrivers are ashamed.

I asked Lord Lyndhurst if he ever heard Pitt speak. "Yes—
three or four times." Was it like the speaking of our day? "No,
quite different; it was much more artificial, but very grand and
imposing of its kind. Pitt used a great deal of action and often
threw his body upon the table before which he stood. In those days
the ministers always appeared in the house in full dress, and such
was his vehemence that before he had been speaking half an hour
the pomatum and powder from his hair trickled down his face."

"I never," said Lord L., "heard Fox when he was great. His
speeches on the occasions when I chanced to be present were very
lame. What I chiefly remember is that his large protruding paunch
was alternately drawn in and puffed out and in the inward movements his waistcoat hung loose about him as if it was twice too
big for him."

Lord L. again: "There is much more intelligence and knowledge
in the House of Commons now than there was formerly. When I
first entered it there were only three or four speakers on each side,
who were a sort of professed retainers for their respective parties.
Now and then a country gentleman was told that if he would express
his opinion it would have great weight but he only uttered a few
sentences." Was the speaking as animated under the old system as
under the present? Lord L.: "Yes,—more so I think." This
Brougham confirmed, but added "that the cry which used to be
raised of Canning, Canning,—Brougham, Brougham was no

compliment to them as speakers, nor proceeded from any desire
of the house to hear them, but from the knowledge of the country
gentlemen that until they had spoken there would be no division,
without which they could not go home to supper or bed." To bed
I must go now, for they are about to shut up the coffee-room. So
good bye, dearest Wife, and

> Believe me,
> Your doating husband,
>
> Whitwell Elwin

> 1 o'clock, Dec 3: 1858
> *Newstead, Wimbledon Park*

My most dearly beloved Wife,

I have just returned from the christening and am now going
over to Clapham to see Sir W. Napier.

Parson Adams performed the Baptismal ceremony and he and
Mrs. A. come today. I shook hands with him and had a couple of
minutes conversation. He was exceeding kind.

I forgot to mention in my account of Thackeray's talk that he
said he should carry Warrington to the play in his next number
and give a description of Garrick's acting. "Can you," I said,
"realize to yourself what Garrick was as an actor?" "Yes, as a
comic actor I think I can. I am sure I know his laugh. I have looked
at his portrait till I am positive if I heard his laugh I should
identify it as *his*." I suppose he has observed some connection
between the countenance and the laugh, which is curious, and what
I fancy no physiognomist has ever noticed.

I enclose Brougham's note begging me to go this morning and
see the children. I went of course. His kindness is delicious to me.
He gave me a most pleasant message from Lyndhurst.

Ever your devoted husband

> W. E.

Brougham spoke of some man of the Tory party whom Peel
was compelled to defend. "He did it," said B, "in his usual way."
"That is," joined in Lyndhurst, "half and half. He never defended
any one with heartiness in his life." I give you this as a trait of
Peel's character.

B. & Lyndhurst laughed at Ld. Campbell's clap-trap speeches
from the Bench, & L. mentioned as a specimen that the other day a
Mahometan came to the court of Queen's Bench to be sworn in as
an attorney—the first Mahometan attorney that has ever been in
England. Campbell to humour the cry for religious toleration said,
"I wish you, Sir, success in your profession"—"wished him
success" went on Lord L., "*because* he was a Mahometan, as if
Mahometanism was a merit. He has no good wishes for good
Christians who come to be sworn in as attornies." These trifles

will give you some idea of L's way of talking and will therefore interest you.

The Murrays desire all kind remembrances. They are gratified at my coming.

Old Hummums, Covent Garden
June 13: 1861

My most dearly beloved Wife,

I called upon the big man [Thackeray] at ½ past, found him at home and lunched with him. After lunch we drove to his new house, a handsome red-brick building in the style of Queen Anne— and from thence into London, where I parted with him. He asked me to dinner, which was only to throw bitters into every dish I shall eat elsewhere.

Talking of the two persons at our club who wished to exclude him I said, "You have at some period or other trodden on their corns and in that anguish they kick at you." "That is it," said he; "the only wonder is I have not ten times as many enemies. Many people are rancorous against me because I have got on. Even my mother, worthy soul, cannot quite forgive me. *She* has sunk in the world, and *I* have risen, and she thinks our positions ought to be reversed. She is living near us now and has my carriage to drive in, but always feels that the carriage ought to be her own. I must say though that the old boy (his step-father) rejoices in my prosperity and delights to partake in it. He has his little tip and accepts it with honest, open simplicity and gratitude."

"By Bags I meant Monckton Milnes. If I tumbled into the gutter he would pick me up and wipe my clothes; but he cannot endure my success and I was told that he went about saying 'There is no bearing Thackeray's insolence!' Other people declare on the contrary that I have been a sneak to lords. The lords sought *me*; I never sought them; and they have dropped me because I do not court, or even call upon them. I want to state this charge in the Magazine and comment upon it, but cannot yet see how to bring it in!"

I asked him if Mrs. Brookfield was the person to whom I praised the Lines in the Album. "Yes, and she was the person on whom the lines were written. Your praise of them was more pleasure to her than if you had given her twenty thousand pounds, and it did me some good with her." "Why," I replied, "do you not make up the quarrel?" "Because I cannot. Her husband treated her cruelly and I remonstrated with him for the express purpose of making a breach. I had got so fond of her that it was no longer safe to continue the intimacy. There is my history—the tragedy of my life."

I told him that Lovell began admirably and ended badly, "I intended it," he said, "for a jest." "Then my objection," I answered, "still holds good; for you raise a real interest in the first part, and balk it in the last. If you designed a farce the whole should have been farcical." "Well," he said, "the fact is it was a play turned into a tale. I wrote it at the request of Wigan, who afterwards refused to perform it, because the characters himself and his wife had to play were too like their own. I think of continuing the history of Elizabeth,—a woman without vice, but without the least heart. I shall carry her on through the world, watching warily at every step to set her foot upon a higher round of the ladder, and making her husband an Earl by her exertions. At the close the person shall turn up with whom she was originally in love—some low cad—and for whom she has retained a sneaking affection through life while caring for nobody else."

I praised Philip. "I have told my tale in the novel department. I can repeat old things in a pleasant way, but I have nothing fresh to say. I get sick of my task when I am ill and think, good Heavens, what is all this stuff about! I believe though that Philip will increase in interest as it proceeds and when Philip is done I turn to the History of Queen Anne." He has made some little sketches to sell at a bazaar at which his daughters are to keep a stall, and one of the sketches represents a big black bottle, underneath which is written, "The death of Queen Anne." You are aware that she was a drunkard.

His new house is large and handsome. It costs him £5,000. If he can have capital to yield him £500 a year more than he possesses he can live an idle man for the remainder of his days. I knew you would like me to jot down these little items while they were fresh. It is post-time, and there is nothing more worth repeating. God bless you, my precious wife, and

Believe me your most devoted,

W. Elwin

It was an unspeakable delight to me to see him. He was as kind as possible. He remarked while we were looking over his new House—"An uncle of mine annoyed me by saying, 'It ought to be called Vanity Fair.' The fact is it is too good for me."

Miss Thackeray said, "Do you dine at home today or at a house by a river?" "At a house by a river to be sure. I shall go to Greenwich and write a bit of Philip." "Write Philip at a tavern at Greenwich!" said I. "Yes," he replied; "I cannot write comfortably in my own room. I do most of my composition at hotels or at the Club. There is an excitement in public places which sets my brain working."

He said: "I am only a sham editor. Mr. Smith, the publisher, does most of the work and likes it. He has no confidence in my judgment, and a great deal in his own. He thinks me good for nothing except as a writer of stories."

I said, "The Round-about Papers are delicious." "I think," he replied, "They are pleasant reading. They give me no trouble. When I have hit on a subject, a 'Round-about Paper' is only a day's work."

I asked Miss Thackeray if she would sell, by private contract, one of the sketches her father had made for the bazaar. "Yes," said she. "No," said he: "You cannot afford to buy gimcracks now: you are a dethroned editor: I will draw something for you and give it you."

He said of Forster, "He is a clever fellow but his books are not good. They are not the genuine wine, and in his heart he knows it."

[From a letter of about the same date]

. . . It has often been objected to Lord Macaulay that he was dictatorial in conversation, and that he would suffer no one else to talk. I suppose he occasionally contradicted with rudeness, though I never myself observed any undue dogmatism in him. The charge of monopolising the conversation was just. His teeming knowledge was probably the cause. No subject could be broached that he did not abound in information upon it; no book in any language could be mentioned that he had not read it. I am not easily astonished at the extent of other men's acquirements, knowing how much may be learned by very moderate diligence, and how many volumes may be skimmed in the course of a single twelvemonth. But *his* range was truly astounding. He was not accustomed to select the topics on which he descanted. He took up the first word which other people dropped and seemed from the excess of his knowledge to have made it his own peculiar study. It was the same with books. The obscurest works were as familiar to him as the most famous, and whether reference was to Greek, Latin, German, French, Italian or English authors he showed his perfect acquaintance with them by instantly dealing out their contents. His memory for words as well as for facts was prodigious, and he would quote large passages of prose from second-rate productions, while his stores of verse were endless.

M. Guizot says that he talked in the same style in which he wrote. Nothing can be more incorrect. Marvellous for the variety of matter there was nothing brilliant in the manner. There were none of the short, terse, antithetical sentences which characterise his composition. There was no vivid descriptions, no felicities of phrase, no polish in the construction of his sentences. He talked in an easy, careless, fluent strain without ever uttering a word which struck the mind with its beauty or power. What was still more strange in a man who expresses such strong opinions in his books and who had such clear and well-defined views, his conversation was destitute of sentiment and individuality. He poured out his knowledge in bare statements, which derived no colour from their passage through his brain. He did not lay down principles, or deduce conclusions, or offer critical comments. His delight was in naked facts, and quotations—in detailing what others said, and not in declaring what he himself thought. This was a defect in his conversation and deprived it of much of the interest which would otherwise have belonged to it. Nevertheless enough remained to render it highly instructive and though many thought it wearisome, to *me* it was always a treat. I was never tired because the knowledge was as redundant as the talk, and if on the one hand there was nothing striking in his way of expressing himself, there was on the other an utter absence of effort, or a desire to shine. His mind was full to overflowing and he allowed the waters to run out with a calm equable current without attempting to fling them into cascades, or to make them sparkle as they issued forth.

Macaulay said of Shelley's poems that the language was rich and the lines musical,—that his pieces seemed to have the attributes of beautiful verse, and yet that there was page after page to which it was impossible to affix a meaning. He quoted instances. This was one of the few *opinions* I heard him utter, and the criticism is very just. Shelley has the garb of poetry and it clothes nothing. This vagueness and mysticism has a great charm for young minds, who for some reason prefer the world of dreamy, ill-defined shadows to the world of reality.

When Macaulay was in India he had taken with him Richardson's Clarissa to the Neilgherry Hills. It was borrowed by some of the old statesmen who were recruiting their strength there, and they read it in the dearth of all other amusement. The effect, Macaulay said, was extraordinary. Clarissa was the one topic of conversation. They talked of the incidents as of passing events, followed the fortunes of the heroine with breathless suspense, and wept over the catastrophe. The tribute to the pathos of the story was the more signal that, as M. observed, their hearts were as withered as their skins.

Lord Melbourne said of Macaulay, "I wish I was as cock-sure of *anything* as Tom Macaulay is of *everything*."

His memory sometimes deceived him. Herman Merivale told me that he once quoted a phrase from the Greek Testament and Macaulay maintained that some different expression which he repeated was the real wording. When Merivale got home he referred to the text and the various readings and found that Macaulay and himself were both wrong.

It is a proof of the marvellous range of Macaulay's reading that the only production I ever heard mentioned in his presence of which he was ignorant was Cheselden's paper on the optical phenomena which presented themselves to the blind boy whose sight was restored by touching. Macaulay was greatly interested in the subject and enquired particularly where the paper was to be found.

Macaulay said to Professor Napier that you might always tell the state-paper or essay of a Scotchman because it invariably began "In the earliest ages of the world."

Index